International Climate Finance

T0293520

This book is the first to provide a complete overview of international climate finance. In the Copenhagen Accord of 2009, developed countries jointly committed to mobilize US$100 billion per year to address climate change in developing countries. This book presents the best information available on this subject: an overview of current international climate finance, estimates of the incremental investment and cost of mitigation measures, estimates of the additional funding needed for adaptation, analyses of potential sources of international climate finance, and the institutional and governance arrangements to deliver the funds effectively.

Climate finance will play an increasingly important role in international efforts to address climate change over the next decade and this book is currently the only source of all relevant material on international climate finance for policymakers and researchers.

Erik Haites is President of Margaree Consultants Inc., Canada. He advises clients on economic aspects of climate change, including the design of market mechanisms and international financial mechanisms. He was a consultant to the UNFCCC secretariat during the negotiation of the rules for the Kyoto mechanisms.

International Climate Finance

Edited by Erik Haites

LONDON AND NEW YORK

First published 2013
by Routledge
2 Park Square, Milton Park, Abingdon, Oxfordshire OX14 4RN

Simultaneously published in the USA and Canada
by Routledge
711 Third Avenue, New York, NY 10017

First issued in paperback 2015

Routledge is an imprint of the Taylor & Francis Group, an informa business

British Library Cataloguing in Publication Data
A catalogue record for this book is available from the British Library

Library of Congress Cataloging-in-Publication Data
International climate finance / edited by Erik Haites.
    p. cm.
Includes bibliographical references and index.
1. Climatic changes—Economic aspects. 2. Environmental policy—Finance.
I. Haites, Erik F.
QC981.8.C5I576 2013
363.738'746—dc23
2012039592

ISBN 13: 978-1-138-92586-1 (pbk)
ISBN 13: 978-1-84971-405-1 (hbk)

Typeset in Times
by Cenveo Publisher Services

Contents

Figures

Tables

Contributors

Preety Bhandari is the Principal Climate Change Specialist at the Asian Development Bank. Prior to joining the ADB, Preety spent five years with the United Nations Framework Convention on Climate Change (UNFCCC) Secretariat where her responsibilities included climate finance, including preparation of the report on *Investment & Financial Flows to Address Climate Change*. Preety has over 20 years of experience working on issues related to energy, environment, climate change, and sustainable development including stints with The Energy & Resources Institute (TERI), UNEP's Environment Assessment Programme for the Asia Pacific and the International Institute for Applied Systems Analysis. She holds a Bachelors in Economics and a Masters in Business Economics from Delhi University.

Alex Bowen is a Principal Research Fellow at the Grantham Research Institute on Climate Change and the Environment, London School of Economics, where his research focuses on the macro-economic aspects of climate change, mitigation policies, and green growth. He served as a Senior Economic Adviser for the preparation of *The Economics of Climate Change: the Stern Review*. Prior to joining LSE, he worked at the Bank of England. Alex earned a PhD in economics from the Massachusetts Institute of Technology, where he studied as a Kennedy Scholar.

Milan Brahmbhatt is Senior Adviser to the Vice President of the World Bank's Poverty Reduction and Economic Management (PREM) Network. In this capacity he advises and leads work on a range of macro-economic and structural policy issues, including on fiscal policy and on the economics of climate change and sustainable growth. In previous positions at the Bank, Mr Brahmbhatt has been adviser to the Chief Economist of the World Bank's East Asia and Pacific Region, and was leader of the global economic prospects and forecasting team in the Bank's Development Economics Department. Before joining the Bank, Mr Brahmbhatt was a research manager at Data Resources Inc. (DRI/Standard & Poor's) where he consulted on international economic, trade, and environmental issues with corporate and government clients and was the director for DRI's Asian Economic Service where he focused on macro-economic prospects for Asian economies. Mr Brahmbhatt holds an MSc from the London School of Economics and is a former member of the Institute of Chartered Accountants in England and Wales.

Barbara Buchner is the Head of Climate Policy Initiative Europe and a lecturer at Ca' Foscari University, Venice. Her work focuses on international climate finance to address the question of whether it is adequate and productive. An additional topic of interest is the qualitative and quantitative analysis of market-based mechanisms and of other policy approaches to GHG mitigation. Prior to joining CPI, she worked at the International Energy Agency, FEEM and was a visiting scholar at MIT. She holds a PhD in Economics from the University of Graz.

Ian Burton is Professor Emeritus at the University of Toronto and Scientist Emeritus with Environment Canada. He is also a Visiting Fellow at the International Institute for Environment and Development in London; co-chair of the International Advisory Board of the International Centre for Climate Change and Development (ICCCAD) in Bangladesh; and co-chair of the Working Group on Forensic Investigations of Disasters in the programme International Research on Disaster Risk (IRDR). Ian also shares with Thea Dickinson a boutique consulting partnership. His research and consulting interests are concentrated on climate change adaptation and disaster risk reduction, and he is currently a Lead Author of a chapter on 'Climate Resilient Pathways' for the IPCC 5th Assessment Report.

Pradeep Dadhich is currently working as a Director in Deloitte India and looks after clean energy and energy efficiency. He was with TERI, New Delhi till May 2011. He was associated with key studies like the *National Energy Map: Technology Vision 2030* and *National Action Plan on Climate Change* for the Government of India. He was a member of IEA's GHG RD&D Executive Committee (1999 to 2011) and a member of India's Environmental Impact Assessment committee. He is a Lead Author in the AR5 of IPCC. He has a Bachelor's degree (Andhra University) in chemical engineering and a PhD (IIT Bombay).

Thea Dickinson is a partner in Burton Dickinson Consulting and a PhD Candidate at the University of Toronto. She has over 10 years' experience in environmental and biomedical research and has authored and co-authored several publications including *Climate Change Adaptation in Canada: A Multi-Level Mosaic*; *Climate Change and Human Health in Cities*, and *The Compendium of Adaptation Models for Climate Change*. Thea has worked with, and consulted, for the UNDP and UNEP, Red Cross/Red Crescent, Danida, Environment Canada and many others. She administers multi-disciplinary consultancy and research projects and has been the reviewer of over 100 proposals for funding from multilateral institutions. She actively writes, edits, and reviews papers, books, and publications targeting local, national, and international issues and audiences.

Joseph Donahue is a senior policy analyst at Stratus Consulting, an environmental research and consulting firm based in Boulder, Colorado. Mr Donahue specializes in analysing the climate change impacts associated with short-lived climate pollutants (especially black carbon and hydrofluorocarbon refrigerants), identifying best practices in clean energy policy and programme development, and evaluating risks associated with carbon dioxide capture and sequestration technologies. The majority of his research and analytical work is conducted in support of US Environmental Protection Agency programmes. Mr Donahue has a Master of Public Policy degree from Georgetown University.

Tim Essam is an economic consultant focusing on international development and impact evaluation in Washington, DC. He currently serves with Summit Consulting providing sampling and econometric technical services to the US Department of Labor. Mr Essam has provided consulting services to Multilateral Development Banks, UN agencies, and other development organizations. He has published numerous research working papers and peer-reviewed journal articles. Mr Essam is a PhD Candidate in Agricultural and Resource Economics at the University of Maryland, and holds an MS in the same field from the University of Maryland and an MA in International Development from American University.

Angela Falconer is an Analyst with Climate Policy Initiative, Venice where she focuses on climate finance and tracking emissions and mitigation actions. Prior to joining CPI, she worked for AEA Technology as a climate change and energy consultant, primarily on behalf of the European government. Angela holds an MSc in Environmental Change and Management from the University of Oxford.

Samuel Fankhauser is Co-Director at the Grantham Research Institute on Climate Change and the Environment at the London School of Economics. He is also a Director of economics consultancy Vivid Economics. Sam is a member of the Committee on Climate Change, an independent public body that advises the UK government on its carbon targets, and the CCC's Adaptation Sub-Committee. Previously, he has worked at the European Bank for Reconstruction and Development (EBRD), the World Bank and the Global Environment Facility. Sam's research interests include climate-change policy, carbon markets, and the economics of adaptation to climate change. He studied economics at the University of Berne, the London School of Economics, and University College London

Michael Grubb is Chair of Energy and Climate Policy at Cambridge University, and Senior Advisor on Sustainable Energy Policy to the UK Energy

Regulator Ofgem. His former positions include Chair of the international research organization Climate Strategies; Chief Economist at the Carbon Trust; Professor of Climate Change and Energy Policy at Imperial College London; and head of Energy and Environment at Chatham House, and he continues to be associated with these institutions. In 2008 he was appointed to the UK Climate Change Committee, established under the UK Climate Change Bill to advise the government on future carbon budgets and to report to Parliament on their implementation. He is author of seven books, fifty journal research articles, and numerous other publications and has been a Lead Author for several reports of the IPCC on mitigation.

Erik Haites is President of Margaree Consultants Inc. He advises clients on economic aspects of climate change including the design of market mechanisms and international financial mechanisms. He was a consultant to the UNFCCC secretariat during the negotiation of the rules for the Kyoto mechanisms, served as the lead consultant for its report on Investment and Financial Flows to Address Climate Change, and has subsequently assisted the secretariat with negotiations on climate finance. He was guest editor for a special issue of *Climate Policy* devoted to climate finance. Dr Haites has contributed to several IPCC reports and is a Lead Author of the chapter on climate finance in AR5. He holds an MBA from McGill and a PhD from Purdue University.

Morgan Hervé-Mignucci is a Senior Analyst with Climate Policy Initiative, Venice where he deals with climate finance issues. His previous research focused on the impacts of carbon pricing on utilities investment decisions, carbon asset prices, and climate change adaptation impacts in the power sector. Prior to joining CPI, he worked for JPMorgan, EDF, and Caisse des Depots/CDC Climat. Morgan holds a PhD in Economics from Université Paris-Dauphine (France) and a Chartered Financial Analyst (CFA) certification.

Richard Klein is a Senior Research Fellow at the Stockholm Environment Institute, an Adjunct Professor at Linköping University, and Co-director and Chief Scientist of the Nordic Centre of Excellence NORD-STAR. Much of his current work addresses the role of adaptation in the design and implementation of a global climate-policy agreement, but he is also interested in social and institutional adaptation in Sweden and other European countries. Richard is the founder and editor-in-chief of the academic journal *Climate and Development*. Before moving to Sweden in 2006, Richard spent almost eight years at the Potsdam Institute for Climate Impact Research. He began his career at the VU University in Amsterdam in 1992.

Sergio Margulis is currently Special Advisor to the Minister of Environment in Brazil. He has previously worked for the World Bank as an Environmental Economist beginning in 1990. His last responsibility at the World Bank was as the task team leader of the Economics of Adaptation to Climate Change study. This was a very large multi-disciplinary study involving the major sectors affected by climate change (infrastructure, agriculture, water, social, and environment) and seven developing country case studies (Vietnam, Samoa, Bangladesh, Ethiopia, Ghana, Mozambique, and Bolivia). From 2007 to 2009, Dr Margulis was Coordinator of the Brazil Economics of Climate Change Study in partnership with the British Government. He had previously worked for the World Bank's Africa Region, Latin America Region, and in the Bank's Environment Department. He was President of the Rio de Janeiro Environmental Agency between 1995 and 1996 and previously a researcher at IPEA, Ministry of Planning in Brazil. He earned his PhD in Environmental Economics from the University of London, Imperial College of Science and Technology.

Carol Mwape is currently completing a Master of Environmental Management degree at the University of Queensland. Previously she had worked for the Zambian Ministry of Tourism, Environment, and Natural Resources and negotiated climate change finance for Zambia and the Least Developed Countries Group. She served as a member of the Transitional Committee for the design of the Green Climate Fund. Carol also assisted the Zambian CDM Technical Expert in promoting the CDM in the private sector and worked with the Zambian DNA in evaluating proposed CDM projects. She now serves as Adviser to the LDC's Green Climate Fund Board member.

Urvashi Narain is a Senior Environmental Economist at the World Bank and part of the Wealth Accounting and Valuation of Ecosystem Services (WAVES) team. WAVES is a global partnership that aims to promote sustainable development by ensuring that the national accounts used to measure and plan for economic growth include the value of natural resources. Prior to joining WAVES, she co-led a three-year study at the World Bank on the Economics of Adaptation to Climate Change which provided estimates of costs of adaptation for developing countries and developed methodologies for countries to develop climate resilient development plans. Prior to joining the World Bank in 2008, she was a Research Fellow at Resources for the Future, where her research focused on poverty and environment linkages in rural economies and on global climate change policy. She earned her PhD from the Department of Agriculture and Resource Economics at the University of California at Berkeley.

Susanne Olbrisch has worked with UNDP in New York since 2008, focusing on investment and financial flows assessments for mitigation of and adaptation to climate change in Latin America, Africa, and Asia. Before that she worked on adaptation to climate change with UNESCO in Bangkok and in various African countries on water and sanitation questions with the Bremen Overseas Research and Development Association (BORDA). Earlier she worked with UNEP in Nairobi on environmental education and training and with GIZ in Chennai on water and sanitation. Her work led her to more than 20 countries worldwide.

Anand Patwardhan is currently Visiting Professor of Public Policy at the University of Maryland, College Park, USA, on leave from the Indian Institute of Technology, Bombay where he is the Shailesh J. Mehta Chair Professor. He served as the Executive Director of the Technology Information, Forecasting and Assessment Council (TIFAC), in the Ministry of Science & Technology, Government of India from 2004 to 2008. Anand's research interests are in the area of environment–climate studies, focusing on mitigation and adaptation responses to climate change; including the diffusion and adoption of clean technology and broader issues of science, technology and innovation policy.

Mattia Romani is a Visiting Senior Fellow at the Grantham Research Institute on Climate Change and the Environment, London School of Economics and Political Science and Director of the London Office of the Global Green Growth Institute (on secondment from McKinsey), where he leads a portfolio of 15 projects across seven countries focused on the transition to a low-carbon, sustainable economic model. In 2010 he served with Lord Nicholas Stern on the UN Secretary General's High-Level Advisory Group on Climate Finance. Previously Mattia worked for McKinsey's Sustainability and Resource Productivity department, the UK Government on the Stern Review, Royal Dutch Shell, and the World Bank. Mattia obtained his DPhil from the University of Oxford (St. Antony's College).

Matthew Savage is Director of Oxford Consulting Partners, and a specialist in climate-change policy and finance. He has worked extensively for the multilateral development banks on the development of climate funds and investment strategies in Asia and Africa. He is leading adaptation finance reporting on behalf of the MDBs, and contributed to the Investment and Financial Flows (IFF) analysis for UNDP. He provided expert input to the Stern Review, and was previously an energy economics researcher at the University of Sunderland. He holds degrees from the Netherlands Business School and the University of Oxford.

Manish Kumar Shrivastava is Associate Fellow with The Energy and Resources Institute and a PhD Scholar at Jawaharlal Nehru University, New Delhi. He specializes in global environmental justice, institutional economics (particular focus on institution of market) and technological change in the context of national and global climate policy. His MPhil dissertation looked into transfer and convergence of environmental institutions across countries and its impact on technological choices made by firms. The focus of his PhD is on examining implications of market-based environmental diplomacy for 'environmental justice'. He has also worked on issues related to Free Trade Areas, non-tariff barriers, impacts of trade on gender and resettlement of communities from protected forests.

Joel B. Smith, a Principal with Stratus Consulting, has been analysing climate change impacts and adaptation issues for over 25 years. He is an author on the

Third, Fourth and Fifth IPCC Assessment reports. He is a member of the US National Climate Change Assessment Federal Advisory Committee and was a member of the National Academy of Sciences 'Panel on Adapting to the Impacts of Climate Change'. He has provided technical advice, guidance, and training on assessing climate-change impacts and adaptation to people around the world and to international organizations, the US government, states, municipalities, and the non-profit and private sectors.

Andrew Steer is President and CEO of the World Resources Institute. Until recently he was Special Envoy for Climate Change for the World Bank Group where he guided the Group's efforts on climate change in more than 130 countries, oversaw the $7 billion Climate Investment Funds, and led the Bank's engagement on international climate negotiations. He was a member of Ban Ki-moon's High Level Panel on Sustainable Energy for All, and on the B20 Board on Green Growth. Previously he served as Director General at the UK Department of International Development (DFID) in London. Earlier, Andrew held senior posts at the World Bank, including Country Director in Vietnam and Indonesia, and Director of the Environment Department, where he oversaw a number of important innovations, including natural capital accounting and the introduction of carbon trading at the World Bank. Andrew has a PhD in Economics from the University of Pennsylvania, and is a Professor of Practice at the Fletcher School of Tufts University.

Nicholas Stern (Lord Stern of Brentford) is I.G. Patel Professor of Economics and Government, London School of Economics, Chairman of LSE's Asia Research Centre and Chairman of LSE's Grantham Research Institute on Climate Change and the Environment. From 2000 to 2003, World Bank Chief Economist and Senior Vice President; Head of the Government Economic Service, 2003–2007; Second Permanent Secretary to Her Majesty's Treasury, 2003–2005; and Director of Policy and Research for the Prime Minister's Commission for Africa, 2004–2005. Lord Stern led the Stern Review on the Economics of Climate Change, 2005–2006. He was knighted for services to economics in 2004 and made a cross-bench life peer as Baron Stern of Brentford in 2007. Lord Stern was elected President of the British Academy in July 2012 (effective July 2013).

Chiara Trabacchi is a Fellow with Climate Policy Initiative, Venice where she deals with climate finance issues. She is currently enrolled in a PhD programme on the 'Science and Management of Climate Change' at Ca' Foscari University where her research will focus on adaptation finance. Before joining CPI, Chiara worked as business strategy consultant at the The European House-Ambrosetti, KPMG and Datamonitor. Chiara holds a Master's Degree in Business Administration from the Catholic University of Milan.

Simon Zadek works on sustainability issues worldwide and is an independent advisor and author. He is Senior Advisor at the International Institute for Sustainable Development, Senior Fellow at the Global Green Growth Institute, and advisor to the World Economic Forum on sustainability issues. He is founder, and was until recently the chief executive, of AccountAbility. He is author of the award winning book, *The Civil Corporation*, and of the *Harvard Business Review* article, 'Paths to Corporate Responsibility'.

1   International climate finance

Erik Haites

Finance has been one of the key issues in climate change negotiations over the past few years. The Bali Action Plan (December 2007) called for enhanced action on the provision of financial resources as part of a new climate change agreement. In the Copenhagen Accord (December 2009), developed countries committed themselves to providing new and additional resources approaching US$30 billion for 2010–2012 and to mobilizing US$100 billion per year by 2020 from a wide variety of sources. In Cancun (December 2010), countries decided to establish a Green Climate Fund (GCF) to provide increased financial support for mitigation, adaptation and technology cooperation in developing countries. The GCF began operation in 2012.

This book provides a comprehensive overview of international climate finance. This chapter provides the essential background. An overview of current climate finance is provided in Chapter 2. Estimates of the resources needed for future mitigation and adaptation actions in developing countries are reviewed in Chapters 3, 4 and 5. Economic considerations related to raising climate finance are discussed in Chapter 6. Studies, of options for mobilizing US$ 100 billion per year by 2020, by the High-level Advisory Group on Climate Change Financing (AGF), the World Bank and other organizations, for the G20 finance ministers, are summarized in Chapters 7 and 8 respectively. A border tax funding option is presented in Chapter 9. Different estimates of potential funding sources are compared in Chapter 10. Issues associated with the delivery of significantly increased funding for adaptation are discussed in Chapter 11. Chapter 12 argues that mitigation and adaptation must be integrated into each country's sustainable development plan and that this will require new financing arrangements. Finally, Chapter 13 reviews recent developments related to climate finance under the UNFCCC.

1.1 Background

In 2006, the Stern review on the economics of climate change estimated that the costs of reducing emissions to avoid the worst impacts could be restricted to 1 per cent of global GDP per year – high but manageable – while failure to act could lead to a loss of 5 to 20 per cent of global GDP per year (Stern, 2006). Investment and Financial Flows to Address Climate Change (UNFCCC, 2007) attempted to quantify the financial resources needed to address climate change in more detail. It estimated that additional global investment and financial flows of US$200 – $210 billion would be needed in 2030 to return global greenhouse gas (GHG) emissions to current levels.[1] In addition, it estimated that several tens of billions of dollars would be needed in 2030 for adaptation.[2]

Partly as a result of that analysis, the Bali Action Plan, adopted in December 2007, called for enhanced action on the provision of financial resources and investment as part of a future climate change agreement. Finance then became one of the keys to a new agreement. This stimulated more efforts to estimate the resources needed for various sectors and regions and to identify options to generate these resources.

In the Copenhagen Accord (December 2009), developed countries committed to 'provide new and additional resources, including forestry and investments through international institutions, approaching US$30 billion for the period 2010–2012 with balanced allocation between adaptation and mitigation'.[3] In addition, they committed to 'a goal of mobilizing jointly US$100 billion a year by 2020 to address the needs of developing countries … from a wide variety of sources, public and private, bilateral and multilateral … including alternative sources of finance' in the context of meaningful mitigation actions and transparency on implementation.[4]

The UN Secretary General established a High-Level Advisory Group on Climate Change Financing (AGF) in February 2010 to assess how best to mobilize US$100 billion per year by 2020 to support actions to address climate change in developing countries (United Nations, 2010). The AGF assessed a variety of options in terms of the amount they might generate and several qualitative criteria. The Group concluded that it is challenging but feasible to meet that goal. However, it could not agree on a recommended mix of sources.

In Cancun (December 2010), countries noted the Copenhagen Accord commitment by developed countries to provide US$30 billion of 'fast-start' finance for 2010–2012 and recognized their commitment to the goal of jointly mobilizing US$100 billion annually by 2020 to address the needs of developing countries.[5] Countries decided to establish a Green Climate Fund as a vehicle to provide increased financial support for mitigation, adaptation and technology cooperation in developing countries.[6] A committee was established to design the fund during 2011.[7]

Activity picked up during 2011. G20 finance ministers requested that the World Bank Group, in partnership with the IMF, the OECD and the regional development banks, explore options for scaled-up finance for climate change adaptation and mitigation in developing countries building upon and extending the work of the AGF (World Bank *et al.*, 2011). The Climate Policy Initiative published an estimate of current climate finance (Buchner *et al.*, 2011). And the Transitional Committee prepared a governing instrument for the Green

Climate Fund. At the end of the year, UNFCCC parties adopted the governing instrument and interim arrangements to make the Green Climate Fund operational.

1.2 Current climate finance

There is no agreed definition of, or comprehensive data on, climate finance. Buchner *et al.* (Chapter 2) attempt to estimate financial flows to mitigation and adaptation activities in developing countries. They pieced together data from numerous sources to arrive at an estimate of US$ 97 billion per year for current (2009/2010) climate finance. This is the funding for climate actions in developing countries, not the total cost of those actions.[8] Most of the finance (US$ 55 billion) is private. Of the US$ 39 billion of public funding, most (US$ 24 billion) is distributed bilaterally. Only a very small share of the total, US$ 4 billion, goes to adaptation.

Although current climate finance is estimated at US$ 97 billion per year, this does not mean the Copenhagen Accord commitment of US$ 100 billion per year by 2020 has already been met. The commitment is for additional funds while most of the current flows pre-date the commitment. The current flows include some funds from developing countries so the flows from developed countries are smaller. However, the current flows indicate that processes and institutions to generate and deploy significant amounts of climate finance exist and can be utilized as climate finance is scaled up to deliver the Copenhagen commitment.

Climate finance under the United Nations Framework Convention on Climate Change (UNFCCC) also is not well defined. Developed-country Parties agreed to cover the 'agreed full incremental costs' of implementing mitigation measures (Article 4.3) and to 'assist the developing-country Parties that are particularly vulnerable to the adverse effects of climate change in meeting costs of adaptation' (Article 4.4). These commitments are reaffirmed by the Kyoto Protocol (Article 11). Developed-country (Annex II) parties periodically report the financial resources they provide to developing countries through bilateral and multilateral channels for climate change action.

The latest summary of the Annex II reports on the climate finance they have provided indicates that they provided a total of US$ 58.4 billion for the period 2005 through 2010, an average of less than US$ 10 billion per year (UNFCCC, 2011a).[9] Thus, climate finance under the UNFCCC accounts for only about 10 per cent of total climate finance. In contrast to the overall pattern, much more of the finance under the UNFCCC (US$ 44 billion) flows through multilateral than bilateral (US$ 14.4 billion) channels. The mitigation/adaptation split is only available for bilateral funds, but like climate finance overall, is dominated by mitigation (85 per cent).

A third perspective on climate finance is the support provided by multilateral funds that are operating entities of the financial mechanism of the UNFCCC – the Trust Fund of the Global Environment Facility (GEF), the Special Climate Change Fund (SCCF) and the Least Developed Countries Fund (LDCF)[10] – and the Adaptation Fund under the Kyoto Protocol. Annex II Party contributions to the GEF Trust Fund, SCCF and LDCF amounted to about US$ 3.3 billion for 2005 through 2010, an average of less than US$ 0.6 billion per year. Most of the funds are used for mitigation. The Adaptation Fund derives most of its funds from the sale of CERs issued for CDM projects.[11] Thus, the operating entities of the financial mechanism of the UNFCCC deal with less than 10 per cent of the climate finance under the Convention and less than 1 per cent of total climate finance. That is likely to change once the Green Climate Fund becomes operational.

1.3 Accounting issues

Efforts to measure climate finance are also complicated by unresolved 'accounting' issues. Some types of finance provide more benefit to the recipient; a grant is more attractive than a market rate loan because the latter needs to be repaid with interest. Although developed countries consistently promise to provide 'new and additional' funds, there is no agreed definition of this term. As well, the 'full incremental costs' of mitigation measures have not been defined. The last two issues are specific to climate finance under the UNFCCC.

The estimates of current climate finance reported are the 'gross' amounts; the value of the investment, loan or grant regardless of the terms (Buchner *et al.*, 2011). Most of the finance (US$ 76 billion) is provided on commercial terms compared with US$ 13 billion of concessional loans and US$ 4 billion in grants. The 'net' resource transfer is highest for grants, lower for concessional loans and lowest for commercial loans and equity investments. The AGF considered different ways to calculate the 'net' value of different types of finance, but could not agree on appropriate methods or even whether climate finance should be measured in 'gross' or 'net' terms (AGF 2010; Chapter 7).

The Convention (Article 4), Kyoto Protocol (Article 11) and Copenhagen Accord all state that developed countries will provide 'new and additional' financial resources. There is no agreed definition of 'new and additional'. Annex II parties are expected to include their definition when they report the financial resources they provide to developing countries. Some do not report the definition they use and the rest employ several different definitions (UNFCCC 2011a). In the context of the fast start finance (US$30 billion for 2020–2012) pledged in the Copenhagen Accord, researchers have proposed various criteria, which when applied to the pledges, indicate that proportions ranging from virtually none to almost all are new and additional.[12]

A definition of the 'full incremental costs' has not yet been agreed, so the financial resources that should be provided to developing countries for mitigation measures under Article 4.3 of the Convention cannot be estimated accurately. Similarly, the share of the costs of adaptation that should be covered by international assistance has not been agreed, so the financial resources that should be provided to developing countries for adaptation measures under Article 4.4 of the Convention cannot be estimated accurately. Nevertheless, the available estimates of mitigation and adaptation costs provide useful information on the order of magnitude of the financial resources that may be needed.

1.4 Costs of mitigation

Energy efficiency measures illustrate the difficulty of determining the full incremental costs of mitigation measures. Every analysis of options for stabilizing atmospheric concentrations of GHGs indicates that energy efficiency plays a major role. Economic analyses of energy efficiency measures indicate that they are good investments, but a variety of barriers impede their adoption. The full incremental cost could be argued to be zero (or even negative) as the measures are economically attractive. Or the cost of government programmes to stimulate adoption of the measures could be argued to be the incremental cost. Or the incremental cost could be argued to be the incremental capital cost of the measures. Each of these approaches yields a significantly different estimate of the full incremental cost and hence the scale of the financial resources to be provided.

Renewable energy, another significant component of any stabilization strategy, raises a similar issue. Renewables typically have a higher capital cost and lower operating costs than the fossil-fired sources they replace. The full incremental cost could be argued to be the higher capital cost or the higher capital cost less the present value of the operating cost savings. Grid-connected renewables may require higher (or lower) transmission and distribution system investment, which may be borne by a utility rather than the owner of the renewable generating unit. Similarly, energy efficiency measures typically reduce transmission and distribution system investment. Should the change in the transmission and distribution system investment be reflected in the incremental cost?

These examples illustrate that it is important to specify from whose perspective the incremental cost is to be calculated: the owner of the specific measure, a larger entity (such as the electricity system), or the country as a whole. Adopting a national perspective further complicates the calculations.[13] Demand for fossil fuels will be lower, so the investment needed for facilities to produce, process, transport and store those fuels will be reduced. Those savings should then be reflected in lower incremental costs to the country for the mitigation measures it implements. In practice, it may not be possible for a government to capture those savings from the fossil-fuel suppliers and use them to stimulate mitigation measures, in which case the financial support provided for the mitigation measures may not be sufficient to promote their implementation.

The literature is extensive on the cost of climate change mitigation is extensive reflecting a variety of baseline projections, reduction targets, discount rates and other assumptions, as well as different bottom-up and top-down methodologies. Successive reports of the Intergovernmental Panel on Climate Change (IPCC) assess that literature.[14] These studies usually adopt a societal perspective. Some studies report the distribution of costs by country or region. The net cost to a developing country/region could be interpreted as an estimate of the incremental cost to the country/region. That assumes governments are able to capture any savings and apply the funds to the incremental costs of mitigation measures in the country/region.

Some climate finance analyses focus on the incremental *investment* associated with the mitigation measures, while other analyses focus on the incremental *cost* (Olbrisch *et al.*, Chapter 3). When financial incentives are offered they are often linked to the capital cost and paid when the investment is made. Incremental *investment* analyses therefore provide information on the possible scale and timing of the finance needed for mitigation measures. Investment analyses are also much simpler because they do not need data on equipment lifetimes and operating costs or an assumption as to the appropriate discount rate. However, investment analyses ignore the operating cost savings associated with many mitigation measures, such as energy efficiency and renewables.

The operating cost savings are captured by estimates of the incremental *cost*. The calculation of the incremental cost is much more complex than calculating the incremental investment, but the methods and experience of the mitigation cost literature can be applied. The incremental cost estimates depend on a variety of assumptions about the future and on the discount rate used. The estimated incremental cost is usually much lower than the corresponding incremental investment due to the operating cost savings.

1.5 Costs of adaptation

Determining the 'costs of adaptation' is even more challenging (Smith *et al.*, Chapter 4; Narain *et al.*, Chapter 5). Unlike mitigation, there is no operational definition that can be used to specify adaptation measures and then estimate the associated capital and operating costs. Instead, estimates are prepared separately by sector by comparing the cost under a scenario based on the current climate with the cost under a scenario based on the projected future climate – for example, water supply given the current and the projected future climate – which is uncertain.

The list of sectors covered and their definitions vary, but usually include infrastructure, coastal zones, water supply, agriculture, fisheries, forests and human health.[15] Some studies also include extreme weather events, storm-water management, natural ecosystems and tourism. Estimates are almost always limited to the costs of 'hard' adaptation measures such as the construction of sea walls. The costs of 'soft' adaptation measures, such as capacity building and information systems, are rarely estimated but are probably small relative to the 'hard' costs.

The baseline assumes that each sector is, or will be, well adapted to the current climate. The adaptation needed to cope with the projected future climate must be specified. Adaptation measures that are economically optimal or that maintain welfare can be specified. Economically optimal adaptation measures yield marginal benefits (reduced damages) equal to their marginal costs. This can be difficult to apply in sectors where damages, such as loss of ecosystems, are difficult to value. Identifying adaptation measures that enable residents to enjoy the same level of welfare that they would have without climate change is easier.[16]

Additional difficulties arise in moving from the specified adaptation measures to the cost of adaptation. The adaptation measures specified provide some degree of resilience to the uncertain future climate. What is the appropriate level of climate resilience? Is increased resilience an adaptation cost or a benefit? Regardless of the measures specified, residual damage may (be expected to) occur; are these damages an adaptation cost? Climate change may generate benefits in some sectors; should those benefits offset adaptation costs in another sector?

The close link between adaptation and development adds further complications. Adaptation may help achieve development ends and development may facilitate adaptation (McGray *et al.*, 2007; Fankhauser and Burton, Chapter 11; Smith *et al.*, Chapter 4). Conceptually, it is possible to define a 'development deficit' in terms of appropriate infrastructure, coastal protection, water supply, healthcare and other facilities and services, and an 'adaptation deficit' in terms of infrastructure, coastal protection, water supply, healthcare and other facilities and services that are not suited to the current climate variation (Burton, 2004). In practice, it can be difficult to determine whether a specific activity is a development activity or an adaptation measure, and hence whether the cost is an adaptation cost.

Adaptation, unlike mitigation, does not have a large body of literature to draw on to help answer these questions. Recent analyses include estimates of investment (UNFCCC, 2007) as well as costs (Narain *et al.*, Chapter 5). The relationship, if any, between estimates of investment and costs is not yet known. Any assessment of costs must specify 'to whom'. To deal with this issue, the Economics of Adaptation to Climate Change (EACC) study presents costs using three aggregation methods – gross (no netting of costs), net (benefits are netted across sectors and countries), and X-sums (positive and negative items are netted within countries but not across countries) (Narain *et al.*, Chapter 5).[17]

1.6 Range of the estimates

Given the differences in scope, methodology and assumptions, it should not be a surprise that the available estimates of mitigation and adaptation investment/costs span a wide range. Estimates of the incremental investment needed for mitigation action in developing countries range from US$175 billion to US$565 billion in 2030. Although there are fewer estimates of the incremental cost, they are substantially lower: US$140–175 billion per year in 2030. The studies assessed by the IPCC translate into a range of approximately US$50– 625 billion for developing country mitigation costs in 2030.[18]

The UNFCCC estimated that in 2030 developing countries will need US$30–60 billion per year of incremental investment for adaptation (UNFCCC, 2007). The EACC estimated that costs for the developing world of adapting to an approximately 2°C warmer world by 2050 are in the range of US$75–100 billion a year (Narain *et al.*, Chapter 5). Parry *et al.* (2009) found that adaptation costs in developing countries will be substantially higher than estimated by previous studies, but their estimate includes significant amounts for reduction of the development deficit, residual damages and adaptation of natural ecosystems.

As an order of magnitude, then, the current estimates suggest that climate finance of at least US$200 billion per year is needed by 2030, roughly balanced between mitigation and adaptation. To put this into perspective, official development assistance currently totals about US$120 billion per year. In the Copenhagen Accord, developed countries committed to a goal of mobilizing US$100 billion dollars per year by 2020 to meet the needs of developing countries.

1.7 Generating the financial resources

As discussed in section 1.2 current climate finance–financial flows to mitigation and adaptation activities in developing countries– amounts to almost US$100 billion per year. If climate finance of the order of US$200 billion per year is needed by 2030, it could be largely met by fulfilling the Copenhagen Accord commitment to mobilize US$100 billion annually by 2020 if all of that funding is new and additional.

The UN Secretary General's High-Level Advisory Group on Climate Change Finance (AGF) was tasked with assessing potential options to generate another US$100 billion per year of climate change funding by 2020 to meet the Copenhagen Accord commitment (AGF, 2010; Chapter 7). The AGF assessed a number of potential sources in terms of the amount they might generate and against several qualitative criteria including political and technical feasibility. The AGF concluded that no single source is able to generate US$100 billion per year, but that it is feasible, but challenging, to meet the goal with a portfolio ('bundle') of sources. However, it could not agree on a recommended mix of funding sources. The AGF recognized that different sources will be needed for different types of actions; for example, grants and highly concessional loans are crucial for adaptation in the most vulnerable developing countries. It also noted that funds could be mobilized more quickly from some sources than from others.

G20 Finance Ministers requested the World Bank Group, in partnership with the IMF, the OECD and the Regional Development Banks, to build upon and extend the work of the AGF (World Bank and others 2011: Chapter 8). The report recommends the removal of subsidies for fossil fuel use in Annex II countries; implementation of a comprehensive carbon charge or emissions trading with full auctioning of allowances in Annex II countries; a global carbon charge or emissions trading with full auctioning of allowances for international aviation and maritime bunker fuels; expanded carbon offset markets, such as the Clean Development Mechanism; a modest package of public sources, multilateral development bank flows and carbon offset flows to leverage climate-related private flows; and increased capital contributions to multilateral development banks.

Grubb (Chapter 9) proposes a new option: revenue from border levies imposed by developed countries on products imported from developing countries. The levies would deter production shifts to developing countries that do not have

GHG emission control policies and so would address competitiveness and emissions leakage concerns. With levies on imported products, developed countries could raise revenue from domestic producers through a carbon tax or auctioned allowances. Those revenues would be much larger than those raised by the levies, so developed countries might agree to dedicate the revenue from the border levies to financing mitigation and adaptation actions in developing countries.

Bowen (Chapter 6) discusses principles for raising public funds for climate finance in a world where some countries have emissions limitation commitments and others don't. Those principles include imposing a tax on (or auctioning allowances for) greenhouse gas emissions and removing subsidies that encourage emissions. Such policies raise revenue while helping to reduce emissions. Measures, such as border tax adjustments, likewise can raise revenue and reduce the emissions 'leakage' due to the shift of emitting activities to countries without commitments thus making the mitigation policies more effective. Applying a tax or auctioned allowances to international aviation emissions also raises revenue and helps to deter leakage. These principles underlie many of the potential options analysed by the AGF and the report for the G20 finance ministers.

Chapter 10 compares the estimates of different groups by source. The amounts that could be generated by public sources range from US$1 billion to US$40 billion per year. Funds generated by many of these sources will flow into national treasuries. Then the amounts to be provided for climate finance in developing countries, and the channels through which the funds are delivered, will be subject to national budgetary processes. Much of the revenue raised is likely to be retained by developed countries for domestic purposes. Regulation of international aviation and shipping emissions is the only option with the potential to raise significant funds internationally.

Although the economic crisis makes fulfillment of commitments to increase climate finance more difficult, the resources are still needed by developing countries where rapid economic growth continues. Funding sources that put a price on greenhouse gas emissions are particularly well suited to be put in place during periods of low economic growth. They increase the overall efficiency of the economy and are counter-cyclical so they have a modest impact on prices during periods of crisis. They would also generate much needed revenue beyond that required for climate finance; as much as US$150–200 billion per year for developed country national treasuries. The treasuries could use this revenue to help reduce their deficits and debt or to reduce existing distortionary taxes and so help stimulate economic growth.

1.8. Delivering climate finance

At present, climate finance is delivered on a project basis–funding is provided for implementation of specific mitigation or adaptation projects by the bilateral/multilateral funding entities or the CDM (OECD, 2011). A significant increase in the scale of climate finance will require a different approach to delivery; funds will need to be provided for mitigation or adaptation plans with sectoral or national scope, such as a National Adaptation Programme (NAP) or a Nationally Appropriate Mitigation Action (NAMA). The decision adopted in Cancun encourages developing countries to develop low-carbon development strategies or plans in the context of sustainable development.[19]

Bowen (Chapter 6) implicitly makes the same point when he notes that the most efficient way to finance mitigation measures is for governments to adopt policies that address GHG emissions and other market failures.[20] Emitters, mainly the private sector, will then finance and implement measures to reduce their emissions. There may be a net cost to developing countries that adopt such policies that, in principle, would be covered by international financial support. In practice, calculating the cost would be difficult.

With limited financial resources to address climate change, it is important that they be used efficiently and effectively. Fankhauser and Burton (Chapter 11) discuss how to allocate adaptation funding and suggest that further institutional reform may be needed. National governments are better able to address regional and temporal equity of adaptation measures than international bodies (OECD, 2010). That suggests funding national adaptation programmes or low-carbon development strategies or plans. The close link between adaptation and development points in the same direction. However, funding national programmes implies country funding allocations, which have been very difficult to agree internationally.

Mitigation funding is currently tied largely to actual or projected emission reductions. Emission reductions are calculated using assumptions that vary with the measure, so the amounts can be manipulated. Ultimately, successful mitigation means there are no further emission reductions, so this 'product' disappears. Zadek (Chapter 12) argues that instead of continuing to fund this obsolete 'product' it is better to link mitigation funding to desirable goods, such as electricity produced by renewable sources, in the context of a sustainable development plan.

1.9 New institutional arrangements

At Cancun (2010) and Durban (2011) parties agreed on a new institutional architecture for international climate finance under the UNFCCC (Chapter 13). Both the Standing Committee and the Green Climate Fund should become operational in 2013. The Standing Committee's mandate to organize a forum for exchange of information among the bodies and entities dealing with climate change finance may improve coherence and efficiency across the numerous bilateral and multilateral funding channels both under and outside the UNFCCC. All would benefit from better information on the climate finance needed, the climate finance currently provided and coordination of activities.

The size of the Green Climate Fund is not yet clear. With dedicated sources of international funding, such as revenue from regulation of international aviation and shipping emissions, the GCF could be the largest single source of international climate finance by a substantial margin. Then the GCF could adjust its funding allocation to complement that of other channels, so its policies would influence the overall pattern of climate finance. But if the GCF is funded through voluntary contributions from developed country governments it will be just one of many small funds. It will need to compete for funds with each country's bilateral agencies and with other multilateral agencies.

1.10 Conclusions

Work on climate finance is clearly just beginning. Some rough estimates of the cost of mitigation and adaptation in developing countries are available. However, many conceptual and methodological issues remain to be resolved, especially for adaptation.

Agreement has not yet been reached on what portion of the cost should be financed internationally, how the funds should be delivered, or the sources of the funds. Information on the scale of existing finance is sketchy. However, there is agreement that much more funding is needed and a commitment to increase funding significantly.

Increased funding will require a shift away from funding specific projects to supporting sectoral or national mitigation and adaptation programmes. The close links between development and adaptation and mitigation and economic growth will present new challenges in terms of effective programme design and funding decisions.

Notes

 1 UNFCCC (2007: 172).
 2 UNFCCC (2007: 176).
 3 UNFCCC (2010, Article 8).
 4 UNFCCC (2010, Article 8).
 5 UNFCCC (2011, paras. 95 and 98).
 6 UNFCCC (2011, para. 102).
 7 UNFCCC (2011, para. 109).
 8 Data on the total cost of climate change action is not available for any developed or developing country.
 9 Although there is an agreed reporting format, the UNFCCC secretariat notes that many data gaps and inconsistencies persist in the reporting approaches of Annex II Parties. Annex II Parties also report how they have engaged the private sector in mobilizing additional resources, particularly for mitigation.
10 The SCCF and LDCF are managed by the GEF.
11 CERs are issued for certified emission reductions achieved by clean development mechanism (CDM) projects in developing countries. Two per cent of the CERs issued for most CDM projects are provided to the Adaptation Fund. The Fund sells the CERs and uses the proceeds for adaptation projects in developing countries.
12 Brown *et al.* (2010); Stadelmann *et al.* (2010).
13 Narain *et al.* (Chapter 5) illustrate this effect for adaptation costs by reporting the gross sum, net sum and X-sum. The X-sum is the net sum within each country but not across countries.
14 See Metz *et al.* (2007) for the latest assessment.
15 To illustrate differences in sectoral definitions, food processing may or may not be included in the agriculture sector.

16 The water supply system could be designed to provide the same volume of potable water, for example. However, in a warmer climate more water might be needed for irrigation. Also, equivalent service might be provided using a variety of conservation measures. Thus, equivalent welfare can also be difficult to specify in operational terms.

17 This does not, of course, address other issues such as the use of different discount rates for private and public entities.

18 Metz *et al.* (2007, Table SPM.4) report a range of global GDP reduction in 2030 for stabilization at 535–590 ppm CO_2e of 0.2–2.5 per cent. Global GDP in 2030 is projected to be of the order of US$ 50 trillion. So the global costs would be US$ 100–1,250 billion, of which approximately half would occur in developing countries.

19 UNFCCC (2011b, para. 65). Countries also agreed that developed countries should develop low-carbon development strategies or plans (para. 45).

20 Other market failures include barriers that inhibit the adoption of energy efficiency measures and underfunding of research and development.

References

Brown, J., N. Bird and L. Schalatek, 2010, *Climate finance additionality: emerging definitions and their implications*, Heinrich Böll Foundation, North America.

Buchner, B., A. Falconer, M. Hervé-Mignucci, C. Trabacchi, and M. Brinkman, 2011, *The Landscape of Climate Finance*, Climate Policy Initiative, Venice.

Burton, I., 2004, 'Climate change and the adaptation deficit', in: A. French *et al.* (eds), *Climate Change: Building the Adaptive Capacity*, Environment Canada, Ottawa, 25–33.

McGray, H., A. Hamill, R. Bradley, E.L. Schipper and J.-O. Parry, 2007, *Weathering the Storm: Options for Framing Adaptation and Development*, World Resources Institute, Washington, DC.

Metz, B., O.R. Davidson, P.R. Bosch, R. Dave and L.A. Meyer, (eds), 2007, *Climate Change 2007: Mitigation of Climate Change*, Contribution of Working Group III to the Fourth Assessment Report of the Intergovernmental Panel on Climate Change, Cambridge University Press, Cambridge, UK.

OECD, 2011, *Development Perspectives for a Post-Copenhagen Climate Financing Architecture*, OECD, Paris (available at www.oecd.org/47/52/47115936.pdf).

Parry, M., N. Arnell, P. Berry, D. Dodman, S. Fankhauser, C. Hope, S. Kovats, R. Nicholls, D. Satterthwaite, R. Tiffin and T. Wheeler, 2009, *Assessing the Costs of Adaptation to Climate Change: A Review of the UNFCCC and Other Recent Estimates*, International Institute for Environment and Development and the Grantham Institute for Climate Change, Imperial College London, London.

Stadelmann, M., J.T. Roberts and A. Michaelowa, 2010, *Keeping a big promise: options for baselines to assess 'new and additional' climate finance*, Center for Comparative and International Studies (CIS), University of Zurich, Zurich.

Stern, N., 2006, *Stern Review on the Economics of Climate Change*, HM Treasury, London.

United Nations, 2010, *Report of the Secretary-General's High-Level Advisory Group on Climate Change Financing*, United Nations, New York [available at www.un.org/wcm/content/site/climatechange/pages/financeadvisorygroup/pid/13300].

UNFCCC, 2007, *Investment and Financial Flows to Address Climate Change*, UNFCCC Secretariat, Bonn.

UNFCCC, 2010, *Copenhagen Accord*, Decision 2/CP.15, UNFCCC Secretariat, Bonn [available at http://unfccc.int/resource/docs/2009/cop15/eng/11a01.pdf].

UNFCCC, 2011a, Subsidiary Body for Implementation, 'Compilation and Synthesis of Fifth National Communications', Addendum, Financial Resources, Technology Transfer, Vulnerability, Adaptation and Other Issues Relating to the Implementation of the Convention by Parties included in Annex I to the Convention', FCCC/SBI/2011/INF.1/Add.2, Bonn, 6–16 June 2011.

UNFCCC, 2011b, Outcome of the Work of the Ad Hoc Working Group on Long-Term Cooperative Action Under the Convention, Draft Decision 1/CP.16, UNFCCC Secretariat, Bonn [available at http://unfccc.int/files/meetings/cop_16/application/pdf/cop16_lca.pdf].

World Bank, International Monetary Fund, Organization for Economic Cooperation and Development, African Development Bank, Asian Development Bank, European Bank for Reconstruction and Development, European Investment Bank and Inter-American Development Bank, 2011, *Mobilizing Climate Finance*, Paper prepared at the request of G-20 Finance Ministers. [Available (together with background papers) at http://climatechange.worldbank.org/content/ mobilizing-climate-finance].

2 The landscape of climate finance

Barbara Buchner, Angela Falconer,
Morgan Hervé-Mignucci, and
Chiara Trabacchi

2.1 Introduction

Climate finance has been a key topic in recent international climate negotiations, resulting in a 2009 Copenhagen commitment by developed countries to jointly mobilize US$100 billion per year by 2020 to address the needs of developing countries.

A number of organizations and initiatives actively monitor, track and analyse different pieces of climate finance, and since Copenhagen, these efforts have multiplied. Nevertheless, it remains difficult to obtain a clear picture of how *much* climate finance is flowing, from *where* and to *whom* it is flowing, and what *types* of finance are flowing.

A better understanding of current flows is critical to build trust among countries that there is adequate support is being provided where it is needed. Shedding light on the current situation can also inform the debate on the definitional scope of commitments. For instance, it is still not clear whether all North-South financial flows for mitigation and adaptation activities should be counted against commitments, including both incremental support ('free money' in the form of grants, concessional components of concessional loans and policy incentives) and capital investment flows (in the form of commercial loans and equity). Moreover, information on current flows is needed to assess whether the right mix of finance is being provided to put countries on low-carbon, climate-resilient development pathways and, as such, whether limited financial resources are being spent in the most productive way. Information on how much finance is being delivered, in what forms, by whom and to which activities provides the basis from which we can start to understand how public (domestic and foreign) incremental cost support can best be aligned with private investment capital.

This chapter describes the current status of the climate finance landscape, mapping its magnitude and nature along the life cycle of finance flows, i.e. the sources of finance, intermediaries involved in distribution, financial instruments, and final uses. It first outlines the methodology and framework used for the analysis, then presents estimates of current flows based on available data, before making recommendations to improve future data-gathering efforts.

2.2 Methodology

The analysis aims to paint as comprehensive a picture as possible of the landscape of climate finance by compiling data from a wide range of sources: from international organizations like the Organization for Economic Cooperation and Development (OECD), to private sector sources like Bloomberg New Energy Finance (BNEF), as well as Non-Government Organizations (NGOs) like the Overseas Development Institute (ODI). The analysis uses three major sources of information: 1) existing databases, tracking initiatives, and studies compiled by various organizations; 2) third-party expertise, when official numbers were lacking or did not appropriately portray the related flow; 3) our own estimates, when no satisfactory official/third-party numbers were available.

Combining data from different sources presents a number of methodological difficulties, some of which we have been able to account for (e.g. double counting of the same flows), others less so (e.g. differing definitions and time periods).

The analysis captures the following types of climate finance:

- Financial flows from developed to developing countries (North-South), predominantly. Despite their growing importance, flows from developing to developing countries (South-South) and domestic climate finance flows in developing countries are captured to a limited extent due to data availability constraints.
- Public, private, and public-private flows.
- Incremental cost and investment capital: both are an important lens on climate finance flows. The former refers to financial resources provided to compensate the difference between a less costly, more polluting option and a costlier, more environmentally-friendly and/or climate-resilient one. Investment capital refers to tangible investment in mitigation or adaptation projects. Incremental costs are like revenues to recipients, whereas capital investment needs to be paid back. Incremental costs often make the difference in the final investment decision, influencing where investors decide to put their money, and are generally funded by public climate finance resources through policy support or concessional finance. Almost all costs associated with REDD+[1] measures are incremental costs (see Chapter 3).
- Gross not net flows; due to lack of data on the latter. The gross approach reflects the full volume of financial flows delivered through all instruments and is limited by the fact that it also includes money that has to be paid back by recipients i.e. concessional and non-concessional loans and equity.
- Annual commitments not disbursements, due to limited availability of disbursement data. Commitments are likely to be higher than annual disbursements, and data are usually not adjusted *ex-post* for cancellations or amendments to the actual value of support provided, leading to potential overestimates of financial amounts.
- Financial support for mitigation and adaptation activities, including capacity-building and R&D, as well as broader efforts to enable the transition towards low-carbon, climate-resilient development.

To make the analysis as relevant as possible, annual estimates of financial flows are presented for the most recent year for which data were available. Figures presented are often calculated using multi-year data and by aggregating annual estimates of climate finance from different years. While far from ideal, the estimates provide an indication of the scale of current flows. The data presented mostly relate to flows in 2009/2010, based on analysis carried out between October 2010 and October 2011 (Buchner *et al.*, 2011a[2]). Future studies should aim for consistency in reporting years and definitions to allow trend analysis.

The authors therefore acknowledge that there remains ample room for improvement in the estimates presented, often due to the lack of readily available or consistent data sources. For instance, only a selection of bilateral and multi-lateral development banks is currently included in our estimates, and the contribution of global capital markets to climate finance through bilateral and multilateral agencies and climate funds has not yet been quantified due to data availability and methodological difficulties.

2.3 Framing the landscape of climate finance

A comprehensive picture of climate finance is multi-dimensional, involving many pieces of information both on the type of finance and how finance flows from the donor to the recipient and, ultimately, within the recipient structure.

Two dimensions can help structure and systematize this information:

- A horizontal dimension that represents the life cycle of financial flows. How is finance flowing from the source to the final use? How are these flows assembled by source of finance and country of origin? How are they transferred and disbursed?
- A vertical dimension that describes what types of financial flows and inter-mediary channels are being used. Are they public finance, private finance or public–private finance flows? Climate-specific vehicles or general bilateral flows? Flows managed by International Finance Institutions or directly by the government/private sector? Incremental finance or investment finance?

Figure 2.1 illustrates this framework and taxonomy of climate finance, highlight-ing the categories along these dimensions.

2.4 The landscape of climate finance

Figure 2.2 – the 'spaghetti diagram' – summarizes the analysis of the current landscape of climate finance flows along their life cycle. The width of the arrows in the diagram represents the relative size of the flows. Our estimate includes predominantly developed to developing country flows, capturing only to a very limited extent developing to developing country and domestic developing country flows.

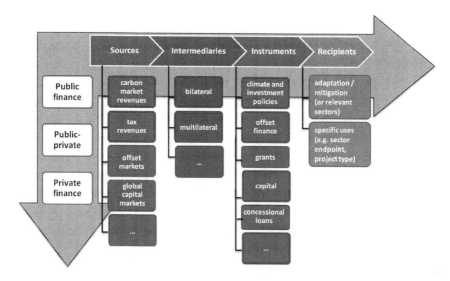

Figure 2.1 The dimensions of climate finance.
Source: Buchner *et al.*, 2011b.

The analysis suggests that at least US$97 billion per annum of climate finance is currently being provided to support low-carbon, climate-resilient development activities, with US$74–87 billion provided in the form of investment capital and US$7–20 billion as support for incremental costs.

The following sections of this chapter describe in more detail each element of the landscape and include estimated volumes of flows where data are available.

2.5 Sources of climate finance

Current sources of climate finance include both public money from general taxes and carbon pricing mechanisms, philanthropy, offset markets and private finance. Estimates of the current volume of finance provided by each source are presented in Table 2.1.

Carbon market revenues comprise proceeds from sales and auctions of carbon assets to cap-and-trade compliance buyers, and originate from carbon constrained economic sectors or countries. The current scale of these revenues can be esti-mated taking into account auctions organized in countries with cap-and-trade systems, most importantly the EU Emissions Trading System (EU ETS) and sales from Assigned Amount Units (AAUs) between countries bound by the Kyoto Protocol. Based on the available data, we estimate that carbon market revenues reached US$1.98 billion in 2010, US$1.40 billion of which was derived from EU ETS auctioning[3] and US$0.58 billion from AAU transactions.

Carbon taxes can be both explicit (i.e. applied on greenhouse gas emissions) and implicit (e.g. energy taxes or fuel taxes). No effort to produce an aggregate

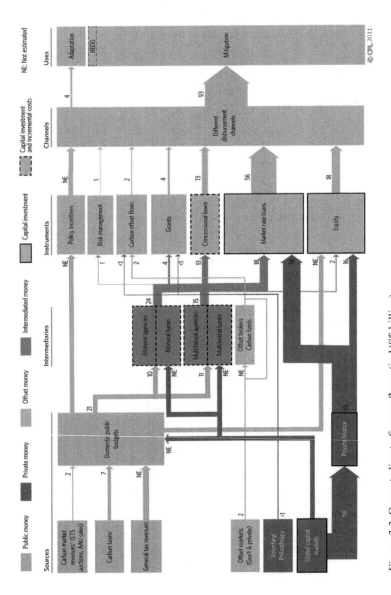

Figure 2.2 Current climate finance flows (in US$ billion).

Source: Climate Policy Initiative (CPI).

Note: Figures presented are indicative estimates of annual flows for the latest year available, 2009/2010 (variable according to the data source). Figures are expressed in US$ billion and are rounded to produce whole numbers. Estimates spanning multiple years are adjusted to produce annual-equivalent estimates. Where ranges of estimates are available, the mid-point is presented. All flows are incremental except for those identified as full or partial 'capital investment'. Most data presented relate to commitments in a given year, due to limited availability of disbursement data.

*Estimated carbon pricing revenues indicated are not necessarily wholly hypothecated for climate finance.

Table 2.1 Sources of climate finance

Source	Annual flow (2009/2010, US$ billion)
Carbon market revenues (EUAs auctioning, AAU transactions)	2.0
Carbon taxes	7.0
General tax revenues	Not estimated
Offsets markets	2.3
Voluntary/philanthropy	0.5
Global capital markets	Not estimated
Private finance	37–72.2
Domestic public budgets	21.2

Note: EUA, European Union Allowance; AAU, Assigned Amount Unit.

figure of carbon or energy tax revenues and earmarking has been identified so far. According to Chaire Economie du Climat (CEC, 2011), annual carbon tax revenues from Finland, Norway, Sweden, Denmark, Switzerland, and Ireland are estimated to be close to US$7 billion.[4]

General tax revenues generally pass through domestic public budgets before being allocated to particular objectives, such as international climate finance. As such, it is difficult to calculate precisely the extent of general tax revenues directed towards international climate finance, and this study refrains from providing an estimate for this source.

All of the sources discussed above flow through *domestic public budgets* in developed or developing countries (i.e. finance from national taxes, including traditional taxes, and from carbon pricing mechanisms and sovereign bond issuances). Moreover, general budget support–which by definition is not earmarked in any way–could represent a potential additional source of climate finance. Climate finance originating from domestic public budgets can flow through intermediaries (i.e. bilateral and multilateral agencies, banks, or climate funds), or flow directly to policy incentives and to capital instruments in the case of direct government ownership and state-owned banks active in climate finance investments.

The best systematic source of data on public North-South flows of climate finance is the OECD's Creditor Reporting System Aid Activities (OECD CRS) database (OECD, 2011a) which provides an estimate of US$9.5 billion *bilateral aid* with climate mitigation objectives provided by 22 DAC countries in 2009.[5] Financial contributions made by Annex II Parties to multilateral institutions over the 2005–2010 reporting period, reported in 5th National Communications, total US$44 billion, or an estimated US$11 billion per annum, however this could be an underestimate as many Parties have experienced difficulties in identifying what share of their multilateral contributions are climate related.

The OECD also monitors *export credit volumes*. Export credits support export transactions by hedging risks for investors. While most forms of export credit are paid to the exporter and do not represent a North–South flow themselves, they can however play a key role in stimulating private low-emission investments in developing countries, and are therefore counted in the landscape of climate finance. The OECD (2011b) estimates the value of export credits directed to renewable energy and co-generation/district heating sectors at US$0.7 billion in 2009 (OECD statistics on export credits, 2010, as cited in Buchner *et al.*, 2011b).

Based on the available data, the volume of the annual domestic public budget flowing into the climate finance system is estimated to be at least US$21.2 billion, including donor reporting of contributions to multilateral institutions in the 5th UNFCCC National Communications and bilateral contributions reported through the OECD CRS system, plus an estimate of the volume of green export credits.

We estimate *voluntary/philanthropic* contributions flowing in the climate-finance landscape to be at least US$450 million per annum. Estimates of global philanthropic donations to tackle climate change in developing countries are not yet available. A 2007 report by California Environmental Associates estimated that US foundations provide approximately US$210 million per annum towards climate change-related interventions (CEA, 2007). Alongside pre-compliance activity, corporate social responsibility is one of the main drivers of the voluntary carbon market, an additional dimension of the climate finance landscape. In 2010, organizations' and individuals' purchases of voluntary carbon offsets – known as Voluntary Emission Reductions (VERs) – contributed approximately US$240 million to 'North–South' climate finance flows (Ecosystem Marketplace, 2011).

Offset markets as a source aggregates public and private money that supports emission reduction commitments or voluntary objectives through various offset projects. Most of these projects are currently related to the Kyoto Protocol's Clean Development Mechanism (CDM) and Joint Implementation (JI). We estimate only the incremental cost linked to carbon offsets, not the investment costs of corresponding emissions reduction projects which should theoretically be captured in other private investment estimates. As a first indication, we estimate the value of carbon offset finance flow between US$2.2[6] and US$2.3[7] billion in 2010. This range is calculated using data from the World Bank, the UNFCCC, and IGES to apply surveyed average annual primary carbon offset prices to the annual volume of offsets issued.[8]

Global capital markets raise money from institutional and individual investors through various forms of investment vehicles (equity, debt, and structured finance), thereby providing capital to governments, MDBs, BFIs, and multinational companies (including those labelled 'private finance', specifically investing in climate finance). Estimating global capital markets' contribution to climate finance flows is however difficult because of the large amount of information needed as well as data confidentiality issues.

There is no agreement on what exactly counts as *private climate finance*, given that profit-making is the main objective of private sector activity and capital flows. However, key outcomes and objectives can also include greenhouse mitigation and climate adaptation, and capital flows to activities with such outcomes should be counted as climate finance. An important component of private climate finance is the flows leveraged by the public sector.

Dedicated systems to track private climate finance are not currently in place. Hence, we consider 'green' Foreign Direct Investments (FDIs) estimates and investments in the renewable energy sector as proxies for private finance flows.

FDIs are defined as investments made by a resident entity in one economy with the objective of establishing a long-term interest in an enterprise located in another economy (UNCTAD, 2010; OECD, 2010a). The OECD (2011d) states that FDIs represent the biggest source of financing across private and public sources, and can play an important role in addressing climate change by favouring the transfer of environmentally-friendly technologies and know-how.

According to the United Nations Conference on Trade and Development (UNCTAD, 2010), from 2003 to 2009 global FDI flows in renewable electricity generation, recycling, and manufacturing of environmental technology products (such as wind turbines, solar panels, and biofuels)[9] reached a cumulative US$344 billion of which, US$90 billion occurred in 2009. Developing countries attracted approximately 40 per cent of these green FDI flows during the 2003–2009 period. Hence, we estimate 2009 'green' FDIs to developing countries to be approximately US$37 billion.

Meanwhile, the United Nations Environment Programme (UNEP) and BNEF (UNEP and BNEF, 2011) suggest that renewable energy investments in developing countries amounted to US$72.2 billion in 2010 (from developed countries, other developing countries, and private investment from national investors). Removing available data relative to public equity markets (initial public offerings, seasoned equity offering, etc.) would result in a US$66.2 billion flow.[10] We therefore use a range of US$66.2–72.2 billion.

Based on available data, we therefore estimate private finance to be between US$37.0 and 72.2 billion, or on average US$55 billion. It thus represents the largest component in the climate finance landscape, and directly flows into the 'capital' instrument categories (market rate loans and equity).

It is worth mentioning that pension funds are showing a greater yet still cautious interest in investments in environmentally-friendly infrastructure projects, but it is difficult to identify the investments by individual pension funds in the climate change sector as a number of them are not required to disclose this information.

2.6 Intermediaries

Most climate finance is not distributed directly by governments to end-users, but is distributed through government agencies and development banks. Agencies mostly rely on public money, while banks typically leverage public money with debt financing.

The principal intermediaries of climate finance are bilateral banks and multilateral banks and agencies. Several information systems currently track the portions of climate finance that flow through these intermediaries. Estimates of the current volume of finance passing through each intermediary are presented in Table 2.2.

Table 2.2 Intermediaries of climate finance

Intermediary	Annual flow (2009/2010, US$ billion)
Bilateral financial Institutions	22.8
Multilateral financial Institutions	12.2–16.5
Climate funds	1.1–3.2
Carbon funds	Not estimated

Bilateral Financial Institutions (BFIs) and bilateral funds are institutions or funds primarily belonging to, or governed by, individual countries. Based on OECD CRS data for bilateral aid (OECD, 2011a), data from individual BFIs where available,[11] and an estimate of green export credits, we estimate that the climate finance currently flowing from bilateral sources is approximately US$22.8 billion per annum.

Multilateral financial institutions (MFIs) and multilateral funds are institutions or funds with multiple governing members, including both borrowing developing countries and developed donor countries. Money that flows to MFIs includes (1) the proceeds of major borrowing programmes, (2) gross income from loans, investments, and shareholdings, and (3) direct contributions from donor countries to specific disbursement programs. Finance raised by MFIs on capital markets can come from a mix of public and private investors (banks, corporate, central banks, official institutions, fund managers, pension funds, insurers, etc.). Sources of finance vary from bank to bank, according to their mandates. Based on latest available estimates from the individual institutions, where available, we estimate the scale of climate finance flowing through multilateral financial institutions and funds to be between US$12.2 billion and US$16.5 billion per annum.[12]

In recent years, a number of bilateral and multilateral organizations have set up specialized *climate funds*. These funds are typically multi-donor, with one or more bilateral or multilateral organizations providing Trustee and administrative services to manage the funds 'off-balance sheet'. Funds tend to have finite life-times and a specific sectoral focus, e.g. renewables, adaptation, forestry, etc. Most existing climate funds are new, and have not yet disbursed large volumes of finance. Based on the ODI/HBF Climate Funds Update, research by the Stockholm Environment Institute (UNEP, 2010), and reporting by the organizations managing the funds themselves, we estimate annual commitments from climate funds and initiatives to range from approximately US$1.05 billion to US$3.2 billion.[13] Note, however, that there are strong overlaps with bilateral and multilateral donor reporting, and the aggregation is subject to various methodological difficulties, including different definitions and reporting years. Therefore, this range should be considered as indicative only of the scale of climate funds within the broader scope of bilateral and multilateral finance.

Carbon funds including those set up by public entities such as the International Finance Corporation (IFC) and private carbon offset brokerage houses such as EcoSecurities, Tricorona, and Camco, also act as climate finance intermediaries, investing in primary offset projects or purchasing secondary offsets from carbon markets on behalf of potential buyers. In 2010, *Carbon Finance* (Environmental Finance, 2011) profiled 97 operational carbon funds and five planned funds, which disclosed a total capitalization of US$15.22 billion, slightly less than what was reported in 2009 (US$15.68 billion). Given the difficulties in identifying an annual financial flow through these intermediaries to the carbon offset finance instrument, we do not include a specific figure in our overview of current finance flows.

2.7 Instruments

Seven major categories of instruments have been identified and the volume of annual flows of climate finance through each has been estimated where possible, as shown in Table 2.3.

Policy incentives include resources directed at regulatory reform and income-enhancing mechanisms, such as feed-in tariffs, tradable certificates, tax incentives, and clean energy subsidies, which are most commonly funded domestically although there are some examples of climate change policy loans supported by bilateral and multilateral agencies. Information available on policy support in developing countries is fragmented, this study does not estimate the volume of support provided annually at this stage.

The *risk management* category includes export credits, guarantees, and finance enhancing instruments. As outlined above, export credits directed at renewable energy and co-generation are estimated at US$0.7 billion for 2009. Guarantees are used to mitigate the risks involved in clean investments (e.g. risks related to non-payment, technology performance, or the fulfillment of obligations by government and affiliated agencies vis-à-vis a given project). Based on our review of donor reporting, we estimate annual guarantees in support of climate mitigation and adaptation to be at least US$347 million, (estimates were only available from the IFC, the Asian Development Bank (AsDB), and

Table 2.3 Climate finance instruments

Instrument	Annual Flow (2009/2010, US$ billion)
Policy incentives	Not estimated
Risk management	1.2
Carbon offset flows	2.5
Grants	4.5
Concessional loans	12.6
Market-rate loans	56.1
Equity	18.0

climate funds). Finance-enhancing instruments help improve the attractiveness of mitigation and adaptation projects by generating better credit ratings and reducing the cost of capital. However, no quantitative data for the flow through this instrument is currently available.

As outlined, US$2.5 billion is estimated to be delivered in the form of *carbon offset flows*, including voluntary offset markets.

Grants are transfers in cash or in kind for which no legal debt is incurred by the recipient (OECD, 2007a). Grants also include knowledge management programs (e.g. technical assistance, capacity building, knowledge hubs, etc.). There is no single source of information on the volume of climate finance provided through grants. Instead, estimates must be taken from the reporting of individual sources, including international finance institutions.

According to the OECD CRS database, 43.6 per cent of bilateral climate funding committed by DAC countries in 2009 was directed to ODA grants. In addition to OECD reporting (OECD, 2011a), individual international financial institutions (IFIs) provide information on the amount of their funding given as grants. We also assume that philanthropic sources of climate finance are channeled entirely through grant instruments. Based on available data, we estimate that annual climate finance flows delivered as grant instruments amount to approximately US$4.5 billion.

Concessional loans, also referred to as soft loans, include debt provided at an interest rate below the prevailing market rate. Concessional loans can be measured as either the total volume of finance provided at concessional rates or as the grant equivalent value of the concessional loan, reflecting the financial terms of the finance provided. However, comprehensive estimates of the grant equivalent value of concessional climate finance are not available, due at least in part to methodological difficulties. This paper therefore presents gross financial flows without taking into consideration the level of concession involved. There is no centralized source of information about financial flows provided through concessional instruments. Based on individual donor reports, we estimate annual concessional loan flows to be around US$13 billion per annum. Concessional loans are typically provided by bilateral and multilateral banks. While the principal loan amount needs to be paid back, the interest rate payments are significantly discounted. The discount can be characterized as 'aid'. Concessional loans can therefore be considered as both incremental and investment contributions, and include ownership interests where public bodies take on risk-return positions that a private investor would not bear.

Capital instruments include the transformation of capital contributions into shareholder ownership (equity), creditor claims (debt, loans, bonds, credit lines, etc.), and hybrid capital instruments. While we acknowledge the important distinction between market-rate loans and equity, the current data makes it challenging to disentangle the various capital contributions made by all actors from the broader capital class. Basic information is often confidential or not readily available, and complex ownership structures add further complications. Our estimates of loans and equity are based on information about the two main contributors to these instruments: IFIs and private finance. The breakdown of IFI finance between loans and equity is gleaned from IFI reporting and indicates a 92 per cent to 8 per cent split. Private finance estimates do not provide any indication of the split. As a proxy, we therefore apply a project finance debt-equity ratio of 70:30,[14] recognizing that this assumption has a significant impact, because the private finance flow is the largest in the landscape.

Overall then, we estimate that US$57–92 billion is channeled as capital instruments; a very rough proxy suggests that US$44–69 billion of this is channeled through market-rate loans and the remainder through equity.

2.8 Channels

Disbursement channels are those organizations that work directly to disburse funds for climate mitigation and adaptation projects, including those from the public sector, public–private partnerships (PPPs), multilateral organizations, NGOs, and civil society. They may be local, regional, national, or international organizations. There are few aggregated estimates of the split of finance by type of disbursement organization. Source–channel relationships could be investigated further to determine the types of partnerships being formed to deliver climate finance.

2.9 Uses

Climate finance is directed toward both mitigation (energy efficiency, renewable energy, forestry and agriculture, transport, industrial processes, and waste) and adaptation (water management, sanitation, forestry and agriculture, health, fishing, disaster prevention and preparedness, and capacity building) activities. Few estimates are available of the portion of total climate finance going to mitigation versus adaptation, or of the portions going to individual sectors of the economy. Estimates generated from this study are shown in Table 2.4.

Note that recent figures not accounted for in this analysis suggest that much more finance is flowing to adaptation activities: US$9.3 billion in 2010 from bilateral sources alone.[15]

The estimates presented above are calculated by:

- aggregating the reports of individual IFIs (including climate funds) on the portion of finance directed to mitigation versus adaptation;[16]

Table 2.4 Uses of climate finance

Use	Annual Flow (2009/2010, US$ billion)
Mitigation	92.5
REDD	0.7–1.9
Adaptation	4.4

- assuming that all private finance outflows and carbon offset flows (including finance generated on the voluntary carbon markets) are directed to mitigation;
- assuming that philanthropic contributions are directed to adaptation.

An attempt has also been made to estimate the scale of climate finance currently being directed to REDD+ schemes.

A bottom-up aggregation of estimates of bilateral, forest carbon market, and REDD+ fund flows suggests that current REDD+ flows could be in the region of US$0.7 billion per annum. Other organizations have, however, produced larger estimates. The World Bank (2008), for example, estimated *annual* bilateral and multilateral flows to forests to be approximately US$1.9 billion in 2005–07.[17]

2.10 Update for 2010–2011

The update has a broader geographic scope, expanded coverage of players, more detailed representation of private sector flows, an improved representation of uses by economic sector and a better understanding of the final users of climate finance (Buchner et al, 2012). Global climate finance commitments amounted to US$ 343–385 billion per year based on a mix of 2010 and 2011 data. Of that total, developing country climate finance commitments amounted to US$ 162 to 202 billion of which US$ 120 to 141 billion, including public funds of US$ 48 to 50 billion, was raised in developing countries. Developed countries raised US$ 213 to 255 billion, including US$ 43 to 50 billion from public sources, of which US$ 160 to 208 billion was committed to developed countries.

When the 2011 Landscape methodology and focus is applied to the 2010–2011 data the total climate finance flows predominantly directed toward developing countries amount to US$ 112 billion per year compared with US$ 97 billion per year for 2009–2010.

2.11 Conclusions

The analysis suggests that about US$97 billion per annum of climate finance is currently being provided to support low-carbon, climate-resilient development activities.

Of the estimated US$97 billion in global climate funding, on average US$55 billion is provided by the private sector in the form of direct equity and debt investments. The relatively small role of the public sector compared to the private sector is remarkable, in light of the debate in the global climate change negotiations where many have emphasized the need for developed countries to fund mitigation and adaptation in developing nations. The dominant role of the private sector is a reminder of the fact that capital investment is crucial for any mitigation and adaptation activities. The role of investment/ownership finance is striking. One can explain the large investment component in international climate finance as due to the lack, in many developing countries, of developed capital markets required to raise investment capital. The poorest countries must rely on development banks.

Indeed, most climate finance, US$74–87 billion out of US$97 billion, can be classified as investment or more generally including ownership interests. Around US$56 billion is in the form of market rate loans; of this amount, US$18 billion is through bilateral and multilateral institutions like IFC and AsDB while US$38 billion is through the private sector. Another US$18 billion is provided as equity, of which US$16 billion comes from the private sector. Because these loan and equity instruments must be paid back to investors over the investment horizon, they are not considered 'aid'.

The remainder of climate finance, between US$8 and 21 billion, is comprised of instruments such as policy incentives, risk management facilities, carbon offset flows and grants. These types of financing, which do not have to be (fully) paid back or enjoy a reduced interest rate, can be seen as 'aid' in the technical sense of the word. A surprisingly low volume of climate finance is provided in the form of grants (just US$4 billion), much more through concessional loans (US$13 billion) and the remainder through carbon offset flows (US$2 billion) and risk management mechanisms (US$1 billion). Policy incentive instruments are increasing in importance but their magnitude is not estimated as information tends to be fragmented. The relatively small role of carbon finance in the overall landscape stands in contrast to the high ambitions for carbon markets when the Kyoto Protocol came into force.

Intermediaries have a key role in climate finance, distributing around US$39 billion of climate finance a year (40 per cent of the total). Most of the public climate finance (US$24 billion) is currently provided by bilateral institutions (those sponsored by one nation) rather than multilateral institutions (like World Bank/IFC or AsDB), which distribute US$15 billion a year. The remainder of climate finance either flows directly through the capital markets, or is provided directly by governments. Important changes to the landscape of intermediaries are anticipated, however, as recipient countries increasingly seek to access sources of climate finance more directly and to limit the role of intermediaries.

The estimated split between mitigation and adaptation spending (95:5) contrasts with some of the rhetoric in global climate change negotiations where many countries and commentators have remarked that climate finance should be split 50:50.

Finally, it should be stressed that the estimates of current flows produced by this analysis cannot easily be compared to international climate finance pledges since a definition of 'full incremental costs' has not been agreed (Chapter 1). It is also difficult to put the estimates in the context of investment or incremental cost requirements as estimates of the latter are made on different methodological bases. In the case of investment requirements, existing estimates tend to refer to incremental (over and above an estimated baseline) rather than absolute investment requirements. However we can see that the estimate of current *total* capital investment in mitigation activities of US$74–87 billion is well below even the ranges of *incremental* investment requirements presented in Chapter 3 (US$117–565 billion in 2030). Estimates of current incremental cost support for mitigation, US$2.6–15.6, are also very low in comparison to existing estimates of incremental costs presented in Chapter 3 (US$139–175 billion).

2.12 Recommendations for climate finance tracking

The analysis of current climate finance flows highlights a number of key issues in climate finance tracking, and suggests that multiple improvements are required to overcome these challenges:

- The complex nature of climate finance and lack of agreed-upon definitions hamper tracking efforts. Inconsistencies in labeling and definitions of what constitutes climate finance exist. There needs to be a common set of definitions spanning all types of climate finance to allow data tracking and comparison.
- The various objectives of climate tracking efforts complicate the analysis. Various goals often require specific methods of analysis. Transparency and clarification regarding the objectives of specific climate finance tracking systems help to focus analytical and data-gathering efforts for global climate finance tracking.
- While there is a wealth of data on elements of the climate finance landscape, there is limited coordination and some gaps in data gathering. An expansion of our and others' efforts, and a platform to bring existing tracking initiatives together, could support a close dialogue between organizations active in this area, and improve the consistency, comprehensiveness, and overall quality of data.
- Several information gaps impede a better understanding of what is needed to enhance the effectiveness of climate finance. Inaccessible and inconsistent data on private finance flows, limited information on domestic and 'South–South' flows, and a lack of data at the instrument, disbursement, and use levels limit our understanding of the scale and effectiveness of climate finance efforts. New efforts to fill in those gaps are required.

A comprehensive picture of climate finance flows is essential for the success of international climate policy. Our study provides a first overview of the climate finance landscape and stimulates thinking and action on next steps in developing a comprehensive tracking system that ultimately helps countries learn how to spend money wisely.

Acknowledgements

This paper is adapted from the analysis presented in Buchner (2011a), to which we gratefully acknowledge the close dialogue and interaction sustained during that work with a number of organizations active in these areas, including, in alphabetical order, Agence Française de Développement, AidData.org, Asian Development Bank, Bloomberg New Energy Finance, Chatham House, Development Bank of Southern Africa, Ecofys, European Bank for Reconstruction and Development, European Climate Foundation, E3G, Global Canopy, Global Environmental Facility, International Finance Corporation, KfW Entwicklungsbank, McKinsey & Company, Organisation for Economic Co-operation and

Development, Overseas Development Institute, Stockholm Environmental Institute, The Nature Conservancy, UNEP, UNFCCC Secretariat, World Resources Institute, and the World Bank. Experts in these organizations were critical in helping us better understand the available data, and our work has benefited substantially from these many discussions. In particular the authors would like to acknowledge the helpful comments from Philippe Ambrosi, Julia Benn, Alexis Bonnel, Jessica Brown, Jan Corfee-Morlot, Pierre Forestier, Liz Galagher, Valerie Gauveau, Kirsty Hamilton, Jochen Harnisch, Ari Huthala, Celine Kaufmann, Johanna Lutterfelds, David McCauley, Ariane Meier, Chantal Naidoo, Charlie Parker, Clarisse Kehler-Siebert, Martin Stadelmann, Stacy Swann, Dennis Tirpak, Guy Turner, Eric Usher, Delia Villagrasa, Christiane Weber, and Ming Yang.

Notes

1 Reducing Emissions from Deforestation and forest Degradation, the sustainable management and conservation of forests, and the enhancement of carbon stocks.
2 2012 update forthcoming.
3 Some 67 million allowances are auctioned on average per annum, multiplied by an average price of EUR 15.80 per ton in 2010 implies revenues of US$1.40 billion.
4 CEC (2011) and data from the Ministries of Environment of the aforementioned countries. For countries with taxes that involve both an energy – and a CO_2 – component, only the share accruing to carbon taxes was considered in the estimate. Calculations are country specific. For an example using Denmark see Sumner *et al.* (2009).
5 Preliminary figures for 2010 show that total bilateral climate change-related aid (for both mitigation and adaptation) by members of the OECD's Development Assistance Committee (DAC) was US$22.9 billion in 2010. This significant jump compared to 2009 data may be due to the introduction of reporting of finance for climate change adaptation in addition to mitigation as well as the fact that 2010 is the first year of the Fast Start Finance 2010–2012 commitment period.
6 Based on (1) CDM: US$14.09/ton (the average primary CER price of the past 3 years in 2010 – using World Bank (2010b) data) and 132.4 million CERs issued in 2010 according to the UNFCCC and (2) JI: US$13.49/ton (the average primary ERU price of the past 3 years in 2010 – using World Bank (2010b) data), and an estimated issuance of ERUs of 23.4 million in 2010 (based on IGES issuance figures for track 2 projects and expected issuance of track 1 projects).
7 Based on (1) CDM: US$14.09/ton (the average primary CER price of the past 3 years in 2010 – using World Bank (2010a) data) and 143.2 million CERs issued in 2010 according to IGES and (2) JI: US$13.49/ton (the average primary ERU price of the past 3 years in 2010 – using World Bank (2010b) data) and an estimated issuance of ERUs of 23.4 million in 2010 (based on IGES issuance figures for track 2 projects and expected issuance of track 1 projects).
8 Details of actual primary carbon offset purchase prices are confidential and included in Emission Reduction Purchase Agreements. Estimates for unit prices of primary carbon offset include the World Bank (2010a), news and analytics providers (IDEAcarbon pCER index – http://www.ideacarbon.com/services/pcerindexnew.htm and PointCarbon – www.pointcarbon.com). Data on the amount of offsets issued can be found in the UNEP/RISØ, IGES, and UNFCCC Registry databases (http://cdmpipeline.org/ http://www.iges.or.jp/en/cdm/report.html and http://cdm.unfccc.int/Registry/index.html respectively).
9 Identifiable in the database of Greenfield projects. In its analysis, UNCTAD also examined and considered FDI data from cross-border M&A operations in renewable electricity generation.

10 'Public Markets' is excluded because money raised this way also covers overhead costs, can cover a single element of a renewable technology's value chain (solar PV cells), can go to R&D, can support investment in developed countries, can support refinancing operations, etc.

11 Including the French Development Agency (AFD), the German Development Bank (KfW), and the Japan International Cooperation Agency (JICA), the Brazilian Development Bank (BNDES), the China Development Bank, the Indian Renewable Energy Development Agency (IREDA), and the Overseas Private Investment Corporation.

12 The lower bound of the range is based on estimates from the IFC, IBRD, IDA, the AsDB, the AfDB, EIB, EU institutions, EBRD, IDB, the Nordic Development Fund, and the Nordic Investment Bank. The upper bound estimate is taken from the preliminary version of the Joint MDB Climate Financing Report (June 2010) and refers to 2009 MDB mitigation financing.

13 The lower bound estimate is taken from a UNEP (2010) report that includes: the Climate Investment Funds 2009 commitment of US$0.47 billion; US$0.24 billion channeled by the Global Environment Facility for climate change; US$0.15 billion made available by the Special Climate Change Fund and the Least Developed Countries Fund; and a lower bound estimate for commitments from other international specialized funds dedicated to climate change of US$0.19 billion. The upper bound estimate is based on a bottom-up aggregation of individual fund values.

14 This estimate is based on a survey of financial experts. The panel provided a range from 60 per cent to 80 per cent of debt. It was highlighted that the gearing level depended on several parameters relative to risks and returns (countries, sector, technologies, and investment stages notably). Moreover, this range would rather relate to renewable energy projects and might distort other mitigation projects a bit (energy efficiency investment for instance) or climate change adaptation.

15 Preliminary figures for 2010 show that total bilateral climate change-related aid by members of the OECD's Development Assistance Committee (DAC) was US$22.9 billion in 2010, representing about 15 per cent of total official development assistance. Of this total, two-thirds was for mitigation, and one-third for adaptation (OECD, 2011c).

16 Some assumptions are also involved in this aggregation, e.g. that all climate-marked flows reported in the CRS database in 2009 relate to mitigation, since the climate adaptation Rio Marker will be used only for reporting on flows from 2010 onwards. Furthermore, where the reporting of organizations is aggregated, variable definitions of mitigation or adaptation finance applied by individual organizations are relied upon.

17 This represents an increase of almost 50 per cent over 2000 levels, particularly due to increased multilateral activity, which accounted for US$0.8 billion in 2005–07. In the same study, Foreign Direct Investment (FDI) to forest industries were estimated to be approximately US$0.5 billion in 2003–05, however such flows are not necessarily related to mitigation activities.

Bibliography

AGF (2010) *Report of the Secretary-General's High-level Advisory Group on Climate Change Financing*, United Nations, New York, November 2010.

Buchner B., Brown L., and Corfee-Morlot J. (2011b) *Monitoring and Tracking Long-Term Finance to Support Climate Action*, OECD, COM/ENV/EPOC/IEA/SLT(2011).

Buchner, B., Falconer, A., Hervé-Mignucci, M., Trabacchi, C., and Brinkman, M. (2011a) *The Landscape of Climate Finance*, A CPI Report, 27 October 2011.

Buchner, B., Falconer, A., Hervé-Mignucci, M., and Trabacchi, C., (2012) The Landscape of Climate Finance 2012, A CPI Report, December 2012.

CEC (2011) 'Twenty years of carbon taxation in Europe: some lessons learned', Chaire Economie du Climat, Université Paris-Dauphine CDC Climat, *Information and Debates Series* No. 9, April 2011, available at: http://www.chaireeconomieduclimat.org/wp-content/uploads/2011/04/11-04-20-Cahier-IDn9-Elbeze-and-De-perthuis-EN.pdf

Ecosystem Marketplace (2011) Back to the Future: State of the Voluntary Carbon Markets 2011, Bloomberg New Energy Finance and Ecosystem Marketplace.

Environmental Finance (2011) 'Carbon Funds 2011', Environmental Finance, Carbon Finance, London, 2011 http://siteresources.worldbank.org/INTCC/Resources/Mapping_study_Final_for_FIP_Design_Meeting_Oct_16-17_08.pdf

OECD (2007a) *Reporting Directive for the Creditor Reporting System*, DCD/DAC(2007) 39/Final, Organisation for Economic Co-operation and Development (OECD), Paris, September 2007.

OECD (2011a) *Creditor Reporting System* _Full download file 'CRS 2009.zip', DAC Creditor Reporting System database, data downloaded 5th April 2011, http://stats.oecd.org/Index.aspx?DatasetCode=CRSNEW

OECD (2011b) *Financing Climate Change Action and Boosting Technology Change*, Organisation for Economic Co-operation and Development (OECD) Paris, flyer update March 2011, http://www.oecd.org/dataoecd/34/44/46534686.pdf

OECD (2011c) *First-Ever Comprehensive Data On Aid For Climate Change Adaptation*, November 2011, http://www.oecd.org/dataoecd/54/43/49187939.pdf

OECD (2011d) 'Defining and measuring Green FDI: An Exploratory Review of Existing Work and Evidence', (Note by the Secretariat) Organisation for Economic Co-operation and Development (OECD), *OECD Working Papers on International Investment*, No. 2011/2.

Sumner, J., Bird L., and. Smith, H. (2009) *Carbon Taxes: A Review of Experience and Policy Design Considerations, Technical Report* NREL/TP-6A2-47312, National Renewable Energy Laboratory, Golden, Colorado. http://www.nrel.gov/docs/fy10osti/47312.pdf

UNCTAD (2010) *World Investment Report 2010. Investing in a Low-Carbon Economy,* June 2010, United Nations, New York and Geneva.

UNEP (2010) *Bilateral Finance Institutions and Climate Change: a Mapping of 2009 Climate Financial Flows to Developing Countries*, United Nations Environment Programme.

UNEP and BNEF (2011) *Global Trends in Renewable Energy Investment 2011 Analysis of Trends and Issues in the Financing of Renewable Energy*, United Nations Environment Programme and Bloomberg New Energy Finance.

World Bank (2008) *Climate Investment Funds: Mapping of Existing and Emerging Sources of Forest Financing.* First Design Meeting on the Forest Investment Program, CIF/FDM.1/ 2, Washington, DC.

World Bank (2010a) *State and Trends of the Carbon Markets 2010*, Washington DC.

World Bank (2010b) World Development Report 2010: Development and Climate Change, Washington DC.

3 Estimates of incremental investment for, and cost of, mitigation measures in developing countries

Susanne Olbrisch, Erik Haites,
Matthew Savage, Pradeep Dadhich and
Manish Kumar Shrivastava

3.1 Introduction

This chapter reviews estimates of the incremental investment and incremental cost of mitigation action in developing countries. Numerous global, country and sectoral estimates have been prepared in recent years. The figures vary widely for a number of reasons. Mitigation measures to reduce projected 'business-as-usual' emissions are identified, and the associated investment or cost is estimated. The estimates are sensitive to the business-as-usual projection, the scale of the emission reductions targeted, the time horizon, the range of mitigation measures considered, the rate of technological change assumed, the discount rate and other factors.

Mitigation measures typically have a higher capital cost than the higher-emitting technologies they are assumed to replace. Some climate finance analyses focus on the incremental investment, whereas others focus on the incremental cost of the measures. When financial incentives are offered, they are often linked to the capital cost and paid when the investment is made. Analyses that focus on the incremental investment provide information on the possible scale and timing of the incentives needed to encourage adoption of mitigation measures. Investment analyses are also much simpler, because cost estimates need data on lifetimes and operating costs and an assumption regarding the appropriate discount rate. Many mitigation measures, such as energy efficiency and renewables, reduce operating costs, thus offsetting some or all of the higher capital cost. The incremental cost, then, is usually much lower than the incremental investment.

In the United Nations Framework Convention on Climate Change (UNFCCC), developed country Parties agreed to cover the 'agreed full incremental costs' of implementing mitigation measures (UNFCCC, 1992, Article 4.3).[1] A definition of the 'full incremental costs' has not yet been agreed, so the financial resources that should be provided to developing countries for mitigation measures cannot be determined precisely. Neither the incremental investment nor the incremental cost is likely to be equal to the agreed full incremental costs of mitigation action by developing countries. Given the operating cost savings for many measures, it should not be necessary to fund the full incremental investment. However, the adoption of measures with a negative cost may still require incentives or programme costs. The incremental cost implicitly applies cost savings from some measures against the higher costs of other measures. In practice, cost savings are unlikely to be available to finance other measures; an electricity utility is unlikely to be able to use costs saved by its customers as a result of energy efficiency to help finance more renewable generation.

Thus, the estimates of incremental investment and cost for mitigation measures can inform, but do not determine, the amount of international financial support needed by developing countries. The international financial support needed is likely to lie between the estimates of incremental cost and the incremental investment. The estimates of the incremental cost and investment reviewed in this chapter are much higher than the current level of international financial support for mitigation. This suggests that more international financial support will be needed for mitigation action in developing countries. However, the additional amount that will be needed cannot be determined from the available analyses.

Developed countries have committed to provide more funding for mitigation by developing countries. The Copenhagen Accord, now supported by 137 countries, commits developed countries to provide 'scaled up, new and additional, predictable and adequate funding approaching US$30 billion for the period 2010–2012 with balanced allocation between adaptation and mitigation' and the 'goal of mobilizing jointly US$100 billion a year by 2020 to address the needs of developing countries' (UNFCCC, 2009, Article 8).

The next section discusses the analytical issues that arise when estimating incremental mitigation investment or cost. Global estimates are reviewed in Section 3.3. Country and sectoral estimates are reviewed in Sections 3.4 and 3.5, respectively. Sections 3.6 and 3.7 review current mitigation funding and funding promised under the Copenhagen Accord. Conclusions are drawn in Section 3.8.

3.2 Estimating incremental mitigation investment or cost

The basic methodology is simple: the emissions for a reference or business-as-usual scenario are estimated, proposed mitigation measures to achieve an emissions reduction target are identified, and the incremental investment or cost of those mitigation measures is estimated. Most of the analyses reviewed cover the period to 2020 and/or 2030 and adopt a target roughly consistent with 2°C global warming. Differences in the business-as-usual scenario and/or the target reduction will affect the estimates.

Mitigation actions broadly comprise the reduction of greenhouse gas (GHG) emissions and enhancement of carbon sinks. These broad categories are usually subdivided further. Emission reduction measures can be grouped by gas: energy-related carbon dioxide (CO_2), process-related CO_2 and other GHGs. They can also be grouped by sector: electricity generation, buildings, industry and transportation. Actions to enhance carbon sinks include measures to maintain and enlarge the carbon stocks of forests and agricultural soils.

A model is often used for the analysis to develop the business-as-usual scenario and to identify the mitigation measures needed to achieve the emissions target. The model can be simple, such as a marginal abatement cost curve, or highly complex, covering many regions and sectors. The scope of the analysis, often determined by the scope of the model, can affect the estimates. For example, an analysis limited to the electricity sector where business-as-usual consumption is maintained will differ from one where energy efficiency measures by customers reduce electricity demand from the business-as-usual level.

The level of aggregation also matters. With more disaggregation, mitigation measures may interact, thereby making the calculations more complex. Reduced waste heat in commercial buildings due to more efficient lighting reduces the potential savings from more efficient air conditioners. More aggregation yields net estimates that may not be relevant for policy purposes. For example, if independent generators provide electricity from renewables and electric utilities own the coal-fired generation, then the net increase in investment/cost understates the scale of the incentives needed to promote renewables.

Geographic aggregation may also understate the incentive needed. A region may include fossil-fuel exporters whose investments/costs are lower than in the business-as-usual scenario, as well as fossil-fuel importers whose investment/costs increase due to the mitigation measures. The regional figure then understates the needs of the countries whose investment/costs increase.

Investment is the initial (capital) cost of a physical asset with an expected life of more than one year. Vehicles and appliances are considered investments, although they are consumer durables in national accounts. Some analyses consider increased funding for research and development an investment, but it is not a large share of the total. The manner in which the incremental investment is financed – debt and equity, domestic or foreign – is generally not analysed.

The extensive literature on the cost of climate change mitigation is periodically assessed by the Inter-governmental Panel on Climate Change (Barker *et al.*, 2007). Analyses of mitigation costs usually adopt a societal perspective. With a few exceptions, they assume that the capital and operating costs of mitigation measures remain constant at their current levels in real terms. Technological improvement would reduce the estimates. Some models only calculate cost savings during the period modelled, even though some measures continue to generate savings after that date, thus overstating the cost. Differences in a variety of other assumptions, such as the discount rate and base year, also affect the estimates.

3.3 Global estimates

The literature includes several studies and reviews of the macroeconomic impacts of various emission reduction targets (e.g. Stern, 2007; IPCC, 2007a; OECD,

2008; Russ *et al.*, 2009; van Vuuren *et al.*, 2009). They estimate the change in gross domestic product (GDP) in a specified year as a result of actions to reduce global GHG emissions. Those studies are not reviewed here because the change in GDP is very difficult to relate to the need for international financial support.

Studies that estimate the incremental investment/costs of mitigation identify four categories of measures:

1   energy efficiency (buildings, industry and transportation);
2   low-carbon energy supply (biofuels and renewables, nuclear) and CO_2 capture and storage (CCS) for electricity supply;
3   reduction of other GHG emissions, including CCS for industrial emissions;
4   carbon sinks (agriculture and forestry).

Many of the studies do not address the last two categories. With societal discount rates (up to 10 per cent), the incremental investment for energy efficiency measures can be recovered through lower energy bills.[2] Low-carbon generation technologies are relatively capital-intensive and the incremental capital cost is only partially offset by lower operating costs, leading to higher electricity prices (IEA, 2009; McKinsey & Co., 2009a). Measures to enhance carbon sinks are not very capital-intensive, so they need relatively little incremental investment, but may have ongoing operating costs (UNFCCC, 2007; McKinsey & Co., 2009a).

Estimates of incremental global investment and cost prepared by the UNFCCC Secretariat, McKinsey & Company and the International Energy Agency (IEA) are summarized in Table 3.1. The UNFCCC and McKinsey estimates cover all mitigation options, whereas the IEA figures are for mitigation of energy-related CO_2 emissions. The UNFCCC includes annual costs for measures, such as reduced forest degradation, that do not require incremental investment.

The UNFCCC study combined several estimates of the mitigation potential for different categories of emissions to reduce projected emissions in 2030 from 61.5 to 29.1 gigatonnes (Gt) of CO_2 equivalent[3] ($GtCO_2e$); 20 per cent below 1990 emissions (UNFCCC, 2007, 2008). The additional investment and financial flows in 2030 were estimated at US$380 billion, of which US$177 billion (47 per cent) would be needed in developing countries.[4]

McKinsey developed a GHG abatement cost curve which includes mitigation measures covering 10 sectors in 21 regions with each measure reducing emissions at a cost less than US$90/$tCO_2e$ (McKinsey & Co., 2009a). Implementing all of the measures to their full potential could reduce projected emissions in 2030 from 70 to 32 $GtCO_2e$, 10 per cent below 1990 emissions.[5] Higher-cost measures and behavioural changes could reduce emissions by another 9 $GtCO_2e$. McKinsey estimates that the incremental investment needed to implement these mitigation measures would be US$1,215 billion per year during the period 2026–2030, of which US$695 billion (57 per cent) would be in developing countries (McKinsey & Co., 2009a). The total cost of the mitigation measures globally is estimated at US$300–525 billion, assuming a discount rate of 4 per cent.

36 Susanne Olbrisch et al.

Table 3.1 Summary of global incremental mitigation investment estimates for 2030 (billions of US$ per year)

	Global			Developing countries		
	UNFCCC[a]	McKinsey[a]	IEA[a]	UNFCCC[a]	McKinsey[a]	IEA[a]
Fossil-fuel supply	– 59[b]	27	– 128	– 32[b]		
Electricity supply	148[c]	222	142[d]	73[c]		72[d]
Biofuels			38			9
Buildings	51	297	206	14		87
Industry	36	142	88	19		57
Transportation	88	450	334	36		152
Agriculture	35	0		13		
Forestry	21	65		21		
Other	1	12		1		
Total	380[e]	1215	808[e]	177[e]	695	377

Notes:

a In 2030 for UNFCCC; annual average for 2026–2030 for McKinsey; annual average for 2021–2030 for IEA. 2005 US$ for UNFCCC; 2008 US$ for IEA; McKinsey estimates reported in euros converted to US$ at the rate of euro 1 equals US$1.50.

b Global (developing country) investment for fossil-fuel supply in 2030 drops from US$322 (156) to US$263 (124) billion.

c Global (developing country) investment in fossil-fired generation and transmission falls by US$156 (79) billion while investment in renewables, nuclear and CCS rises by US$148 (73) billion.

d Power generation only: transmission and distribution are not included.

e Excludes reduced investment in fossil-fuel supply.

Sources: UNFCCC (2007), IEA (2009) and McKinsey & Co. (2009a).

The IEA have analysed options for reducing energy-related CO_2 emissions. These emissions are projected to amount to 40.2 $GtCO_2e$, 71 per cent of the global GHG emissions of 56.6 $GtCO_2e$, in 2030 (IEA, 2009). In its 450 Scenario, global emissions decline to 37.1 $GtCO_2e$ in 2030, approximately equal to 1990 emissions, and energy-related CO_2 emissions are cut by about 35 per cent to 26.4 $GtCO_2e$.

The average annual incremental investment for 2021–2030 is US$808 billion globally, of which US$377 billion (47 per cent) is needed in developing countries. This figure does not reflect the reduced investment for fossil-fuel supply of approximately US$135 billion per year globally, nor the reduced investment for transmission and distribution, which is not reported but could be of the order of US$90–100 billion per year.[6] The energy efficiency measures yield net cost savings over their lifetimes.[7] Electricity prices rise due to the shift to renewables and addition of CCS to fossil-fired generation.

The IEA and McKinsey estimates are relatively close once differences in methodology are taken into account. The incremental investment for mitigation of emissions other than energy-related CO_2 adds US$50–100 billion to the

McKinsey figure. Investment needs increase over time, so the IEA's 2030 figure (not reported) would be substantially higher than the 2021–2030 annual average in Table 3.1. On the other hand, expressing the IEA estimates in 2005 dollars would reduce them by about US$50 billion.

The World Bank (2010a) has compiled several estimates of the incremental costs and financing requirements for the mitigation efforts needed in developing countries in 2030 to ultimately stabilize atmospheric concentrations of CO_2e at 450 parts per million (ppm). These are presented in Table 3.2, together with the estimates reported in Table 3.1. The McKinsey and UNFCCC estimates include all sectors; the other figures only include mitigation efforts in the energy sector.

Estimates of the incremental investment needed for mitigation action in developing countries range between US$175 and US$565 billion. Although there are fewer estimates of the incremental cost, they are substantially lower (US$140–175 billion) in 2030 due to the lower operating costs of the energy efficiency measures and renewables.

Finally, the World Bank (2006) estimated that the annual investment needed for the power sector in developing countries would rise from US$160 to US$190 billion over the period 2010–2030, assuming stabilization at 450 ppm. The incremental investment of US$30 billion per year appears low compared with the estimates in Table 3.1. This may be largely due to the temporal profile of the estimates. All analyses find that the incremental investment/cost increases substantially over time. Then the incremental investment/cost calculated as an average over a period (2010–2030 or 2021–2030) is much lower than the incremental investment/cost for the last year of the period (2030).

Table 3.2 Estimates of incremental mitigation investment/costs for developing countries in 2030 (2005 US$ billions per year)

Study/model	Incremental investment	Incremental cost
IEA Energy Technology Perspectives[a]	565[a]	
IEA World Energy Outlook 2009[b]	377[b]	
McKinsey[c]	563[c]	175[c]
MESSAGE	264	
MiniCAM[d]		
REMIND	384	139[d]
UNFCCC 2007[b]	177[b]	

Notes:
a Annual average up to 2050 (IEA, 2008).
b See notes to Table 3.1.
c Using a dollar-to-euro exchange rate of US$1.25 to 1 euro. The McKinsey figure in Table 3.1 reflects an exchange rate of US$1.50 to 1 euro. After adjusting for the different exchange rate, the figures are essentially the same.
d MiniCAM reports US$168 billion in mitigation costs in 2035, in constant 2000 dollars; this figure has been interpolated to 2030 and converted to 2005 dollars.

Sources: UNFCCC (2007), IEA (2009) and World Bank (2010a).

3.4 Country estimates

In addition to these global studies, a number of studies have analysed the abatement potential and associated incremental investment and/or cost for large developing countries. These studies include:

- World Bank Low Carbon Growth studies (WB);
- Regional Economics of Climate Change Studies (RECCS);
- Project Catalyst, facilitated by McKinsey & Company (PC).

The basic methodology is the same – identify mitigation measures to reduce projected business-as-usual emissions to a target level and then estimate the associated incremental investment and/or cost. The emission reduction targets are usually linked to a global stabilization target. The estimates are summarized in Table 3.3.

Table 3.3 Summary of incremental mitigation investment and cost estimates for developing countries (billions of currency units per year)

Country	Period	Incremental investment	Incremental cost
Brazil	2010–2030		US$5.7 (PC)
China	2010–2030	€150–200 (PC)	US$20 (WB)
	2010–2030		
	2011–2015	€35 (PC)[a]	
	2026–2030	€300 (PC)[a]	
India	2021–2030	US$167 (IEA)	US$12.5 (PC)
	2010–2020	US$18 (PC)[b]	
	2020–2030	US$42 (PC)[b]	US$23 (PC)
	2021–2030	US$49 (IEA)	
Indonesia	2020	US$4.3 (RECCS)	
Mexico	2011–2015	US$7.2 (PC)	US$4.9 (PC)
	2026–2030	US$18 (PC)	US$2.8 (PC)
	2008–2030	US$3 (WB)	
Philippines	2020	US$1.6 (RECCS)	
Thailand	2020	US$1.5 (RECCS)	
Vietnam	2020	US$1.8 (RECCS)	

Notes:
a These figures are from the China country study (McKinsey & Co., 2009c). They differ from the estimates for China (€57 for 2011–2015 and €211 for 2026–2030) in the global study (McKinsey & Co., 2009a).
b These figures are from the India country study (McKinsey & Co., 2009d). They differ from the estimates for India (€8 (US$12) for 2011–2015 and €61 (US$92) for 2026–2030) in the global study (McKinsey & Co., 2009a).

Sources: Project Catalyst (PC): CMM (2008) and McKinsey & Co. (2009b, 2009c, 2009d). Regional Economics of Climate Change Studies (RECCS): ADB (2009) and Heaps (2009). World Bank (WB): Johnson *et al.* (2008) and IEA (2009) and World Bank (2010b).

The studies identify significant potential for low-cost mitigation (less than US$25/tCO$_2$e) in these countries. Such measures account for over 80 per cent of the reductions in Brazil, Indonesia and Mexico and over 60 per cent of the reductions in China and India. A high share of low-cost emissions reduction potential tends to be associated with a relatively large potential for agroforestry and REDD+.[8]

The country study estimates for China and India are broadly consistent with the estimates for those countries in the IEA and McKinsey global analyses. They account for approximately 45 per cent and 13 per cent of developing country incremental investment, respectively, in those analyses. It is not surprising then that the estimates of incremental investment for the other countries are smaller than for India. As in the global analyses, the incremental cost is lower than the incremental investment. However, the difference is less pronounced due to the prevalence of agriculture and REDD+ measures, which are not very capital-intensive.

A regional study of the energy sector for East Asia covering China, Indonesia, Malaysia, the Philippines, Thailand and Vietnam reduces emissions through more energy efficiency, renewables and nuclear generation and less fossil-fired generation (World Bank, Australian Government, AusAid, 2010). The average annual incremental investment required over the period 2010–2030 is US$85 billion for energy efficiency, US$25 billion for renewables and US$10 billion for nuclear generation. Annual investment for fossil-fired generation is reduced by US$40 billion, so the net incremental investment is US$80 billion per year. Fuel cost savings, discounted at 10 per cent per year, average US$145 billion per year. China accounts for 85 per cent of the incremental investment and roughly the same share of the fuel cost savings.

In the UNDP project 'Capacity Development for Policy Makers to Address Climate Change', countries assess the investment and financial flows necessary to address climate change mitigation in selected key sectors.[9] In the UNFCCC 'National Economic, Environment and Development Study (NEEDS) for Climate Change' project, countries also estimate mitigation costs associated with specific national sectors. The Centre for Clean Air Policy's (CCAP) project, 'Assisting Developing Country Climate Negotiators through Analysis and Dialogue' also produced estimates for selected sectors in several countries. Table 3.4 provides available estimates for countries participating in these projects.

The estimates for the Philippines (US$30.5 billion), Indonesia (US$16.8 billion) and Costa Rica (US$7.8 billion) seem high relative to those given for the other countries, which are mostly less than US$1 billion. The estimates for the Philippines and Indonesia are also much higher than those reported in Table 3.3 (US$1.6 and 4.3 billion, respectively). For other countries the estimates appear to be broadly consistent with those from the country studies (Table 3.3), which typically cover more sectors.

The estimates for Indonesia and the Philippines also appear high relative to the estimates from the World Bank study of the energy sector for East Asia, which also covers China, Malaysia, Thailand and Vietnam. That study estimates

Table 3.4 Mitigation cost estimates for selected countries and sectors for 2030 (US$ billions per year)

Country	Period	Sectors and Discount Rate	Incremental Cost	
			Total	Annual Average
Capacity development for policymakers to address climate change				
Bangladesh	2005–2030	Energy (6%)	24.807	0.954
Colombia	2005–2030	Agriculture (0%)	2.078	0.080
Dominican Republic	2005–2030	Energy (1.58% & 5%)	10.728	0.413
Ecuador	2010–2030	Transport (0.1%)	2.551	0.121
	2011–2030	Forestry (0.1%)	2.618	0.131
Gambia	2005–2030	Energy (19%)	0.423	0.016
Honduras	2005–2030	Forestry (0%)	3.894	0.150
	2005–2030	Transport (0%)	1.555	0.060
Liberia	2005–2030	Energy (9%)	1.301	0.050
	2005–2030	Forestry (0%)	0.186	0.007
Namibia	2005–2030	Energy (8%)	2.212	0.085
Niger	2005–2030	Forestry (4.95%)	2.170	0.083
Paraguay	2010–2030	Forestry (0%)	0.098	0.005
Togo	2005–2030	Energy (2 rates)	0.883	0.033
Turkmenistan	2003–2030	Electricity produc. (10%)	0.676	0.024
	2008–2030	Electricity demand (10%)	0.041	0.002
Uruguay	2006–2030	Energy (1%)	5.531	0.221
NEEDS project				
Costa Rica	2010–2030	Land use, land use change and forestry (LULUCF)	0.488	0.023
	2010–2030	Agriculture	0.210	0.010
	2010–2030	Total – LULUCF, agriculture, energy and solid waste management (12%)	7.80	0.371

Country	Years	Sector		
Egypt	2010–2020	Energy (discount rate not specified)	4.200	0.420
Ghana	2006–2020	Energy (37.5%)	Total:{0.340	0.023
	2003–2020	Transport (37.5%)		
	2006–2020	Forestry (37.5%)		
Indonesia	2009–2020	Total of energy, transport, industrial processes, agriculture, forestry, waste, peat (discount rate not specified)	12.020[a,b]	1.002
Jordan	2010–2020	Energy (discount rate not specified)	3.220	0.292
		Waste (discount rate not specified)	0.125	0.011
Maldives	2010–2020	All measures to achieve carbon neutrality by 2020	1.100	0.100
Mali	2010–2020	Forestry and agriculture (discount rate not specified)	11.010	1.000
Nigeria	2010–2020	Energy sector measures to cut emissions by 25% (discount rate not specified)	9.614	0.874
		Afforestation (discount rate not specified)	2.900	0.263
		Agroforestry (discount rate not specified)	1.780	0.162
		Establishing forest units	0.444	0.040
Philippines	2008–2030	Energy (10%)	30.51[c]	1.327
Center for Clean Air Policy (CCAP)				
Brazil	2020	Electricity (0%)		−0.141[d]
		Transportation (0%)		0.580
		Cement (0%)		−0.737[d]
		Total		−0.298[d]
China	2020	Electricity (0%)		10.886
		Transportation (0%)		−2.308[c]
		Iron and steel (0%)		3.667
		Cement (0%)		0.440
		Total		12.685

(*Continued*)

Table 3.4 (Continued)

Country	Period	Sectors and Discount Rate	Incremental Cost	
			Total	Annual Average
India	2020	Electricity (0%)		−0.556[d,e]
		Transportation (0%)		−55.973[d,e]
		Iron and steel (0%)		1.611[e]
		Cement (0%)		−0.076[d,e]
		Pulp and paper (0%)		−0.012[d,e]
		Total		−55.006[d,e]

Notes:
a Exchange rate used: 1 IDR ¼ US$0.000111694.
b Estimates reflect costs associated with increasing efforts to reduce emissions from the planned 26 to 41%.
c Value of the 'Maximum Renewable Energy Scenario'.
d A negative amount means a net saving.
e The figures in Table 5.18 of the CCAP report do not match those in the accompanying text. The estimate for transportation, and hence the total, is obviously incorrect.

Sources: Reports of the UNDP project 'Capacity Building for Policy Makers to Address Climate Change' available at www.undpcc.org/content/project–en.aspx; reports of the UNFCCC 'NEEDS' project available at http://unfccc.int/cooperation_and_support/financial_mechanism/items/5630.php; CCAP (2006) reports available at www.ccap.org/index.php?component=resources&by=program.

the incremental investment at US$80 billion, of which 85 per cent was for China, leaving US$12 billion for the remaining five countries. The NEEDS studies estimate the incremental cost (which is generally much lower than the incremental investment) for the energy sector at US$8 billion and US$30 billion, respectively, for Indonesia and the Philippines.

3.5 Sectoral estimates

Most of the analyses presented above are limited to the energy sector. The United States Environmental Protection Agency (US EPA) has developed marginal abatement cost curves for non-CO_2 emissions for all regions for the period 2000–2020, and the World Business Council on Sustainable Development (WBCSD) has analysed options to reduce industrial process CO_2 emissions (WBCSD, 2002; US EPA, 2006). McKinsey and the UNFCCC included agricultural emission reduction and sink enhancement measures in their analyses, but there are no independent analyses of the agriculture sector.

Several studies have estimated the costs for REDD+.[10] Virtually all of the potential is in developing countries. REDD+ measures require little investment, so virtually all of the costs are operating costs and essentially all of the costs are incremental to current spending. The incremental cost estimates for REDD+ are summarized in Table 3.5.

Most analyses project the business-as-usual emissions due to deforestation to remain roughly constant. The target then becomes a reduction of this rate. The marginal cost increases as the reduction target rises, because deforestation needs to be halted on land with increasingly more profitable alternative uses.

3.6 Current mitigation funding

The types of funding that qualify as financial resources provided by developed countries for mitigation measures in developing countries have not been agreed. It is generally agreed that grants and concessional loans qualify, but there is disagreement over the inclusion of credit (offset) purchases and private investment. The net benefit to developing countries differs for revenues from these sources. The High-Level Advisory Group on Climate Change Financing (AGF) estimated both the 'gross' amount – the amount of revenue generated – and the 'net' amount – the grant-equivalent value of concessional public flows and the net benefit to developing countries for non-concessional public and private flows such as offset purchases, commercial loans and equity investments (United Nations, 2010). AGF members disagreed whether revenue should be measured in gross or net terms and on how to estimate the net revenue for different sources.

Unfortunately, the amounts of different types of international funding currently provided to developing countries for mitigation, adaptation, technology development and transfer, and capacity building cannot be determined accurately. Efforts are being made to improve reporting on international funding

Table 3.5 Mitigation cost estimates for REDD+ (billions of currency units per year)

Study	Target date	Mitigation measures	Cost
UNFCCC	2030	Reduced deforestation (5.7 GtCO$_2$/yr)	US$12
		Forest management (6.5 GtCO$_2$/yr)	US$8
		Afforestation/reforestation	US$1
McKinsey	2030	Avoided deforestation (3.6 GtCO$_2$/yr)	€43 (US$65)
		Afforestation/reforestation (2.4 GtCO$_2$/yr)	
		Other measures (1.8 GtCO$_2$/yr)	
IWG-IFR	2015	25% reduction of emissions REDD+ (1.5 GtCO$_2$/yr; 5.5 total)	€3–5 incentives €0.3–0.5 for other costs
		Peat-related reductions (1.5 GtCO$_2$ total)	
Isenberg & Potvin		50% reduction of emissions	US$14.2
Stern		Deforestation halted in countries responsible for 70% of emissions	US$3–11
Grieg-Gran		Deforestation halted in countries responsible for 70% of emissions	US$4–8
Kindermann *et al.*	2030	50% reduction of emissions	US$17.2–28
European Commission	2020	50% reduction of emissions	US$20–33

Sources: Stern (2007), UNFCCC (2007), European Commission (2008), Grieg-Gran (2008), Kindermann *et al.* (2008), IWG-IFR (2009), McKinsey (2009a) and Isenberg and Potvin (2010).

(Atteridge *et al.*, 2009). Several sources estimate the total at US$10–15 billion per year, of which 70–90 per cent is for mitigation.[11] The available data are summarized in Table 3.6.

Developed countries are expected to provide information on the bilateral and multilateral assistance they provide to developing countries for climate purposes in their national communications. As a result of the gaps and inconsistencies in the reporting approaches of different countries, it is not possible to calculate the financial support provided using information from these documents (UNFCCC, 2007; Tirpak *et al.*, 2010). The information provided relates to different periods (fiscal and calendar years), consists of annual and cumulative amounts, includes both commitments and disbursements, and treats bilateral and multilateral support inconsistently.

The Organisation for Economic Co-operation and Development's (OECD) Development Assistance Committee gathers harmonized data on financial assistance provided to developing countries by member countries and a number of multilateral agencies. The data include 'markers' that identify projects that

Table 3.6 Current international funding for mitigation measures in developing countries (US$ billions per year)

Source	Amount	Notes
Bilateral assistance	5.8	Average bilateral assistance for projects that had climate change mitigation as a 'principal' (US$3.3 billion) or 'significant' (US$2.5 billion) objective during 2006–2008; concessional loans expressed as grant equivalents
Multilateral climate funds	<0.3	Global Environment Facility Trust Fund
	<2.0	Climate Investment Funds, REDD funds and other funds outside the Convention
Multilateral assistance	3	Funding for projects with mitigation as a 'principal' or 'significant' objective estimated as 6.1% of multilateral assistance during 2006–2008; concessional loans expressed as grant equivalents
CDM	3–10	Estimated payments for current and future credits during 2009; market value of credits issued was US$2 billion and value of estimated reductions for all existing and planned projects was US$11 billion; only part of the revenue is a financial benefit to the host country
Private investment	35	Global foreign direct investment in 2009 of US$90 billion in alternative/renewable energy, recycling activities and environmental technology manufacturing, of which 40% occurred in developing countries; only part of the investment is a financial benefit to the host country
	>30	Asset finance for renewable energy projects during 2009 in China; the global total was US$101 billion (data for other developing countries not reported); only part of the investment is a financial benefit to the host country

Notes: Figures should not be summed due to possible double counting; foreign direct investment may include some asset finance, and multilateral assistance may include some projects supported by multilateral climate funds.

Sources: OECD (2011), REN21 (2010) and UNCTAD (2010).

have climate change mitigation as a principal or significant objective. Reporting is incomplete, and the accuracy of the coding has been questioned (Michaelowa and Michaelowa, 2010; Roberts *et al.*, 2010). Funding for projects that had mitigation as a principal or significant objective averaged about US$5.8 billion per year for 2006–2008 (about 6.1 per cent of bilateral development assistance during this period). Because this is the total value of these projects, the funding provided for mitigation measures would be less.

Mitigation measures have been funded through the Global Environment Facility since 1991. Several new funds were launched during 2007 and 2008. The financial support provided by these climate funds during 2009 is not known, but it is expected to grow to over US$2 billion per year. International financial institutions, UN agencies and other multilateral institutions provide grants and concessional loans for a variety of development projects. If 6.1 per cent of the multilateral assistance went to projects with mitigation as a 'principal' or 'significant' objective, the funding would amount to roughly US$3 billion per year for 2006–2008. The funding provided for mitigation measures would be less.

The Clean Development Mechanism (CDM) issues credits for emission reductions (CERs) achieved in developing countries. The credits can be sold to firms and governments in developed countries. The number of credits issued for each project is known and the market price of CERs is readily available, so it is possible to calculate the market value of the credits issued for each project. However, buyers often contract to purchase credits generated over a number of years early in the life of a project at a price below the market price, so the financial support received can differ both in timing and amount from the market value of the credits issued.

The CDM relies on the market for credits to generate financial support for mitigation actions, while the other channels provide grants and concessionary loans. The AGF estimated the net contribution at 20–33 per cent of the credit revenue (United Nations, 2010). The investment in CDM projects, estimated at US$11–27 billion in 2009, is more than double the revenue from the sale of credits; the investment will be repaid from revenue from the sale of credits and other outputs, such as electricity, over the life of the project. The CDM has been criticized because most of the projects are located in China and India (54 and 19 per cent of the projected emission reductions, respectively), so the revenue and investment are similarly concentrated in these countries. As a market mechanism, the CDM is not very effective for some types of mitigation actions, including energy efficiency in buildings and transportation, geothermal, solar and tidal energy, and forestry. These projects face non-price barriers (energy efficiency), become only marginally more profitable due to the sale of credits (geothermal, solar and tidal), or earn temporary credits for which there is only a limited market (forestry) (Schneider *et al.*, 2010).

Data on foreign direct investment and asset finance suggest that a significant amount of private investment in renewables is occurring in developing countries. It is not known how much of the asset finance is also counted as foreign direct investment. These investments are made on commercial terms. The AGF has estimated the net contribution at 10 per cent of the private investment (United Nations, 2010).

3.7 Future mitigation funding

The estimates of incremental investment and cost for mitigation measures inform, but do not determine, the amount of international financial support needed by developing countries. Given the operating cost savings for many measures, it should not be necessary to fund all of the incremental investment. However, the adoption of measures with negative costs may still require incentives. Although the amount of international funding needed cannot be determined from the available analyses, it is likely to lie between the estimates of incremental cost and the incremental investment.

The literature reviewed has more estimates of the incremental investment needed than of the incremental cost. For developing countries, only two estimates of the incremental cost are available: US$139 and 175 billion for 2030 (Table 3.2). The incremental cost of the mitigation measures implemented during the intervening years would be much lower. To achieve a given target, the mitigation effort, and the associated incremental investment and cost, rises substantially over time. Thus, the incremental cost in 2015 or 2020 would be much lower than in 2030.

Developed countries have promised more funding to address climate change in developing countries. In the Copenhagen Accord they promised 'new and additional' funding of US$30 billion for 2010–2012, with balanced allocation between adaptation and mitigation and a goal of mobilizing jointly US$100 billion dollars a year by 2020. The announced fast-start (2010–2012) pledges to date total US$27–33 billion.[12] The pledges are almost all public funds that will be disbursed bilaterally or multilaterally as grants and loans (Fallasch and De Marez, 2010; Project Catalyst, 2010). It appears that more money will go to mitigation than to adaptation (Project Catalyst, 2010).

Several baselines could be used to assess whether the fast-start finance commitments are 'new and additional' (Stadelmann *et al.*, 2010). However, there is no agreed baseline, so each country is free to adopt its own criteria. Independent assessments conclude that some pledged funding is not new and additional.[13] Nevertheless, the additional funding represents a significant increase to current bilateral and multilateral mitigation funding.

The 2020 goal of mobilizing US$100 billion per year falls within the low end of incremental mitigation cost estimates, but only if this is an annual average for 2012–2020 rather than a goal for 2020 (GCN, 2010). The UN Secretary General's High-Level Advisory Group on Climate Change Financing (2010) assessed a range of options as possible sources of climate finance (Romani and Stern, Chapter 7). The group concluded that a combination of sources, including an expanded carbon market, will probably be required to achieve the target of US$100 billion per year.

The ability of carbon markets to finance mitigation measures in developing countries depends on the demand for the credits. The demand is driven primarily by the emissions limitation commitments of developed countries and the rules they adopt regarding the use of credits. Developed country commitments are currently under negotiation, so the future size of the market and the funding it might generate for mitigation in developing countries is uncertain (Kossoy and Ambrosi, 2010).

The mitigation measures eligible to generate credits can also have a significant effect on the supply. Some experts believe that REDD+ measures should be allowed to earn credits, whereas others believe they should be funded (Isenberg and Potvin, 2010). The scale of the potential reductions is such that they could dominate the supply of credits. Such considerations yield a very wide range in the estimates of the potential supply of credits in 2020 (2–12 $GtCO_2e$; Alberola and Stephan, 2010).

3.8 Conclusions

This chapter presents estimates of the incremental investment/cost of mitigation measures in developing countries. The estimates are sensitive to the business-as-usual projection, the scale of the emission reductions targeted, the time horizon, the range of mitigation measures considered, the rate of technological change assumed, the discount rate and other factors. Investment analyses are much simpler, because cost estimates need data on lifetimes and operating costs and an assumption as to the appropriate discount rate. Many mitigation measures, such as energy efficiency and renewables, reduce operating costs, thus offsetting some or all of the higher capital cost. The incremental cost is therefore usually much lower than the incremental investment.

The estimates of incremental investment and cost for mitigation measures inform, but do not determine, the amount of international financial support needed by developing countries. There is no agreed basis for determining how much international financial support should be provided and the studies reviewed do not specify how the incremental investment/costs will be funded. Although the amount of international funding needed cannot be determined from the available analyses, it is likely to lie between the estimates of incremental cost and the incremental investment.

The few estimates of incremental mitigation costs available suggest that these costs will rise substantially over the next two decades and exceed US$100 billion by 2030. The promises to increase international climate funding significantly over the next decade are encouraging, but it is not yet possible to determine whether the promised funding will be sufficient.

Acknowledgements

The authors would like to thank Rebecca Carman, Tim Clairs, Carlos Salgado, Matt Spannagle, Sasanka Thilakasiri, Bhujang Dharmaji, James Tee and three anonymous reviewers for their valuable input. We also acknowledge the MISTRA supported CLIPORE program for supporting part of the research presented in this paper. The views presented in this chapter are those of the authors and do not represent the views of parent or affiliated organizations.

Notes

1 The commitment is reaffirmed in Article 11 of the Kyoto Protocol. Funds are to be provided by Annex II Parties.
2 This may not hold for private discount rates over 10 per cent.
3 CO_2e means all greenhouse gases expressed in terms of their carbon dioxide equivalent over a 100-year horizon. A gigatonne is a billion metric tonnes.
4 UNFCCC (2007), Table IX-64, with the amounts adjusted for the reduced investment for fossil-fuel supply from Table IX-61.
5 The McKinsey analysis has both higher reference scenario emissions and a larger mitigation potential than the UNFCCC analysis, yet it would still have higher emissions in 2030, illustrating the impact of the reference scenario.

6 IEA (2009). Reduced investment for fossil-fuel supply estimated from Figure 7.12. Cumulative investment in transmission and distribution in the reference scenario is US$6.6 trillion over 2010–2030 inclusive, about US$314 billion per year. The 450 Scenario reduces electricity growth over 2007–2030 from 14,536 to 10,183 TWh, about 30 per cent. This suggests a reduction of US$90–100 billion per year for transmission and distribution investment.

7 IEA (2009). With a 10 per cent discount rate there are net savings of US$450 billion.

8 REDD means reducing emissions from deforestation and forest degradation in developing countries. REDD+ also includes sustainable management of forests and enhancement of carbon stocks.

9 Some countries also cost adaptation measures for selected sectors.

10 Pagiola and Bosquet (2009) provide a good conceptual overview of the issues involved in estimating the cost of REDD+.

11 World Bank (2010a, Figure 6.2) shows US$9 billion in 2005 dollars and the text states 'roughly $10 billion' presumably current dollars. Atteridge *et al.* (2009) estimate the climate finance channelled through four bilateral and multilateral agencies during 2008 to be about US$10 billion, of which about US$3 billion was for adaptation. Roberts *et al.* (2010) estimate total climate-related aid during 2007 at almost US$15 billion, with a five-year average, from 2003 to 2007, of over US$11 billion per year.

12 Climate Funds Update (2010) estimates US$29 billion; Fallasch and De Marez (2010) estimate US$31.2 billion; Project Catalyst (2010) estimates US$28 billion; World Development Movement (2010) estimates US$27.5 billion; and World Resources Institute (2010) estimates US$31.32 billion. A partial list of pledges and commitments is also available at www.faststartfinance.org/content/contributing-countries.

13 Project Catalyst (2010: 14) states 'it is clear from our preliminary analysis that only a share of this total funding will be new and additional'. Fallasch and De Marez (2010) evaluate the commitments against two base-lines and find that US$8.2 or US$17.8 billion is new and additional. WRI states that '[a] number of pledges are restated or renamed commitments already made in the past'. Available at www.wri.org/stories/2010/02/summary-climate-finance-pledges-put-forward-developed-countries.

Bibliography

Alberola, E., Stephan, N., 2010, *Carbon Funds in 2010: Investment in Kyoto Credits and Emissions Reductions*, CDC Report No. 23, CDC Climat, Paris [available at www.cdcclimat.com/IMG/pdf/etude_climat_23-Carbon_Funds_in_2010.pdf].

Asian Development Bank (ADB), 2009, *The Economics of Climate Change in Southeast Asia: A Regional Review*, Asian Development Bank, Manila.

Atteridge, A., Kehler Siebert, C., Klein, R.J.T., Butler, C., Tella, P., 2009, *Bilateral Finance Institutions and Climate Change: A Mapping of Climate Portfolios*, Working Paper 2009, Stockholm Environment Institute, Stockholm [available at http://sei-international.org/mediamanager/documents/Publications/ Climate-mitigation-adaptation/bilateral-finance-institutions-climate-change.pdf].

Barker, T., Bashmakov, I., Alharthi, A., Amann, M., Cifuentes, L., Drexhage, J., Duan, M., Edenhofer, O., Flannery, B., Grubb, M., Hoogwijk, M., Ibitoye, F.I., Jepma, C.J., Pizer, W.A., Yamaji, K., 2007, 'Mitigation from a cross-sectoral perspective', in *Climate Change 2007: Mitigation of Climate Change. Contribution of Working Group III to the Fourth Assessment Report of the Intergovernmental Panel on Climate Change* (B. Metz, O.R. Davidson, P.R. Bosch, R. Dave, L.A. Meyer, eds), Cambridge University Press, Cambridge, UK.

Bowen, A., 2011, 'Raising climate finance to support developing country action: some economic considerations', *Climate Policy 11*(3), 1020–1036.

Center for Clean Air Policy (CCAP), 2006, *Greenhouse Gas Mitigation in Brazil, China and India: Scenarios and Opportunities Through 2025*, CCAP, Washington, DC [available at www.ccap.org/index.php?component=resources&by=program].

Centro Mario Molina (CMM), 2008, *Low-Carbon Growth: A Potential Path for Mexico*, Discussion Draft, Centro Mario Molina, Mexico City, Mexico.

Climate Funds Update, 2010, *Fast Start Finance* [available at www.climatefundsupdate.org/fast-start-finance].

European Commission, 2008, *Addressing the Challenges of Deforestation and Forest Degradation to Tackle Climate Change and Biodiversity Loss, European Commission*, Brussels [available at http://eur-lex.europa.eu/LexUriServ/LexUriServ. do?uri=COM:2 008:0645:FIN:EN:PDF].

Fallasch, F., De Marez, L., 2010, *New and Additional? An Assessment of Fast-Start Finance Commitments of the Copenhagen Accord, Climate Analytics*, 7 October 2010 Version, Potsdam [available at www.climateanalytics.org/.climateanalytics.org/].

GCN (Global Climate Network), 2010, *Investing in Clean Energy: How Can Developed Countries Best Help Developing Countries Finance Climate-Friendly Energy Investments?*, Discussion Paper 4, Global Climate Network [available at www. globalclimatenetwork.info/ecomm/files/Investing%20in%20Clean%20Energy%20 Nov2010.pdf].

Grieg-Gran, M., 2008, *The Cost of Avoiding Deforestation: Update of the Report Prepared for the Stern Review of the Economics of Climate Change*, International Institute for Environment and Development, London [available at www.iied.org/pubs/pdfs/G02489. pdf].

Heaps, C., 2009, A Deep Carbon Reduction Scenario for China, Stockholm Environment Institute, Sommerville, MA, USA [available at www.energycommunity.org/documents/ DCRSFinal.pdf].

Informal Working Group on Interim Financing for REDD (IWG-IFR), 2009, *Report of the Informal Working Group on Interim Finance for REDD+*, Discussion Document, Informal Working Group on Interim Finance for REDD, Helsinki [available at www. unredd.net/index.php?option=com_docman&task=doc_details&gid=1096&Ite mid=53].

Intergovernmental Panel on Climate Change (IPCC), 2007, *Climate Change 2007 Synthesis Report* (Fourth Assessment Report), IPCC, Geneva [available at www.ipcc. ch/pdf/assessment-report/ar4/syr/ar4_syr.pdf].

International Energy Agency (IEA), 2008, *Energy Technology Perspectives 2008: Scenarios and Strategies to 2050*, IEA, Paris [available at www.iea.org/w/bookshop/ add.aspx?id=330].

International Energy Agency (IEA), 2009, *World Energy Outlook 2009*, IEA, Paris.

Isenberg, J., Potvin, C., 2010, 'Financing REDD in developing countries: a supply and demand analysis', *Climate Policy 10*(2), 216–231.

Johnson, T., Liu, F., Alatorre, C., Romo, Z., 2008, Mexico Low-Carbon Study – Me´xico: Estudio Para la Disminución de Emisiones de Carbono (MEDEC), World Bank, Washington, DC [available at www-wds.worldbank.org/external/ default/ WDSContentServer/WDSP/IB/2010/01/05/000333037_20100105001113/Rendered/ PDF/524580PUB0low0101Official0Use0Only1.pdf].

Kindermann, G., Obersteiner, M., Sohngen, B., Sathaye, J., Andrasko, K., Rametsteiner, E., Schlamadinger, B., Wunder, S., Beach, R., 2008, 'Global cost estimates of reducing carbon emissions through avoided deforestation', *Proceedings of the National Academy of Sciences of the USA 105*(30), 10302–10307.

Kossoy, A., Ambrosi, P., 2010, *State and Trends of the Carbon Market 2010*, World Bank, Washington, DC [available at http://siteresources.worldbank.org/INTCARBON FINANCE/Resources/State_and_Trends_of_the_Carbon_ Market_2010_low_res.pdf].

McKinsey & Co., 2009a, *Pathways to a Low-Carbon Economy*. Version 2 of the Global Greenhouse Gas Abatement Cost Curve, McKinsey & Company, New York [available at www.mckinsey.com/clientservice/ccsi/pathways_low_ carbon_economy. asp].

McKinsey & Co., 2009b, *Pathways to a Low Carbon Economy for Brazil*, Project Catalyst, Brussels [available at www.project-catalyst.info/images/publications/brazil_pathways. pdf].

McKinsey & Co., 2009c, China's Green Opportunity: Prioritizing Technologies to Achieve Energy and Environmental Sustainability, Project Catalyst, Brussels [available at www.mckinsey.com/locations/greaterchina/mckonchina/reports/china_green_ revolution_report.pdf].

McKinsey & Co., 2009d, *Environmental and Energy Sustainability: An Approach for India*, Project Catalyst, Brussels [available at www.mckinsey.com/clientservice/ sustainability/pdf/India_Environmental_Energy_Sustainability_final.pdf].

Michaelowa, A., Michaelowa, K., 2010, Coding Error or Statistical Embellishment? The Political Economy of Reporting Climate Aid, Working Paper 56, Center for Comparative and International Studies, Universität Zü rich, Zurich [available at www.cis.ethz.ch/ publications/publications/2010_WP56_Michaelowa_Michaelowa.pdf].

Organisation for Economic Cooperation and Development (OECD), 2008, *OECD Environmental Outlook to 2030*, OECD, Paris [available at www.oecd.org/ environment/outlookto2030].

Organisation for Economic Cooperation and Development, 2011, Development Perspectives for a Post-Copenhagen Climate Financing Architecture, OECD, Paris [available at www.oecd.org/dataoecd/47/52/47115936.pdf].

Pagiola, S., Bosquet, B., 2009, *Estimating the Costs of REDD at the Country Level*, Version 2.2, 22 September, World Bank, Washington, DC [available at www. forestcarbonpartnership.org/fcp/sites/forestcarbonpartnership.org/files/Documents/ PDF/REDD-Costs-22.pdf].

Project Catalyst, 2010, *Making Fast Start Finance Work*, Briefing Paper, 7 June 2010 [available at www.project-catalyst. info/images/publications/2010-06-07_project_ catalyst_-_fast_start_finance_-_full_report_-_7_june_version.pdf].

REN21, 2010, *Renewables 2010 Global Status* Report, REN21 Secretariat, Paris [available at www.ren21.net/Portals/97/documents/GSR/REN21_GSR_2010_full_revised% 2Sept2010.pdf].

Roberts, J.T., Weissberger, M., Peratsakis, C., 2010, *Trends in Official Climate Finance: Evidence from Human and Machine Coding*, Version of 14 March, 1 pm [available at http://s3.amazonaws.com/aiddata/Roberts_aiddata. pdf].

Russ, P., Ciscar, J-C., Saveyn, B., Soria, A., Szábó, L., Van Ierland, T., Van Regemorter, D., Virdis, R., 2009, Economic Assessment of Post-2012 Global Climate Policies – Analysis of Greenhouse Gas Emission Reduction Scenarios with the POLES and GEM-E3 models, EUR 23768 EN – 2009, JRC, European Commission, Brussels [available at ftp. jrc.es/ EURdoc/JRC50307.pdf].

Schneider, M., Schmidt, T., Hoffmann, V., 2010, 'Performance of renewable energy technologies under the CDM', *Climate Policy 10*(1), 17–37.

Stadelmann, M., Roberts, J.T., Michaelowa, A., 2010, *Keeping a Big Promise: Options for Baselines to Assess "New and Additional" Climate Finance*, CIS Working Paper 66, Center for Comparative and International Studies, ETH Zurich and University of Zurich, Zurich [available at www.cis.ethz.ch/publications/publications/2010_WP66_Stadelmann_Michaelowa.pdf].

Stern, N., 2007, *The Economics of Climate Change:* The Stern Review, Cabinet Office – HM Treasury, Cambridge, UK [available at www.hm-treasury.gov.uk/independent_reviews/stern_review_economics_climate_change/stern_review_Report.cfm].

Tirpak, D., Ronquillo-Ballesteros, A., Stasio, K., McGray, H., 2010, *Guidelines for Reporting Information on Climate Finance*, World Resources Institute, Washington, DC [available at www.wri.org/publication/ guidelines-for-reporting-information-on-climate-finance].

United Nations Conference on Trade and Development (UNCTAD), 2010, *World Investment Report 2010: Investing in a Low-Carbon Economy*, UNCTAD, Geneva [available at www.unctad.info/en/Surveys/World-Investment-Report-2010/].

United Nations Framework Convention on Climate Change (UNFCCC), 1992, *Framework Convention on Climate Change*, UNFCCC Secretariat, Bonn [available at http://unfccc.int/resource/docs/convkp/conveng.pdf].

UNFCCC, 2007, *Investment and Financial Flows to Address Climate Change*, UNFCCC Secretariat, Bonn [available at http://unfccc.int/files/cooperation_and_support/financial_mechanism/application/pdf/background_paper. pdf].

UNFCCC, 2008, *Investment and Financial Flows to Address Climate Change: An Update*, FCCC/TP/2008/7, United Nations Framework Convention Secretariat, Bonn [available at http://unfccc.int/resource/docs/2008/tp/07. pdf].

UNFCCC, 2009, *Copenhagen Accord*, FCCC/CP/2009/11/Add.1, Decision 2/CP15, UNFCCC, Bonn [available at http://unfccc.int/resource/docs/2009/cop15/eng/11a01. pdf#page=4].

United Nations (Secretary-General's High-level Advisory Group on Climate Change Financing), 2010, *Report of the Secretary-General's High-level Advisory Group on Climate Change Financing*, United Nations, New York [available at www.un.org/wcm/content/site/climatechange/pages/financeadvisorygroup/pid/13300].

United States Environmental Protection Agency (US EPA), 2006, *Global Anthropogenic Non-CO_2 Greenhouse Gas Emissions: 1990–2020*, US EPA, Washington, DC.

van Vuuren, D., Hoogwijk, M., Barker, T., Riahi, K., Boeters, S., Chateau, J., Scrieciu, S., van Vliet, J., Masui, T., Blok, K., Blomen, E., Kram, T., 2009, 'Comparison of top-down and bottom-up estimates of sectoral and regional greenhouse gas emission reduction potentials', *Energy Policy 37*, 5125–5139.

World Bank, 2006, *Clean Energy and Development: Towards an Investment Framework*, World Bank, Washington, DC [available at http://siteresources.worldbank.org/DEVCOMMINT/Documentation/20890696/DC2006-0002(E)-CleanEnergy.pdf].

World Bank, 2010a, *World Development Report 2010: Development and Climate Change*, World Bank, Washington, DC [available at http://siteresources.worldbank.org/INTWDR2010/Resources/5287678-1226014527953/Chapter-6.pdf].

World Bank, 2010b, *Brazil Low-Carbon Country Case* Study, World Bank, Washington, DC [available at http://siteresources.worldbank.org/BRAZILEXTN/Resources/Brazil_LowcarbonStudy.pdf].

World Bank, Australian Government, AusAid, 2010, *Winds of Change. East Asia's Sustainable Energy Future*, World Bank, Washington, DC [available at http://siteresources.worldbank.org/INTEASTASIAPACIFIC/Resources/226262-1271320774648/windsofchange_fullreport.pdf].

World Business Council for Sustainable Development (WBCSD), 2002, *Towards a Sustainable Cement Industry: Climate Change*, WBCSD, Geneva [available at www. wbcsd.org/web/publications/toward-a-sustainable-cement-industry. pdf].

World Development Movement, 2010, *A Long Way to Go. An Update on the State of Fast Start Climate Finance*, World Development Movement, Edinburgh [available at www. wdm.org.uk/sites/default/files/alongwaytogo.pdf].

World Resources Institute, 2010, *Summary of Climate Finance Pledges Put Forward by Developed Countries*, 5 June, Washington, DC [available at http://pdf.wri.org/climate_ finance_pledges_2010-08-12.pdf].

4 Development and climate change adaptation funding

Coordination and integration

Joel B. Smith, Thea Dickinson,
Joseph D.B. Donahue, Ian Burton,
Erik Haites, Richard J.T. Klein and
Anand Patwardhan

4.1 Introduction

The United Nations Framework Convention on Climate Change (UNFCCC, or the Convention) calls on developed countries to provide assistance to developing country parties 'that are particularly vulnerable to the adverse effects of climate change in meeting costs of adaptation to those adverse effects' (Article 4.4; United Nations, 1992). Because climate change can be seen as a global pollution problem caused largely by historical emissions within developed countries, developing countries have always maintained that funds provided by developed countries to meet costs of adaptation should be 'new and additional' and not a diversion of development assistance. Developed countries and multilateral development agencies, while agreeing in principle to the requirement of new and additional funding, have also argued that keeping the adaptation funds separate from development funds could lead to a serious duplication of effort and the misallocation of scarce resources.

Resolution of this issue would be difficult if all adaptation funds were to be disbursed through specialized channels. It is clear, however, that donor countries believe that although some new and additional funds for adaptation will be channelled through climate funds, substantial (perhaps most) funds will probably be channelled through multilateral development banks, bilateral development programmes, non-governmental organizations and civil society. In addition, it is clear that development-oriented investments by the private sector will increasingly need to take climate change risks into account and can therefore be seen, in part, as contributing to 'the costs of adaptation'.

This chapter analyses the context of these issues by reviewing estimates of the adaptation funds needed and currently available. The share of existing Official Development Assistance (ODA) allocated to 'climate-sensitive' activities is assessed, and the proposed adaptation projects under the UNFCCC are chara-cterized. The results indicate that there is much overlap in development, so coor-dination of adaptation and development funding could help avoid duplication of effort or investments that are at cross purposes. The need for coordination is recognized in the ongoing climate negotiations. Initiatives to facilitate better coordination are discussed briefly.

4.2 Adaptation cost estimates

Several attempts have been made in recent years to estimate the cost of adapta-tion. This is a challenging task because there is no operational definition that can be used to specify adaptation measures and then estimate the associated capital and operating costs.

Early estimates used one approach, or a combination of two approaches. The first approach, developed by the World Bank (2006), uses an estimate of the fraction of each type of investment in developing countries (development assis-tance, foreign direct investment, etc.) that is climate-sensitive, and applies a 'mark up' factor to this fraction of the current flow to reflect the cost of reducing the vulnerability of those investments to climate change. The second approach uses estimated costs for adaptation projects identified by the National Adaptation Programmes of Action (NAPAs) of a limited number of countries, and scales that amount up to cover all developing countries.

The adaptation costs estimated by these studies range from a few billion to over US$100 billion per year for the near future: US$9–41 (World Bank, 2006); US$4–37 (Stern, 2007); over US$50 (Oxfam, 2007); and US$86–109 (UNDP, 2007). Agrawala and Fankhauser (2008) note that, although there is a comforting convergence of estimates, they are not substantive studies, they borrow heavily from each other, and they have not been peer reviewed.

Three more recent studies – UNFCCC (2007), Parry *et al.* (2009) and the World Bank (2010a; Narain *et al.*, 2011) – use more elaborate approaches. Estimates were prepared separately by sector by comparing investment under a scenario based on the current climate with investment under a scenario based on the projected future climate; for example, water supply given the current and projected future climate. The list of sectors covered varies.

Each study estimated the adaptations needed to cope with the projected future climate. Adaptation measures that are economically optimal or that maintain same level of service or welfare (whether they are adequate to cope with current climate risks or not) were identified. In principle, economically optimal adapta-tion measures yield marginal benefits (reduced damages) equal to their marginal costs. This can be difficult to apply in sectors where damages, such as loss of ecosystems, are difficult to value. Identifying adaptation measures that enable residents to enjoy the same level of welfare is easier, but still complicated (Narain *et al.*, 2011). For example, more reservoirs could in theory be built to maintain water supplies, but such infrastructure can displace people and cause environ-mental harm.

A critical issue is the degree to which societies are adequately adapted to the current climate. Adaptation to the existing (normal) climate is often less than could be expected or is not economically feasible, so there is an existing 'adaptation deficit' (Burton, 2004). This adaptation deficit, discussed below, is excluded from the baseline and therefore from the cost estimates, with the exception of the Parry *et al.* (2009) study, which explicitly estimates costs to make up for the adaptation deficit.

For most sectors, these studies estimate the investment (capital cost) required for 'hard' adaptation measures such as the construction of sea walls or reservoirs in some future year (e.g. 2030) or period (e.g. 2010–2050). The incremental operating costs of these measures and the costs of 'soft' adaptation measures, such as capacity building, are rarely estimated. Assuming the incremental operating and maintenance costs are positive, the investment is a lower bound for the adaptation cost. However, if assistance is calculated as a share of the capital cost, the estimated investment is sufficient to calculate the funding needed. For some sectors, such as health, the adaptation costs are estimated costs of treating illnesses; for some other sectors, the cost of adaptation is developed using the 'mark-up' approach described above.

The three estimates, from UNFCCC (2007), Parry *et al.* (2009) and World Bank (2010a), are summarized in Table 4.1. The UNFCCC estimated that additional investment of US$28–67 billion per year will be needed by 2030 for adaptation in developing countries.[1] The World Bank estimated that the adaptation costs for developing countries will be approximately US$80–90 billion annually by 2030. Parry and colleagues revised the UNFCCC estimates, but also added estimates for adaptation of natural ecosystems and investments to rectify the adaptation deficit, making their total much higher. None of the estimates includes the cost of 'residual damage', where complete adaptation is not technically feasible or simply too expensive. The rough similarity of the totals when the same sectors are compared and the adaptation deficit is ignored masks considerable variation in the estimates for many of the sectors.

The large estimate for infrastructure in the Parry *et al.* (2009) study illustrates the importance of the assumed baseline. The studies project a considerable amount of economic development, which becomes the baseline. The cost of moving from the current situation to that baseline is not considered an adaptation cost, except for infrastructure in the Parry *et al.* (2009) study.

A recent study by Project Catalyst (2009), which includes costs for soft measures and accounts for the potential co-benefits of adaptation actions, estimated costs of €21–61 (US$30–$90) billion by 2030. Most (65–80 per cent) of the total is the incremental cost of hard adaptation measures.

In contrast, attempts to estimate adaptation costs at a regional level can result in much higher estimates. Watkiss *et al.* (2010) estimated adaptation needs for Africa. They estimated that climate change adaptation requires at least US$25 billion per year in the next two years, and this will increase to US$60 billion per year by 2030. However, the authors note the wide range of estimates and the incompatibility of many of the studies.[2]

Table 4.1 Comparison of published estimates of developing country adaptation costs (US$ billions per year in 2030)

Sector	UNFCCC (2007)	Parry et al. (2009)	World Bank (2010a)
Agriculture, forestry, fisheries	7	7	6
Water resources	9	Much higher than UN or World Bank	11
Human health	5	At least 10	3
Coastal zones	5	10	29
Infrastructure	22–41	65–154	29
Extreme events	-	-	7
Fisheries	-	-	2
Ecosystem	-	33–40[a]	-
Total	28–67	>134–230	80–90[b]

Notes:

a Parry *et al.* (2009) reported a global estimate of US$65 – 80 billion. We assume that half of this amount is in developing countries.

b Range is from World Bank (2010) report. Estimates by sector are based on reported numbers for 2020s and 2030s.

Sectoral estimates of adaptation costs have been developed in a number of country studies through the UNFCCC 'National Economic, Environment and Development Study (NEEDS) for Climate Change Project' and the United Nations Development Programme (UNDP) project for 'Capacity Development for Policy Makers to Address Climate Change'. Available estimates are presented in Table 4.2. The estimates cover both capital and operating costs, but use different discount rates. If the global estimates presented above are spread over more than 130 developing countries, the average is less than US$1 billion per country per year. The figures in Table 4.2, with the exception of Bangladesh and Nigeria, are of that order of magnitude. All the caveats and limitations that apply to the global estimates apply to these figures as well. However, they cover both capital and operating costs, although often not soft costs.

In summary, the approach to estimating adaptation costs has evolved rapidly from simple multipliers to more detailed assessments, some including operating costs and also costs of soft adaptation measures. In all cases, however, to estimate adaptation needs across the globe, uniform and hence simplifying assumptions are applied. The baseline conceptually distinguishes adaptation from development, but the sensitivity of adaptation costs to the choice of development (baseline) has not been explored. The options for selecting adaptation measures – economic efficiency or welfare maintenance – have been identified, but the cost implications have not been explored. The change in residual damage from the baseline could, in principle, be estimated, but this has not yet been attempted. Nonetheless, the estimates do give an insight into the order of magnitude of adaptation needs in developing countries.

Table 4.2 Adaptation cost estimates for selected countries and sectors for 2030 (US$ billions per year, negative values indicate savings)

Country	Period	Sectors and Discount Rate	Incremental Cost	
			Total	Annual Average
Capacity building for policy makers to address climate change				
Bangladesh	2010–2030	Agriculture (5%)	39.665	1.888
	2010–2030	Water (5.5%)	25.848	1.231
Colombia	2005–2030	Agriculture (0%)	0.728	0.028
Costa Rica	2010–2030	Biodiversity (0.1%)	1.351	0.064
	2010–2030	Water (0.1%)	2.057	0.097
Dominican Republic	2010–2030	Water (5%)	2.793	0.133
	2010–2030	Tourism (1.58%)	0.779	0.037
Ecuador	2011–2030	Food Security (0.1%)	2.377	0.119
Gambia	2010–2030	Agriculture (12%)	0.016	0.0006
	2011–2030	Water (2%)	–0.014	–0.0001
Honduras	2005–2030	Water (0%)	1.112	0.043
Liberia	2005–2030	Agriculture (1.5%)	1.407	0.054
Namibia	2005–2030	Agriculture (8%)	2.888	0.111
Niger	2005–2030	Livestock (4.95%)	0.373	0.014
Paraguay	2010–2030	Health (0%)	0.147	0.007
	2005–2030	Agriculture (3%)	0.161	0.006
Peru	2010–2030	Agriculture (4.3%)	1.125	0.054
	2010–2030	Water (4.3%)	0.953	0.045
	2010–2030	Fisheries (4.3%)	0.280	0.013
Togo	2005–2030	Agriculture (4.5–6.75%)	0.166	0.006
Turkmenistan	2005–2030	Water (10%)	1.732	0.067
Uruguay	2006–2030	Agriculture (1%)	4.598	0.184
NEEDS project				
Egypt	2010–2020	Agriculture, irrigation, coastal zones, observation systems, socio-economic studies of the cost of adaptation, capacity-building and training for adaptation (discount rate not specified)	2.800	0.255
Ghana	2006–2020	Agriculture, coastal zones, health (discount rate not specified)	0.697	0.046
Jordan	2005–2020	Agriculture (discount rate not specified)	0.154	0.010
	2005–2020	Water (discount rate not specified)	2.640	0.165

| Maldives | 2010–2020 | Water, coastal protection, health, flood control, settlements and infrastructure (discount rate not specified) | 0.279 | 0.025 |
| Nigeria | 2010–2030 | Water, agriculture, health, transport (discount rate not specified) | 125.950 | 11.450 |

Source: Compiled from the respective country reports.

4.3 Current adaptation funding

Some bilateral and multilateral assistance includes funding for adaptation. In addition, funding is provided by a few adaptation funds. Developed countries are expected to provide information on the financial assistance they provide to developing countries for climate purposes in their national communications to the UNFCCC. Owing to gaps and inconsistencies in reporting approaches, it is not possible to calculate the financial assistance provided using information from these documents (UNFCCC, 2007). The Organisation for Economic Co-operation and Development (OECD) has monitored aid, targeting the objectives of the UNFCCC and other Rio Conventions, by integrating the 'Rio markers' into its Creditor Reporting System. Adaptation funding will be reported for the first time in 2010 and will be published in 2011.

Despite the limited information available, estimates of current adaptation funding range from US$1 to US$4 billion per year. The World Bank has estimated the current climate change funding at approximately US$10 billion per year, including adaptation funding of less than US$1 billion per year (World Bank, 2010b). The Stockholm Environment Institute has prepared annual reports on the nature and amounts of bilateral climate finance committed in 2008 and 2009 by the French Development Agency (AFD), the European Investment Bank (EIB), the Japan International Cooperation Agency (JICA) and the Development Bank of Germany (KfW); a report for 2010 is in progress. The total amount of climate finance reported by these four organizations for 2008 was US$10.3 billion, of which just over US$3 billion was for adaptation (Atteridge *et al.*, 2009). In 2009, the total amount of climate finance had increased by 25 per cent to US$12.9 billion, while the amount for adaptation had increased by 31 per cent to almost US$4 billion (Kehler Siebert *et al.*, 2010). These numbers suggest that total current adaptation funding may be higher than Project Catalyst's estimates of US$3–4 billion per year (Project Catalyst, 2010a).

Additional information is available on the funding provided by six funds with an adaptation focus: the Least Developed Countries Fund (LDCF), the Special Climate Change Fund (SCCF), the Strategic Priority on Adaptation (SPA) of the Global Environment Facility (GEF), the Adaptation Fund under the Kyoto Protocol, the environment and climate change thematic window of the Millennium

Development Goals (MDG) Achievement Fund, and the Pilot Program for Climate Resilience. Table 4.3 summarizes these multilateral adaptation funds.

Total annual funding for adaptation from these specialized funds amounts to US$100–200 million per year, less than 10 per cent of the estimated annual adaptation funding.

Adaptation funding for 2010–2012 could increase substantially as a result of commitments made by developed countries in the Copenhagen Accord. Developed countries committed to collectively 'provide new and additional resources approaching $30 billion for the period 2010 to 2012 with balanced allocation between adaptation and mitigation' (UNFCCC, 2009). Several organizations

Table 4.3 Summary of adaptation funds

Name of fund	Funding	Status/other
LDCF Became operational in 2002, administered by the GEF	GEF has voluntary pledges of US$224 million for the LDCF, of which US$169 million has been received (June 2010)	Approximately US$140 million has been dispersed by GEF (ODI, 2010)
SCCF (2002) (GEF)	As of June 2010, pledges from 14 participants made, amounting to US$148 million, of which US$110 million has been received (GEF, 2010b)	Although the SCCF has four windows, most of the pledges and funds disbursed are for adaptation
SPA (2004) (GEF)	The SPA received US$50 million, which has been allocated to 22 projects; by September 2009, all SPA funding was allocated	The SPA was a 'one-time-only' initiative; all future adaptation projects of the GEF will be funded through the LDCF and the SCCF (GEF, 2010a)
Adaptation Fund (2009) Administered by Adaptation Fund Board (AFB)	As of November 2010, the total amount pledged including CERs, was US$216.15 million of which US$202.11 million had been deposited	In June 2010, the AFB approved the first four project proposals to receive funding (AFB, 2010)
MDG Achievement Fund, Environment and climate change thematic window (2007) (UNDP)	As of November 2010, pledges amounted to US$90 million all of which had been received	All of the funds received have been committed and about US$62 million has been disbursed
Pilot Program for Climate Resilience (2008) (World Bank)	As of 31 March 2010, pledges for US$975 million made, US$161 million received	About US$9 million disbursed as of July 2010

Sources: AFB (2010), GEF (2010a, 2010b) and ODI (2010).

have tabulated announced pledges (Climate Funds Update, 2010; Fallasch and De Marez, 2010; Project Catalyst, 2010a; World Development Movement, 2010; World Resources Institute, 2010).[3] To date, the pledges total US$27–33 billion.

There is no agreement on the baseline for assessing whether fast-start finance pledges are 'new and additional'. Several possible baselines have been proposed (Brown *et al.*, 2010; Project Catalyst, 2010b; Stadelmann *et al.*, 2010a). Depending upon the baseline chosen, between all and almost none of the amount pledged is new and additional (Project Catalyst, 2010b; Fallasch and De Marez, 2010; Stadelmann *et al.*, 2010b). Current indications are that adaptation will receive less than half of the fast-start funding, and most of the fast-start funding will be disbursed bilaterally (Project Catalyst, 2010b). If most of the fast-start finance is new and additional, and close to half is devoted to adaptation, it would more than double current funding for adaptation.

At the 16th Conference of Parties to the UNFCCC (COP-16) in Cancún, Parties established the Cancún Adaptation Framework to enhance adaptation efforts by all countries and an Adaptation Committee to provide technical support to Parties, facilitate sharing of information and best practices, and advise the Conference of the Parties (COP) on adaptation-related matters. It was also agreed that a significant share of new multilateral funding for adaptation should flow through the Green Climate Fund under the guidance of the COP (UNFCCC, 2010b).

4.4 Future adaptation funding

In the Copenhagen Accord, developed countries committed to 'a goal of mobilizing jointly US$100 billion a year by 2020 to address the needs of developing countries. This funding will come from a wide variety of sources, public and private, bilateral and multilateral, including alternative sources of finance' (UNFCCC, 2009). There is a long-established target for developed countries to provide development assistance equal to 0.7 per cent of their gross national income (GNI) (e.g. Sachs, 2005). In 2008, only five countries met this target, and total development assistance represented 0.31 per cent of total GNI (OECD, 2010).

The long-standing gap between the target and the development assistance provided by developed countries suggests that sources other than developed-country government budgets may be essential for increased climate-change funding. In February 2010, the UN Secretary General established a High Level Advisory Group on Climate Change Financing (AGF) to assess potential sources of revenue. The AGF concluded that a combination of sources will probably be required to achieve the target of US$100 billion per year by 2020 (United Nations, 2010; Romani and Stern, Chapter 7). Different sources will most likely be needed to effectively address different types of climate actions; for example, grants and highly concessional loans are crucial for adaptation in the most vulnerable developing countries.

Historically, adaptation has received much less than half of the climate change funding. Thus, even if the challenge of generating US$100 billion per year is met, less than US$50 billion might be available for adaptation.

Recent estimates of adaptation costs in developing countries after 2020 exceed US$50 billion per year. Of course, the adaptation cost estimates are uncertain and the share of those costs to be covered by international assistance has not been agreed. Agreement on the share of adaptation costs to be funded internationally will require implicit or explicit agreement on issues such as the criteria for specifying adaptation measures (maintenance of welfare or economic efficiency), how cost savings within the country are treated, how the adaptation deficit (discussed later in this chapter) is addressed and whether changes to residual damages are considered.

At present, funders choose from among available projects when providing financial support for adaptation projects. If the level of financial support is increased by an order of magnitude and funding for adaptation and development is coordinated (as discussed in this chapter), more adaptation funding will need to be distributed on a country basis. The share of estimated adaptation costs and the issues this raises could be important when determining country funding allocations.

4.5 Development funding of climate-sensitive activities

Many development activities are sensitive to climate. The authors examined development funding for climate-sensitive activities from selected bilateral and multilateral organizations. ODA's main objective, as defined by OECD (2009), is 'promotion of the economic development and welfare of developing countries'. ODA is provided through bilateral development agencies such as the Danish International Development Agency (DANIDA) and through multilateral organizations such as the World Bank. The World Bank (2006) estimates that 40 per cent of concessional and ODA assistance is invested in climate-sensitive activities.

The authors reviewed information on ODA by sector to obtain an indication of the extent to which development aid is being directed towards projects in sectors that are climate-sensitive, that is, sectors that can be affected (positively or negatively) by climate variability or change. Investments in the climate-sensitive sectors are most vulnerable to climate change, and are therefore a priority for adaptation. For example, agriculture is sensitive because temperature and precipitation directly affect crop growth. The climate-sensitive sectors are agriculture, fisheries, water resources and water infrastructure, human health, forestry, wildlife and ecosystems, transportation infrastructure, energy and tourism.

Data on total development aid to climate-sensitive sectors were collected for the bilateral and multilateral organizations that have the largest contributions to development. The data are presented in Table 4.4. More than US$45 billion was spent by these organizations on development projects in climate-sensitive sectors in 2008. Transportation and infrastructure accounted for the largest component of this amount (US$14.6 billion), followed by energy development (US$10.5 billion).

Development aid for some of the sectors listed in Table 4.4 is potentially over-estimated. This is because many aid organizations report spending in sector clusters, not all of which are climate-sensitive. For example, many of the aid organizations cluster transportation and communications. Although transportation sectors are considered climate-sensitive, communications sectors are less so. The figures in the table include spending on sector clusters that could include sectors with low climate sensitivity.

The World Bank provides substantially more resources to climate-sensitive sectors than any other organization. Indeed, one-third of the funding reported in Table 4.4 is from the World Bank. Two regional banks, the Asian Development Bank (ADB) and the Inter-American Development Bank (IDB), took the next highest funding spots. However, the role of the multilateral agencies is over-stated, because many bilateral aid organizations such as those from the Netherlands, Scandinavian countries and Canada are not included.

4.6 Climate funding of development activities

NAPAs are prepared by developing countries to identify their most 'urgent' adaptation needs. About half of NAPAs (22 out of 45; UNFCCC, 2010c) were examined to divide the proposed projects into three categories: climate proofing (making investments less vulnerable to climate change), vulnerability reduction, and standalone adaptation (addressing emerging climate change impacts), based on McGray *et al.* (2007). Only NAPAs submitted in English were examined. The results are displayed in Table 4.5. It seems unlikely that inclusion of the other NAPAs would substantially change the estimated allocation of projects in the table.

The placement of projects in categories is subjective. Other analysts may come up with a different allocation of NAPA projects. About three-fifths of the projects fit into the vulnerability reduction category. These are investments that are basically for development, but can also reduce vulnerability to climate change. Thus, approximately two-fifths of development funding is for projects in climate-sensitive sectors and approximately three-fifths of climate change adaptation funding appears to be for development. These ratios are rough and could change based on further analysis. The key point is that there is a lot of overlap between what is thought of as development funding and what is thought of as adaptation funding.

This apparent overlap should not be surprising. A great deal of development investment is in projects and activities that are sensitive to climate and hence to climate change. If such investments do not sufficiently consider risks due to climate change, they could increase vulnerability to climate change. Most adaptation funding is for activities that aid development and reduce vulnerability to climate change. If such investments support development, it is important that they be consistent with development goals. With such overlap, there is a need for coordination between adaptation and development funding.

Table 4.4 Total development spending on climate change-sensitive sectors, by sector, in 2008 (US$ million)

Sector	Multilateral organization		Regional organization			Bilateral organization				Sector total
	World Bank	UNDP	ADB	AfDB[a]	IDB	USAID	DFID	JICA and JBIC[a]	AFD[a,b]	
Energy	4,180.3		2,722.4	1,469.6	540.7			1,563.8		10,476.8
Tourism					204.4			0.4		204.8
Agriculture, fishing, forestry and other natural resource management	1,360.6		528.3	282.5	567.1	448.5		239.1	131.6	3,557.7
Health	1,607.9	57.2	226.3		15.0	2,798.5	798.5	2.0	129.2	5,634.6
Transportation and infrastructure	4,829.9		2,903.2	1,196.1	3,460.9	462.7		1,777.1		14,629.9
Water supply, sanitation, waste management and flood protection	2,359.9		461.5	334.2	797.2		105.3	2,006.5	872.8	6,937.4
Urban development					761.1			121.5		882.6
Other environmental, not disaggregated by sector	298.0			15.5	394.0	138.5	55.5	236.1	317.9	1,455.5
Multiple climate-sensitive sectors					727.4				812.3	1,539.7
Organization total	14,338.6	355.2	6,841.7	3,298.0	6,740.4	3,848.3	1,686.6	5,932.7	2,263.8	45,319.0

Notes:

a Data were not available for 2008 at the time the analysis was done. Numbers reflect 2007 amounts. Only ODA is reported.

b Multiple climate-sensitive sector estimates for AFD include energy and infrastructure combined. Data were collected from organizations' annual reports, in particular their fiscal operations analyses, where available. To account for organizational differences in sector classification, broad sector descriptions were used.

Values may not sum correctly due to rounding. Data for GTZ spending by climate-sensitive sector were not available for comparison with other organizations. The GEF provides funding to other multilateral agencies. Although GEF funding for projects in climate-sensitive sectors was analysed, the data are not included in this table to avoid double-counting.

Table 4.5 Placement of NAPA projects in three adaptation categories

Category	Number of projects	Total cost (US$)	Average cost (US$)	% of projects	% of cost
1. Climate proofing	45	105,182,540	2,337,390	22	19
2. Vulnerability reduction	119	339,620,002	2,853,950	58	62
3. Standalone	41	104,199,185	2,541,444	20	19
	205	549,001,727			

The NAPAs included were from Bangladesh, Bhutan, Burundi, Cambodia, Cape Verde, Comoros, Eritrea, Ethiopia, Gambia, Guinea Bissau, Kiribati, Lesotho, Malawi, Maldives, Mauritania, Rwanda, Samoa, Tanzania, Uganda and Zambia. A single Ethiopian proposal on water development was excluded because its size, US$700 million, would dwarf the other projects and distort the analysis.

4.7 The adaptation deficit

An important factor in estimating adaptation costs is whether the adaptation deficit (also referred to as the development deficit; World Bank, 2010a) is a problem for adaptation or for development. This is an example of the issues raised by separating adaptation and development.

Many climate-sensitive sectors in developing countries are currently not well adapted to the risks from current climate. For example, an area may have no or inadequate protection from current climate risks such as floods and drought. This is the adaptation deficit (Burton, 2004). With the exception of the Parry *et al.* (2009) study, the cost of addressing the adaptation deficit is not included in the adaptation cost estimates reviewed earlier; those estimates assume that climate change adaptations return the areas to the present level of vulnerability. They do not include additional costs of reducing present vulnerability to a desired level.

Is the adaptation deficit a problem of adapting to climate change or a problem of development? If all future development is well adapted to the future climate, the adaptation deficit might eventually disappear as development occurs, for example as flood control facilities are built or replaced. The adaptation deficit can then be considered a 'development deficit' (e.g. World Bank, 2010a). Funding to reduce the adaptation deficit would probably flow through traditional development mechanisms such as the bilateral and multilateral development institutions. Currently, the adaptation deficit appears to be growing, as reflected in the rising losses from climate-related extreme weather events (Munich Re, 2008).

Regardless of whether the adaptation deficit is treated as a development issue or an adaptation issue, the deficit exists. At a minimum, it is more evidence of the need for coordination between adaptation and development funding.

4.8 Coordination and integration of adaptation and development funding

Coordination between development funds and adaptation funds could help ensure that all funds support development and adaptation to climate change. Such coordination may require:

- better information on adaptation funding needs, effectiveness and how adaptation funding is distributed;
- mechanisms to coordinate national adaptation (and more broadly climate change) plans with development plans;
- mechanisms to coordinate funding for adaptation with development funding on a national basis;
- an institutional arrangement for international coordination of adaptation (and more broadly climate change) and development funding.

Efforts to address each of these requirements have been initiated. These efforts are happening at both national and international levels. At the national level, mechanisms are being set up to coordinate aid from different sources. At the international level, reporting mechanisms are being used to track adaptation funding from developed countries.

A growing number of developing countries are establishing 'national funding entities' to manage international and domestic climate change funding and to help mainstream programmes and projects into national development strategies and plans at the country level (Gomez-Echeverri, 2010). Existing funds include the Amazon Fund of Brazil, the Bangladesh Climate Change Resilience Fund, the Brazil National Fund on Climate Change, the China CDM Fund, China Funds for the Environment, the Ecuador Yasuni ITT Trust Fund, the Guyana REDD Investment Fund, the Indonesia Climate Change Trust Fund, the Maldives Climate Change Trust Fund and the Thailand Energy Efficiency Revolving Fund (Gomez-Echeverri, 2010). In addition, funds are being developed or are in the process of being established in Costa Rica, Nigeria, India, Indonesia and the Philippines.

As noted above, reporting by developed countries in their national communications on their financial support to developing countries does not yield data that can be aggregated to describe the support provided. In the Cancun Agreements, Parties decided that developed countries shall improve the reporting of information on the provision of financial support to developing countries through enhanced common reporting formats and methodologies for tracking of climate-related support (UNFCCC, 2010a). They also decided that developing countries should submit biennial update reports, inter alia, on needs and support received. In principle, this could create a 'double entry' book-keeping system, with developed countries reporting the climate-related funding provided and developing countries reporting the funds received.

In contrast, but possibly complementary to national-level coordination, the OECD tracks development assistance by developed countries. The OECD monitors aid targeting the objectives of the three Rio Conventions, including the UNFCCC, by integrating the Rio markers into its Creditor Reporting System. To date, UNFCCC reporting has focused on mitigation; adaptation funding will be reported for the first time in 2010, for publication in 2011. The marker identifies funded activities for which climate change mitigation, and now adaptation, is a 'principal' or 'significant' objective. When an activity has multiple objectives, no attempt is made to apportion the funding between the different objectives. Assuming that the reporting is complete and accurate, the adaptation and mitigation markers would provide information on the geographic and sectoral distribution of the development assistance that contributes to mitigation and adaptation, as well as an upper-bound estimate of the total support provided by developed countries.[4]

In the Cancun Agreements, Parties decided to establish a Standing Committee under the COP to, inter alia, assist the COP in exercising its functions with respect to measurement, reporting and verification of support provided to developing countries and improving coherence and coordination in the delivery of climate change financing.

Improved integration of climate adaptation funding with development funding, at the international level, is also occurring through the work of the OECD (Gigli and Agrawala, 2007). The need for better coordination between the Convention Funds, the multilateral development agencies and the bilateral donor is well recognized and is the subject of much discussion both within and outside the Convention negotiations.

Effective coordination of adaptation funding at the national and international level will in all likelihood be a major challenge. National-level coordinating bodies could coordinate the many sources of funding for adaptation, mitigation and other development activities. There are likely to be many impediments including different requirements of donors and the many different government and non-government aid entities. Coordination will also require harmonization of international aid efforts, which also cut across adaptation, mitigation and other development activities. One crucial element will be the reporting of aid data to help show where needs exist and where aid is flowing. An institutional arrangement, such as regular meetings of funders and recipients, could help improve coordination. The type of regime that will emerge post-Durban (COP-17 in 2011) remains to be seen.

4.9 Conclusions

Several recent studies have estimated the cost of adapting to climate change in developing countries. Although the methods and coverage differ, they all show costs of tens of billions of dollars per year, perhaps over US$100 billion per year by 2030. Although developed countries have promised assistance to help meet the costs of adaptation, the share of the cost to be covered by international assistance has not yet been agreed. At present, international financial support for adaptation in developing countries is estimated at US$1–4 billion per year, well below estimated future needs. More has been promised in the Copenhagen Accord and the Cancun Agreement. However, even if the US$100 billion per year committed for 2020 is generated, it is not clear that it will be sufficient to meet adaptation and other climate change needs.

International funding for development is much larger than that for climate change. Of this funding, US$45 billion was invested in climate-sensitive sectors in 2008. The majority of funding needs for adaptation identified by developing countries through their NAPAs can be considered investments in development. Thus, there are some potentially strong benefits in coordinating development funding and climate change adaptation funding.

To facilitate improved coordination, efforts have been initiated to encourage the formulation of low-carbon development strategies or plans in the context of sustainable development. A number of developing countries have established national funding entities to coordinate domestic and international funding for adaptation with development funding, on a national basis. Initiatives to improve the reporting of climate change finance are under way at the UNFCCC and the OECD. The value of a mechanism for improving coherence and coordination in the delivery of climate change financing has also been recognized in the UNFCCC. Together, these initiatives are a start towards coordinating adaptation and development funding for developing countries.

Acknowledgements

We wish to acknowledge the support provided by Jody Jennings, Diane Callow, Erin Miles and Mary Kay Kozyra at Stratus Consulting Inc. in preparing the manuscript. We also wish to acknowledge the research assistance, comments and advice from Tarik Islam, Tom Downing, Susanne Olbrisch, three anonymous referees and the journal's adjudicator.

Notes

1 US$100 billion is approximately 0.75 per cent of projected investment in developing countries in 2030. The World Bank (2006) estimated the climate-sensitive share of concessional and ODA finance at 40 per cent, foreign direct investment at 10 per cent and gross domestic investment at 2–10 per cent.
2 The World Bank (2010a) study also estimates adaptation costs at a national level. Unfortunately, it is difficult to compare the regional and national estimates.
3 A partial list of pledges is also available at www.faststartfinance.org/content/contributing-countries.
4 A few countries and multilateral development banks do not yet use the mitigation marker when they report. The accuracy of the mitigation marker has been questioned by Michaelowa and Michaelowa (2010).

Bibliography

AFB, 2010, *Financial Stats of the Adaptation Fund Trust Fund and the Administrative Trust Fund*, AFB/EFC.1/5, Adaptation Fund Board, Bonn, Germany.

Agrawala, S., Fankhauser, S. (eds), 2008, *Economic Aspects of Adaptation to Climate Change. Costs, Benefits and Policy Instruments*, OECD, Paris.

Atteridge, A., Kehler Siebert, C., Klein, R.J.T., Butler, C., Tella, P., 2009, *Bilateral Finance Institutions and Climate Change: A Mapping of Climate Portfolios*, SEI Working Paper 2009, Stockholm Environment Institute, Stockholm, Sweden [available at http://sei-international.org/mediamanager/documents/Publications/Climate-mitigation-adaptation/bilateral-finance-institutions-climate-change.pdf].

Bowen, A., 2011, 'Raising climate finance to support developing country action: some economic considerations', *Climate Policy 11*(3), 1020–1036.

Brown, J., Bird, N., Schalatek, L., 2010, *Climate Finance Additionality: Emerging Definitions and their Implications*, Climate Finance Policy Brief No. 2, Heinrich Bö ll Stiftung North America and Overseas Development Institute [available at www.odi.org.uk/resources/download/4931.pdf].

Burton, I., 2004, *Climate Change and the Adaptation Deficit*, Environment Canada, Downsview, Ontario, Canada [also in Schipper, E.L.F., Burton, I. (eds), 2009, *Adaptation to Climate Change: The Earthscan Reader*, Earthscan, London].

Climate Funds Update, 2010, *Fast Start Finance* [available at www.climatefundsupdate.org/fast-start-finance].

Fallasch, F., De Marez, L., 2010, *Assessment of Progress on Fast-Start Finance Commitments*, Climate Analytics, Potsdam, 1 December 2010 version [available at www.climateanalytics.org/].

GEF, 2010a, *Adaptation* [available at http://thegef.org/gef/adaptation].

GEF, 2010b, *Progress Report on the Least Developed Country Fund (LDCF) and the Special Climate Change Fund (SCCF)*, GEF/LDCF.SCCF.8/Inf 3, Global Environment Facility, Washington, DC.

Gigli, S., Agrawala, S., 2007, *Stocktaking of Progress on Integrating Adaptation to Climate Change into Development Co-operation Activities*, OECD, Paris.

Gomez-Echeverri, L., 2010, *National Funding Entities: Their Role in the Transition to a New Paradigm of Global Co-operation on Climate Change*, European Capacity Building Initiative, Oxford [available at www.eurocapacity. org].

Kehler Siebert, C., Atteridge, A., Klein, R.J.T., 2010, *Bilateral Finance Institutions and Climate Change: A Mapping of 2009 Climate Financial Flows to Developing Countries*, UNEP Climate Change Working Group for Bilateral Finance Institutions, Paris

McGray, H., Hammill, A., Bradley, R., Schipper, L., Parry, J., 2007, *Weathering the Storm: Options for Framing Adaptation and Development*, World Resources Institute, Washington, DC.

Michaelowa, A., Michaelowa, K., 2010, *Coding Error or Statistical Embellishment? The Political Economy of Reporting Climate Aid*, Working Paper 56, Center for Comparative and International Studies, Universität Zürich, Zurich [available at www.cis.ethz.ch/publications/publications/2010_WP56_michaelowa_michaelowa.pdf].

Munich Re, 2008, *Topics Geo, Natural Catastrophes 2007: Analyses, Assessments, Positions*, Munich Reinsurance Company, Munich.

Narain, U., Margulis, S., Essam, T., 2011, 'Estimating costs of adaptation to climate change', *Climate Policy 11*(3), 1001–1019.

ODI, 2010, *Climate Funds Update*, Overseas Development Institute, London [available at www.climatefundsupdate. org/listing/least-developed-countries-fund].

OECD, 2009, *Official Development Assistance*, Organisation for Economic Cooperation and Development, Paris [available at www.oecd.org/dataoecd/26/14/26415658.pdf].

Oxfam, 2007, *Adapting to Climate Change. What is Needed in Poor Countries and Who should Pay?*, Oxfam Briefing Paper 104, Oxfam, Oxford, UK.

Parry, M., Arnell, N., Berry, P., Dodman, D., Fankhauser, S., Hope, C., Kovats, S., Nicholls, R., Satterthwaite, D., Tiffin, R., Wheeler, T., 2009, *Assessing the Costs of Adaptation to Climate Change: A Review of the UNFCCC and Other Recent Estimates*, International Institute for Environment and Development and the Grantham Institute for Climate Change, Imperial College London, London.

Project Catalyst, 2009, *Adaptation to Climate Change: Potential Costs and Choices for a Global Agreement*, Climate Works Foundation, San Francisco, CA [available at www.project-catalyst.info/images/publications/adaptation_potential.pdf].

Project Catalyst, 2010a, *From Climate Finance to Financing Green Growth*, Briefing Paper, 23 November 2010, European Climate Foundation and Climate Works Foundation, San Francisco, CA [available at www.project-catalyst.info/images/publications/101127_from_climate_finance_to_financing_green_growth_formated.pdf].

Project Catalyst, 2010b, *Making Fast Start Finance Work*, Briefing Paper, 7 June 2010, European Climate Foundation and Climate Works Foundation, San Francisco, CA [available at www.project-catalyst.info/images/publications/2010-06-07_project_catalyst_-_fast_start_finance_-_full_report_-_7_june_version.pdf].

Sachs, J., 2005, *Ending Poverty: How We Can Make it Happen in Our Lifetime*, Penguin Books, New York.

Stadelmann, M., Roberts, J.T., Huq, S., 2010a, *Baseline for Trust: Defining 'New and Additional' Climate Funding*, International Institute for Environment and Development, London [available at www.iied.org/pubs/pdfs/17080IIED.pdf].

Stadelmann, M., Roberts, J.T., Michaelowa, A., 2010b, *Keeping a Big Promise: Options for Baselines to Assess 'New and Additional' Climate Finance*, CIS Working Paper 66, Center for Comparative and International Studies, Zurich, Switzerland [available at www.cis.ethz.ch/publications/publications/2010_WP66_Stadelmann_Michaelowa.pdf].

Stern, N., 2007, *Stern Review: Economics of Climate Change*, Cambridge University Press, Cambridge, UK.

UNDP, 2007, *Human Development Report 2007/08*, Palgrave Macmillan, New York.

UNFCCC, 2007, *Investment and Financial Flows to Address Climate Change*, United Nations Framework Convention Secretariat, Bonn, Germany [available at http://unfccc.int/files/cooperation_and_support/financial_mechanism/application/pdf/background_paper.pdf].

UNFCCC, 2009, *Copenhagen Accord*, Decision 2/CP.15, United Nations Framework Convention on Climate Change Secretariat, Bonn, Germany [available at http://unfccc.int/resource/docs/2009/cop15/eng/11a01.pdf].

UNFCCC, 2010a, *Cancun Agreements*, United Nations Framework Convention on Climate Change Secretariat, Bonn, Germany [available at http://unfccc.int/meetings/cop_16/items/5571.php].

UNFCCC, 2010b, *Outcome of the Work of the Ad Hoc Working Group on Long-Term Cooperative Action Under the Convention*, Draft Decision -/CP.16, United Nations Framework Convention on Climate Change Secretariat, Bonn, Germany [available at http://unfccc.int/files/meetings/cop_16/application/pdf/cop16_lca.pdf].

UNFCCC, 2010c, *NAPAs Received by the Secretariat* – Last Update: 09 November 2010, United Nations Framework Convention on Climate Change Secretariat, Bonn, Germany [available at http://unfccc.int/cooperation_support/least_developed_countries_portal/submitted_napas/items/4585.php].

United Nations, 1992, *United Nations Framework Convention on Climate Change*, FCCC/ INFORMAL/84 GE.05-62220 (E) 200705, United Nations, New York [available at http://unfccc.int/resource/docs/convkp/conveng.pdf].

United Nations, 2010, *Report of the Secretary-General's High-level Advisory Group on Climate Change Financing*, United Nations, New York [available at www.un.org/wcm/ content/site/climatechange/pages/financeadvisorygroup/ pid/13300].

Watkiss, P., Downing, T.E., Dyszynski, J., 2010, *AdaptCost Project: Analysis of the economic costs of climate change adaptation in Africa*, United Nations Environment Programme, with Stockholm Environment Institute and Global Climate Adaptation Partnership, Nairobi.

World Bank, 2006, *Managing Climate Risk: Integrating Adaptation into World Bank Group Operations*, World Bank, Washington, DC.

World Bank, 2010a, *The Costs to Developing Countries of Adapting to Climate Change: New Methods and Estimates*, World Bank, Washington, DC.

World Bank, 2010b, *World Development Report 2010*, World Bank, Washington, DC [available at http://econ.world-bank.org/WBSITE/EXTERNAL/EXTDEC/EXTRE SEARCH/EXTWDRS/EXTWDR2010/0,contentMDK:21969137~ menuPK:5287748~ pagePK:64167689~piPK:64167673~theSitePK:5287741,00.html].

World Development Movement, 2010, *A Long Way to go, an Update on the State of Fast Start Climate Finance*, World Development Movement, Edinburgh [available at www. wdm.org.uk/sites/default/files/alongwaytogo.pdf].

World Resources Institute, 2010, *Summary of Developed Country Fast-Start Climate Finance Pledges*, World Resources Institute, Washington, DC [available at http://pdf. wri.org/climate_finance_pledges_2010-11-24.pdf].

5   Estimating costs of adaptation to climate change

Urvashi Narain, Sergio Margulis and Timothy Essam

5.1 Introduction

As scientific evidence mounts about the deleterious impacts of climate change on economic development, the importance of understanding the likely cost to countries of adapting to climate change has increased substantially. This is particularly true for developing countries, which, historically, have not been the major contributors to greenhouse gas emissions, have nearly 85 per cent of the world's population, and will be affected to a greater extent because of their greater sensitivity to climate change (World Bank, 2010). Although developed countries have financial resources on which to draw to adapt to climate change, developing countries have limited resources available to close their current development deficit as well as to address the additional burden imposed by a changing climate.

Recognizing the inequality of climate change impacts and the need to help the developing world adapt to a warmer climate, policy makers from developed countries adopted the December 2007 Bali Action Plan at the United Nations Climate Change Conference. The plan agreed to allocate 'adequate, predictable, and sustainable financial resources and [to provide] new and additional resources, including official and concessional funding for developing country parties' (UNFCCC, 2007b, p.5) to help them adapt to climate change. Despite the agreement, the level of financial resources and the type of adaptation initiatives needed in many countries remained unclear, in part because the literature on adaptation costs was quite limited and fragmented (IPCC, 2007).

Previous adaptation studies can be divided into two camps, as summarized by Fankhauser (2010). First-generation studies rely primarily on a climate mark-up methodology that scales different types of investment flows sensitive to climate risk. Early studies (World Bank, 2006; Stern, 2006) put costs in the range of US$4–41 billion a year by 2050. However, little attention is devoted to the additional financing needed to climate-proof existing investments or to close the development deficit. Later studies (UNDP, 2007) add considerations for social protection programmes and costs grow to US$109 billion a year by 2015. Bottom-up approaches, such as those of Oxfam International (2007), consider the finances needed for funding prioritized adaptation projects and non-governmental-led adaptation interventions, and report costs in the range of US$8–33 billion a year.

Fankhauser (2010) attests that the major limitation of these early studies is the lack of empirical grounding on the size of the mark-ups for climate-proofing.

Second-generation studies more critically analyse the sectoral breakdown of adaptation costs. The UNFCCC's (2007a) study covers five sectors[1] and accounts for the costs of both planned and private adaptation measures. It estimates costs to be around US$28–67 billion a year by 2030. A recent study (Project Catalyst, 2009), which includes costs for soft measures, accounts for potential co-benefits of adaptation actions and devotes more attention to the sequencing of adaptation measures, estimates costs in the range of US$30–90 billion by 2030.

The wide divergence in adaptation costs, ranging from US$4 to US$109 billion, is not surprising considering the different methodological approaches and assumptions used in each study. However, some have argued that these estimates may be gross underestimates of adaptation costs. The Global Humanitarian Forum (2009) suggests that current adaptation needs to be scaled up 100 times to avert dire outcomes. Moreover, a recent critique by Parry *et al.* (2009) suggests that many of the estimates fall well short of the true costs of adaptation. Specifically, they assert that the UNFCCC estimates may be too low because some sectors were excluded, included sectors were not fully accounted for, climate-proofing of infrastructure stocks ignored the need for additional stocks for handling current climate variability, and the study did not account for residual damages (impacts remaining after adaptation).

With the 2009 Copenhagen climate negotiations looming on the horizon, the World Bank launched the Economics of Adaptation to Climate Change (EACC)[2] study to provide up-to-date and consistent adaptation cost estimates to the international community. In doing so, the EACC study addressed many of the shortcomings found in the adaptation literature. First, adaptation costs are clearly defined in the study as the additional costs of development due to climate change, an assumption that avoids confounding costs of closing the development deficit, and thus the implicit adaptation deficit.[3] Second, the study covers eight major sectors (infrastructure, coastal zones, water supply, agriculture, fisheries, forests and ecosystems, human health and extreme weather events). It embeds within each sector a common trajectory of population and gross domestic product (GDP) growth to establish a development baseline, and a common set of global climate models is used to simulate climate effects. Two climate scenarios are used to capture a full spread of model predictions to represent the inherent uncertainty in climate projections. Finally, the study applies an innovative methodology for aggregating costs at the sector level within a country, and across countries.

Under these assumptions, it is concluded in the EACC study that the costs for the developing world of adapting to an approximately 2°C warmer world by 2050 are in the range of US$70–100 billion a year for the period 2010–2050.

In Section 5.2, the difficulties of operationalizing adaptation costs are highlighted and the concepts that have come to define adaptation cost studies are reviewed. The EACC methodology used to simulate demographic and economic changes and climate impacts up to 2050 is outlined in Section 5.3, while a summary of the costs of adapting to climate change is presented in Section 5.4. The final section concludes and discusses future research topics.

5.2 Operationalizing adaptation costs

Among the challenges adaptation studies face is operationalizing adaptation costs as a concept. Adaptation costs are intuitively understood as those incurred by societies to adapt to changes in climate. The Intergovernmental Panel on Climate Change (IPCC) describes adaptation costs as 'the costs of planning, preparing for, facilitating, and implementing adaptation measures, including transition costs' (IPCC, 2007, p.76). However, this description is hard to operationalize. First, development as usual needs to be conceptually separated from adaptation. That requires deciding on whether the costs of development initiatives that enhance climate resilience ought to be counted as part of adaptation costs. It also requires deciding how to incorporate the adaptation deficit in those costs. Second, a working concept must define how much adaptation is necessary as well as the type of adaptation needed. It must determine how costs reflect the uncertainty about climate projections and impacts, and must specify how potential benefits from climate change in some sectors and countries offset (if at all) adaptation costs in another sector or country. The following section reviews each of these points and concludes with a summary of adaptation costs as defined by the EACC study.

5.2.1 *Links between adaptation and development*

One of the key messages emerging from the climate change literature is that development and adaptation are clearly linked. Schelling (1992) was one of the first to conclude that continued development may be one of the best defences against climate change. Not only does development enable an economy to diversify and become less reliant on sectors that are most likely to be vulnerable to the effects of climate change, it also makes more resources available for abating risk and recovering from disasters. Noy (2009) supports the latter point, showing that countries with advanced education levels, institutions, incomes and government spending are better able to withstand disaster shocks.

Adaptation is also viewed as essential for development: unless agricultural societies adapt to changes in temperature and precipitation, development will be delayed. Adaptation requires a new type of climate-smart development that makes countries more resilient to the effects of climate change. These links suggest that adaptation measures range from discrete adaptation to climate-smart development to development not as usual. McGray *et al.* (2007) highlight the dual relationship between adaptation and development initiatives, noting that adaptation may serve as a means to achieve development ends, and development activities may be a means to achieve an adaptation ends.

Developing countries today face not only a deficit in adapting to current climate variation, let alone future climate change, but also deficits in providing education, housing, health and other services. Thus, many countries face a more general development deficit of which the part related to climate variability and extremes has been termed the 'adaptation deficit' (Burton, 2004). As the adaptation deficit is difficult to operationalize and thus measure (except in the most abstract modelling exercise), the choice was made in the EACC study to estimate only additional adaptation costs. That is, the EACC study assumes that the adaptation deficit should be a part of the development baseline, so that adaptation costs should cover only the additional costs to cope with future climate change.

5.2.2 *How much to adapt? What kind of adaptation?*

The next issue is to decide how much countries should adapt to climate change. They can try to adapt fully, so that society is at least as well off as it was before climate change. They can choose to do nothing – to suffer (or enjoy the benefits from) the full impact of climate change – or they can decide to adapt to the level where the benefits from adaptation equal their costs, at the margin. The EACC study assumes that countries will adapt up to the level at which they enjoy the same level of welfare in the (future) world as they would have without climate change. This is not necessarily the most economically rational decision, but it is a practical rule that greatly simplifies the analysis.

To estimate the cost of actions that restore welfare in a future world with climate change, one must identify adaptation measures that can be classified by the types of economic agent initiating the measure: public or private. The literature (Carter *et al.*, 1994; Fankhauser *et al.*, 1999) distinguishes between autonomous (or spontaneous) adaptation and planned adaptation. The EACC study focuses on planned adaptation. This focus is not to imply that autonomous adaptation is costless. However, because the overall objective of the study is to help governments plan for risks, it is important to have an idea of what problems private markets will solve on their own, how public policies and investments can complement markets and what measures are needed to protect public assets and vulnerable people. For that, an assessment of planned adaptation is needed.

Table 5.1 summarizes each adaptation measure by sector. In all sectors except extreme weather events, 'hard' adaptation options involving engineering solutions are favoured over 'soft' options based on policy changes and social capital mobilization. For adaptation to extreme weather events, the emphasis is on investment in human resources, particularly those of women. The decision to focus on hard options for the global cost assessment was motivated largely by the fact that these are easier to cost.

5.2.3 *Adapt to what? Uncertainty about climate outcomes*

Operationalizing adaptation costs requires dealing with the considerable uncertainty about future climate projections. With a 2°C increase above pre-industrial levels by 2050 now considered highly probable under the business-as-usual assumption (Allen *et al.*, 2009; Meinshausen *et al.*, 2009), studies indicate that annual global mean average temperatures will increase, rainfall will become more

Table 5.1 Types of adaptation measures considered, by sector

Sector	Adaptation measure
Infrastructure	Design standards, climate-proofing maintenance
Coastal zones	River and sea dikes, beach nourishment, port upgrades
Water supply and flood protection	Reservoir storage, recycling, rainwater harvesting, desalination, flood protection dikes and polders
Agriculture	Agricultural research, rural roads, irrigation infrastructure expansion, efficiency improvements
Fisheries	Fisheries buybacks, individual transferable quotas, fish farming, livelihood diversification measures, marine-protected areas
Human health	Prevention and treatment of disease
Extreme weather events	Investment in human resources

Source: EACC study team.

intense in most places and possibly less frequent, sea levels will rise, other extreme climate events (such as hurricanes) will become more frequent and more intense, and regional climate systems such as the El Ninõ Southern Oscillation phenomenon and the Asian monsoon will be altered.

Although there is considerable consensus among climate scientists on these general outlines of climate change, there is much less agreement on how climate change will affect a given location. To capture a full spread of climate model predictions, the EACC study reports adaptation costs resulting from two climate models, one from the Commonwealth Scientific and Industrial Research Organization (CSIRO) and one from the National Centre for Atmospheric Research (NCAR).

5.2.4 Summing potential costs and benefits

The final step to operationalize adaptation costs requires developing a methodology for summing potential adaptation costs and benefits. One possible outcome is that changes in climate lead to lower investment requirements for some sectors in some countries. In such cases, the 'costs' of adaptation are negative. For calculating global costs, this becomes a summation problem. Rather than making an explicit decision on whether to offset potential benefits of climate change against the costs of adaptation, whether across sectors or countries, the study presents costs using three aggregation methods: gross (no netting of costs), net (benefits are netted across sectors and countries) and X-sums (positive and negative items are netted within countries but not across countries). The study opted to use X-sums in reporting most adaptation costs in the interest of space, although similar trends hold for the other aggregation methods.

5.2.5 Adaptation costs are ...

The EACC study defines adaptation costs as the costs of development initiatives needed in the developing world to restore (future) welfare to levels prevailing before climate change and not as optimal levels of adaptation plus residual damage.[4] Adaptation costs do not include the cost of closing the adaptation deficit, but do include planned adaptation measures and are mostly composed of hard adaptation options for nearly all sectors. Costs are also reported over a range of climate scenarios to reflect the inherent uncertainty in climate projections. Finally, costs are calculated using three summation options, each of which places different restrictions on offsetting negative and positive costs.

5.3 Main assumptions

Although the methodology used to estimate both the impacts of climate change and the costs of adaptation is specific to each sector, the sectoral methodologies share several elements.[5] Adaptation costs in most sectors were calculated for 2010–2050 from a common trajectory of population and GDP growth used to establish the development baseline and two common global climate models used to simulate climate effects.

5.3.1 Choosing a timeframe

The choice of timeframe for the analysis of the costs of adapting to climate change will be likely to affect the overall cost estimates, with a longer timeframe producing higher costs than would a shorter one. The EACC study uses a timeframe up to 2050, because forecasting climate change and its impacts on an economy becomes even more uncertain beyond this period, and the complexity of the analysis favours getting more precise estimates in the short term rather than less precise estimates over a more extended timeline. The timing of all investments in the sector models is determined by the outcomes of specific climate projections. Given the expected climate outcome within the useful life of an investment, each new investment must be designed to restore welfare to levels that would have existed without climate change. Owing to the complexity of modelling sectors at a global level, none of the sectoral models is capable of choosing the optimal timing of investments (with the exception of the models used for coastal zones). This implies that time paths of investments are insensitive to changes in the discount rate, and therefore all results are presented for a zero discount rate (although costs have been expressed in 2005 constant prices). Obviously, discounting the time stream of investment costs would lower the net present value of total investment or adaptation costs, but it would not influence the choice of investments or the underlying investment costs. The inability to model policy tradeoffs across time is a clear limitation imposed by the global nature of this study.

5.3.2 Using baseline GDP and population projections to account for continuing development

Most existing adaptation studies consider the present cost of adaptation, which does not allow for the quality changes that accompany economic growth. For example, design standards may change as a country grows and improves existing and new infrastructure. As countries become economically more advanced over the medium term, the economic impact of climate change will be altered, as will the type and extent of adaptation needed. The EACC study accounts for the impact of development on estimates of adaptation costs by establishing development baselines by sector. These baselines establish a fictional growth path in the absence of climate change that determines sectoral performance indicators such as the stock of infrastructure assets, level of nutrition and water supply availability. Climate change impacts and the costs of adaptation are examined in relation to this baseline. Table 5.2 shows the definition of the development baseline adopted for each sector.

Baselines are established across sectors using a consistent set of future population and GDP projections. The population trajectory is aligned with the United Nations Population Division's middle-fertility projections for 2006. The GDP trajectory is based on the average of the GDP growth projections of three major integrated assessment models of global emissions growth – Climate Framework for Uncertainty, Negotiation, and Distribution (FUND[6]; Anthoff and Tol, 2009), PAGE2002 (Hope, 2006) and the Regional Dynamic Integrated Model of Climate and the Economy (RICE99; Nordhaus and Boyer, 2000) – and growth projections used by the International Energy Agency and the Energy Information Administration of the US Department of Energy to forecast energy demand. Unlike the Special Report on Emissions Scenarios' (SRES) GDP projections, which are based on global numbers, all five sources provide growth estimates at a regionally disaggregated level.

The global average annual real GDP per capita growth rate constructed in this way is 2.1 per cent, which happens to be similar to global growth rates assumed in the UNFCCC A2 emissions scenario from the IPCC Fourth Assessment Report (AR4).

Table 5.2 Definition of development baseline, by sector

Sector	Development baseline
Infrastructure	Average sector performance by income groups
Coastal zones	Efficient protection of coastline
Water supply and flood protection	Average municipal and industrial water demand by income groups; efficient protection against monthly flood with given return period
Agriculture	Exogenous productivity growth, area expansion, investment in irrigation
Fisheries	Maintenance of 2010 fish stocks
Human health	Health standards by income groups
Forestry and ecosystem services	Not established
Extreme weather events	GDP-induced changes in mortality and numbers affected

Source: EACC study team.

5.3.3 Choosing climate scenarios and global climate models

Twenty-six global climate models provide climate projections based on the IPCC A2 Scenario from the SRES. The EACC study uses the NCAR Community Climate System Model 3 (CCSM3) and CSIRO Mk3.0 model to model climate change, because they capture a full spread of model predictions to represent inherent uncertainty, and they report the specific climate variables (minimum and maximum temperature changes) needed for sector analyses.

Although the model predictions do not diverge much for projected temperature increases by 2050 (both projecting increases of approximately 2°C above pre-industrial levels), they vary substantially for precipitation changes. Of the models reporting minimum and maximum temperature changes, the NCAR was the wettest scenario and the CSIRO the driest (globally, not necessarily the wettest and driest in every location) based on the climate moisture index. Climate projections for these two models were created with a 0.5 × 0.5 spatial degree scale and a monthly timescale by applying model predictions through 2050 to a historical climate baseline obtained from the University of East Anglia Climate Research Unit's Global Climate Database time series 2.1.

Analysis was limited to two scenarios rather than the mean multiple of the global climate models, because the mean masks extreme values. A model average of near-zero could be the result of models predicting near-zero change, but just as well the result of two opposing changes that differ in sign. Using a group of global climate models (multi-modal ensembles), as opposed to one model, can somewhat correct for biases and errors. The question with an ensemble approach is how to capture the full range of results from model runs.

5.4 Summary of results

The EACC study concludes that the cost between 2010 and 2050 of adapting to an approximately 2°C warmer world by 2050 is in the range of US$70–100 billion a year (Table 5.3). This range is of the same order of magnitude as the foreign aid that developed countries now give developing countries each year, but it is still a very low percentage of the wealth of countries (measured by their GDP).

Total adaptation costs average well over US$10 billion a year more, calculated by the gross sum method rather than by the other two methods. The difference is driven by countries that appear to benefit from climate change in the water supply and flood protection sector, especially in 'East Asia and Pacific' and 'South Asia'. The drier scenario (CSIRO) requires lower total adaptation costs than the wetter one (NCAR), largely because of the sharply lower costs for infrastructure, which outweigh the higher costs for water and flood management. In both scenarios, infrastructure, coastal zones, and water supply and flood protection account for the bulk of the costs. Infrastructure adaptation costs are highest for the wetter scenario, and coastal zone costs are highest for the drier scenario.

On a regional basis, for both climate scenarios, the East Asia and Pacific region bears the highest adaptation cost, and the 'Middle East and North Africa' the

Table 5.3 Total average annual costs of adaptation for all sectors, by region and climate change scenario, 2010 – 2050 (US$ billions at 2005 prices, no discounting)

Cost aggregation type	East Asia and Pacific	Europe and Central Asia	Latin America and Caribbean	Middle East and North Africa	South Asia	Sub-Saharan Africa	Total
NCAR, wettest scenario							
Gross sum	25.7	12.6	21.3	3.6	17.1	17.1	97.5
X-sum	21.7	11.2	18.7	2.4	12.4	15.1	81.5
Net sum	21.7	11.1	18.7	2.3	12.3	14.9	81.1
CSIRO, driest scenario							
Gross sum	20.1	8.1	17.9	3.5	18.7	16.4	84.8
X-sum	17.9	6.9	14.8	2.5	15.0	14.1	71.2
Net sum	17.7	6.5	14.5	2.4	14.6	13.8	69.6

Notes: The gross aggregation method sets negative costs in any sector in a country to zero before costs are aggregated for the country and for all developing countries. The X-sums net positive and negative items within countries, but not across countries, and include costs for a country in the aggregate as long as the net cost across sectors is positive for the country. The net aggregate measures net negative costs within and across countries.

Source: EACC study team.

lowest. 'Latin America and the Caribbean' and 'Sub-Saharan Africa' follow East Asia and the Pacific in both scenarios (Table 5.4). On a sector breakdown, the highest costs for East Asia and the Pacific are in infrastructure and coastal zones; for Sub-Saharan Africa, water supply and flood protection and agriculture; for Latin America and the Caribbean, water supply, and flood protection and coastal zones; and for South Asia, infrastructure and agriculture.

Not surprisingly, both climate scenarios show costs increasing over time, although falling as a percentage of GDP, suggesting that countries become less vulnerable to climate change as their economies grow (Figures 5.1 and 5.2).

Table 5.4 Total annual cost of adaptation and share of costs for NCAR scenario and CSIRO scenario, by region ($ billions at 2005 prices, X-sum, no discounting)

	NCAR		CSIRO	
	Cost	Share (%)	Cost	Share
East Asia and Pacific	21.7	27	17.9	25
Europe and Central Asia	11.2	14	6.9	10
Latin America and Caribbean	18.7	23	14.8	21
Middle East and North Africa	2.4	3	2.5	4
South Asia	12.4	15	15.0	21
Sub-Saharan Africa	15.1	19	14.1	20
Total	81.5	100	71.2	100

Source: EACC study team.

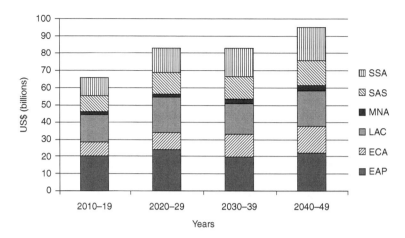

Figure 5.1 Total annual cost of adaptation for NCAR scenario, by region and decade (US$ (billions) at 2005 prices, X-sum, no discounting).

Notes: EAP, East Asia and Pacific; ECA, Europe and Central Asia; LAC, Latin America and Caribbean; MNA, Middle East and North Africa; SAS, South Asia; SSA, Sub-Saharan Africa.

Source: EACC study team.

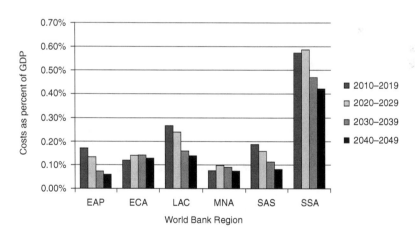

Figure 5.2 Total annual costs of adaptation for NCAR scenario as share of GDP, by decade and region (percent, at 2005 prices, X-sum, no discounting).

Notes: EAP, East Asia and Pacific; ECA, Europe and Central Asia; LAC, Latin America and Caribbean; MNA, Middle East and North Africa; SAS, South Asia; SSA, Sub-Saharan Africa.

Source: EACC study team.

There are considerable regional variations. Adaptation costs as a percentage of GDP are considerably higher in Sub-Saharan Africa than in any other region, denoting greater vulnerability.

5.4.1 Adaptation costs by sector

Table 5.5 contains a complete breakdown of costs by sector and climate scenario. The infrastructure sector has accounted for the largest share of adaptation costs in past studies and takes up a major share in the EACC study. (In fact, it has the biggest share for the NCAR (wetter) scenario because the adaptation costs for infrastructure are especially sensitive to levels of annual and maximum monthly precipitation.) Urban infrastructure (urban drainage, public buildings and similar assets) accounts for about 54 per cent of the infrastructure adaptation costs, followed by roads (mainly paved) at 23 per cent. East Asia and the Pacific, and South Asia face the highest costs, reflecting their relative populations. Sub-Saharan Africa experiences the greatest increase over time, with its adaptation costs rising from US$1.1 billion a year for 2010–2019 to US$6 billion a year for 2040–2049 (Figure 5.1).

Coastal zones are home to an ever growing concentration of people and economic activity, yet they are also subject to a number of climate risks, including sea-level rise and possible increased intensity of tropical storms and cyclones. These factors make adaptation to climate change critical. The EACC study shows that coastal adaptation costs are significant and vary with the magnitude of sea-level rise, making it essential for policy makers to plan while accounting for the uncertainty. One of the most striking results is that Latin America and Caribbean and East Asia and Pacific account for about two-thirds of the total adaptation costs.

Climate change has already affected the hydrologic cycle, a process that is expected to intensify over the century. In some parts of the world, water availability has increased and will continue to increase; in other parts, it has decreased and

Table 5.5 Total average annual costs of adaptation by sector and climate change scenario, 2010–2050 ($ billions at 2005 prices, no discounting)

Sector	NCAR	CSIRO
Agriculture, forestry, fisheries	2.54	3.04
Coastal zones	28.48	27.65
Extreme weather events	6.68	6.38
Human health	1.97	1.45
Infrastructure	27.52	12.96
Water supply and flood protection	14.36	19.69
Total (X-sum)	81.55	71.16

Source: EACC study team.

will continue to do so. Moreover, the frequency and magnitude of floods is expected to rise, because of projected increases in the intensity of rainfall. Accounting for the climate impacts, the study shows that water supply and flood management ranks as one of the top three adaptation costs in both the wetter and drier scenarios, with Sub-Saharan Africa having by far the highest costs. Latin America and the Caribbean also sustain high costs under both models, and South Asia sustains high costs under the CSIRO scenario.

Climate change affects agriculture by altering yields and changing the areas where crops can be grown. The EACC study shows that changes in temperature and precipitation in both climate scenarios will significantly hurt crop yields and production, with irrigated and rain-fed wheat, and irrigated rice the hardest hit. South Asia shoulders the biggest losses in production, but developing countries fare worse for almost all crops compared with developed countries. Moreover, the changes in trade flow patterns are dramatic. Under the NCAR scenario, developed-country exports increase by 28 per cent, whereas under the CSIRO scenario they increase by 75 per cent compared with 2000 levels. South Asia becomes a much larger importer of food under both scenarios, and East Asia and Pacific becomes a net food exporter under the NCAR scenario. In addition, the number of malnourished children rises with the decline in calorie availability brought about by climate change.

The key human health impacts of climate change include increases in the incidence of vector-borne disease (malaria), water-borne diseases (diarrhoea), heat- and cold-related deaths, and injuries and deaths from flooding, as well as in the prevalence of malnutrition. The EACC study, which focuses on malaria and diarrhoea, finds adaptation costs falling in absolute terms over time to less than half the 2010 estimates of adaptation costs by 2050. Why do costs decline in the face of higher risks? The answer lies in the benefits expected from economic growth and development. Although the declines are consistent across regions, the rate of decline is more rapid in South Asia, and East Asia and the Pacific than in Sub-Saharan Africa. As a result, by 2050, more than 80 per cent of health-sector adaptation costs will be shouldered by Sub-Saharan Africa.

In the absence of reliable data on emergency management costs, the EACC study tries to shed light on the role of socio-economic development in increasing climate resilience. It asks 'As climate change increases potential vulnerability to extreme weather events, how many additional young women would have to be educated to neutralize this increased vulnerability?' 'And how much would it cost?' The findings show that by 2050, neutralizing the impact of extreme weather events requires educating an additional 18–23 million young women at a cost of US$12–15 billion a year. For the period 2000–2050 as a whole, the tab reaches about US$300 billion in new outlays. This means that, in the developing world, neutralizing the impact of worsening weather over the coming decades will require educating a large new cohort of young women at a cost that will steadily escalate to several billion dollars a year. However, it will be enormously worthwhile on other margins to invest in education for millions of young women who might otherwise be denied its many benefits.

5.5 Conclusions

This chapter summarizes the EACC and explores the study's contributions to the adaptation literature. An operational definition of adaptation costs, which exclude the costs of closing the adaptation deficit, permits the EACC study to model explicitly the costs of planned adaptation initiatives needed to restore (future) welfare to levels prevailing before climate change. By using a common development baseline and range of climate projections across numerous economic sectors, the study has consistently identified climate impacts and thus future costs of adaptation. The global price tag for the developing world of adapting to an approximately 2°C warmer world by 2050 is in the range of US$70–100 billion a year.

Despite the detailed methodological approach, the study suffers from a number of limitations, many of which require additional research. First, the characterization of government decision-making is greatly simplified in that the study calculates adaptation costs as if decision-makers know with certainty what the future climate will be. In truth, current climate knowledge does not permit even probabilistic statements about country-level climate outcomes and therefore provides virtually no help in informing country-level decision-makers' investment decisions. However, Dessai *et al.* (2009) noted that decision-makers can analyse potential adaptation packages over a wide range of climate outcomes and select strategies that are significantly robust across a range of alternative futures.

Second, the study also greatly simplifies the characterization of human behaviour to make cost estimation tractable. Many adaptive measures are best implemented through effective collective action at the community level. However, the circumstances that elicit effective collective action are complex (Ostrom, 1990). Soft adaptation measures, such as early warning systems, community preparedness programmes, watershed management, urban and rural zoning, and water pricing, generally rely on effective institutions supported by collective action. Since it is easier to cost hard measures and because it is hard to know, in a global study, whether such institutional preconditions exist in a given setting, this study has generally opted to estimate hard adaptation measures that require an engineering response.

Third, economic models normally assume fully rational behaviour. None of the sector models used in this study is capable of intertemporal optimization. Calculations in each sector ensure that service levels are maintained despite climate change, but no effort was made to identify whether the resources invested in one sector to counter the effects of climate change would have yielded a higher benefit – cost ratio in another sector or whether cash transfers would maintain welfare at less cost. This feature imparts an upward bias on adaptation estimates. Recent work by McKinsey (2009) demonstrates that costs can be reduced by using a portfolio of cost-effective adaptation measures.

Finally, the study is limited by the range of climate and growth outcomes. Agrawala and Fankhauser (2008) discuss the importance of this feature, noting that adaptation costs must be taken in context, as measures that improve baseline adaptive capacity may drastically affect estimated adaptation costs. Different growth scenarios may produce vastly different futures. In some, accumulated assets and elevated incomes may reduce future vulnerability and thus adaptation costs; in others, stagnant economic growth and poor institutional development may expose even more people and assets to the deleterious effects of climate change, thus greatly increasing adaptation costs.

These limitations, and others identified in the sector-specific studies, are left for future research to address.

Appendix

Sector methodologies

Infrastructure methodology

The starting point for estimating the costs of adaptation are baseline projections of infrastructure demand in physical units by country at five-year intervals with no climate change. These projections are derived from econometric equations estimated using historic panel data, including GDP per capita at purchasing power parity exchange rates, population structure, urbanization, country characteristics and climate variables as independent variables. Two econometric specifications were used: panel regressions representing average levels of infrastructure and stochastic frontier regressions representing the 'efficient' levels of infrastructure given the values of the independent variables.

In the period from t to t + 1, say from 2010 to 2015, the country will have to invest to meet the new level of infrastructure in t + 1 and to replace infrastructure existing at date t that reaches the end of its useful life during the period. Thus, the total value of investment in infrastructure of type i in country j and period t is

$$I_{ijt} = C_{ijt} \left(Q_{ijt} + 1 - Q_{ijt} + R_{ijt} \right) \tag{1}$$

where Cijt is the unit cost of investment, $Q_{ijt}+1 - Q_{ijt}$ is the quantity of new investment in infrastructure, and Rijt is the quantity of existing infrastructure that has to be replaced. The change in the total cost of infrastructure investment may be expressed as the total differential of Equation (1) with respect to the climate variables that affect either unit costs or efficient levels of provision for infrastructure of type i:

$$DI_{ijt} = DC_{ijt} \left(Q_{ijt} + 1 - Q_{ijt} + R_{ijt} \right) + \left(C_{ijt} + DC_{ijt} \right) \left(DQ_{ijt} + 1 - DQ_{ijt} + DR_{ijt} \right) \tag{2}$$

An equivalent equation may be derived for operation and maintenance costs. The first part of the right side of Equation (2) is referred to as the DP component of the cost of adaptation, and the second part as the DQ component. These components cover several ways in which climate change might cause changes in the costs or quantities of infrastructure services.

The DP component combines the baseline projections of infrastructure assuming no climate change with estimates of the percentage changes in the unit costs of constructing, operating and maintaining infrastructure as a consequence of climate change. The changes in unit costs are derived from dose–response relationships estimated from the engineering-economic literature on the costs of adjusting asset design and operational standards to hold infrastructure performance constant under different climate conditions. The factors that drive the costs include average and maximum monthly temperatures, total annual and maximum monthly precipitation, and maximum wind speed. The dose–response relationships for operating and maintenance costs for existing assets differ from those for newly constructed assets, which are designed to cope with the projected climate over the life of the assets.

The DQ component of Equation (2) captures the impact of climate change on demand for infrastructure services, taking account of the higher unit costs of constructing and operating infrastructure. This has two dimensions. Climate change may change the level or composition of demand for energy, transport and water at given levels of income, so the net impact on capital and operating costs has to be calculated. Climate change will also mean that countries have to invest in additional assets to maintain standards of protection for non-infrastructure activities or services. For water management and flood management and for coastal protection, this dimension of the DQ component is addressed in specific sector studies, whereas for infrastructure the analysis includes the first dimension plus other adjustments that are not captured elsewhere, such as changes in health infrastructure.

The econometric analysis involves estimating a reduced-form equation describing demand for infrastructure:

$$Q_{ijt} = h_i \left(P_{jt}, Y_{jt}, X_{jt}, V_{jt}, t \right) \tag{3}$$

where P_{jt} is the population of country j in period t, Y_{jt} is average income per capita for country j in period t, X_{jt} is a vector of country characteristics for country j in period t (including an index of construction costs), and V_{jt} is a vector of climate variables for country j in period t.

As there are no strong priors on the appropriate functional forms, a standard flexible functional form is used to represent the demand equation hi() in terms of the explanatory variables using a restricted version of the translog specification for variables other than population. Because, in practice, it is often difficult to estimate the full translog specification using the more complex econometric models, the analysis started with the log-linear specification and then tested whether the coefficients on the quadratic and cross-product terms were significant.

To deal with the claim that climate variables – especially average temperature – may act as a proxy for institutional and other factors that shaped past patterns of economic development, the values of demographic variables in 1950 are used in the models as instruments for institutional development, following the approach of Acemoglu *et al.* (2001). Other country fixed effects include country size and the proportions of land area that are desert, arid, semiarid, steep or very steep and the proportion of land with no significant soil constraints for agriculture using standard Food and Agriculture Organization (FAO) land classifications. The use of differently weighted climate variables (population-weighted and inverse population-weighted mean temperature, total precipitation, temperature range and precipitation range) captures the differences between climate conditions in more and less densely populated areas.

Coastal zone methodology

Adaptation costs for coastal zones are derived mainly from the Dynamic and Interactive Vulnerability Assessment (DIVA) model, based on 12,148 coastal segments that make up the world's coast (except for Antarctica) and a linked database and set of interacting algorithms (McFadden *et al.*, 2007; Nicholls *et al.*, 2007; Vafeidis *et al.*, 2008). The sea-level rise scenarios are downscaled with an estimate of the vertical land movement in each segment. The coastal erosion analysis considers only sandy coasts and takes account of the direct effect (Bruun effect) and indirect effects of sea-level rise, as well as beach nourishment where it occurs. The indirect effects occur at major estuaries and lagoons.

The flooding analysis determines the flood areas for different return periods and extreme water levels, including the effects of dikes. Because empirical data on actual dike heights are not available at a global level, 'optimum' dikes heights were estimated for the base year of 1995 using a demand for safety function.[7] Dike heights are then upgraded according to projected sea-level rise to 2050. Increased flooding due to sea-level rise along the coastal-influenced reaches of major global rivers (identified in the DIVA database) is also considered. Damages are evaluated in terms of physical, social and economic indicators such as land lost to erosion or submergence, the number of people expected to be subject to annual flooding, the number of people forced to migrate because of land loss, and the costs of this migration.

DIVA implements the adaptation options according to complementary adaptation strategies. For beach nourishment, a cost–benefit adaptation strategy balances costs and benefits (damage avoided) of adaptation, including the tourist value of beaches. For dike building, the demand function for safety is applied over time, subject to population density. Dikes are built only when population density exceeds one person per square kilometre, with an increasing proportion of the recommended height being built as population density rises – for example, 98 per cent of the dike height is built at densities of 1,000 people per square kilometre. The unit costs of beach nourishment, dikes and port upgrades were derived from the global experience of Delft Hydraulics (now Deltares).

For this analysis, DIVA was extended to include a sensitivity analysis of more intense tropical storms. This influences adaptation costs only for dikes. The maintenance costs of sea and river dikes and port upgrades globally are also computed outside DIVA. Port costs are based on a strategy of continuously raising existing port areas as sea levels rise.[8]

Water sector methodology

The effects of climate change on the water cycle were assessed by running the Climate and Runoff model (CLIRUN-II) on a monthly time step. The key parameters were monthly runoff and the magnitude of the 10- and 50-year maximum monthly runoff. The results were aggregated to the 281 food production units of the International Model for Policy Analysis of Agricultural Commodities and Trade (IMPACT) developed by the International Food Policy Research Institute (IFPRI). The analysis considers industrial and municipal water supply and riverine flood protection.

Water supply

Costs of adaptation are defined as the cost of providing enough raw water to restore future industrial and municipal water demand to the levels that would have existed without climate change. Such demand is assumed to be met by increasing the capacity of surface reservoir storage, except when that would raise withdrawals to more than 80 per cent of river runoff and when the cost of supplying water from reservoir yield is more than US$0.30 per cubic metre. In these cases, supply is assumed to be met through alternative measures, such as recycling, rainwater harvesting and desalination, at a cost of US$0.30 per cubic metre.

Additional reservoir storage capacity to meet future water demand is calculated using storage–yield curves showing the storage capacity needed to provide a given yield and reliability of water supply over the year. The storage–yield curves were developed using simulated time-series of monthly runoff and evaporation from CLIRUN-II. The costs of reservoir construction were based on a method relating topography to cost, and annual operation and maintenance costs were assumed to be 2 per cent of construction costs. Three scenarios were used to estimate the size distribution of future reservoirs: small dams, with all future reservoirs having a storage capacity under 25 million cubic metres; large dams, with all future reservoirs having a storage capacity greater than 12,335 million cubic metres; and best estimate, with future construction assumed to follow the same size distribution as in the twentieth century in the USA. The results in this section are shown for the best estimate scenario.

Flood protection

Costs are defined as the cost of providing flood protection against the 50-year monthly flood (maximum monthly runoff) in urban areas and the 10-year monthly flood in agricultural areas. First, the baseline costs (without climate change) of providing flood protection to all urban and agricultural areas were estimated. Then, the costs of adaptation were estimated by assuming that the costs of providing flood protection rose by the same percentage as the percentage change in the magnitude of the 50- or 10-year monthly flood event. Flood protection was assumed to be provided through a system of dikes and polders, at a cost of

US$50,000 per km² in urban areas and US$8,000 per km² in agricultural areas (these cost estimates were derived from World Bank case studies). Annual operation and maintenance costs were assumed to be 0.5 per cent of construction costs.

Agricultural sector methodology

Climate change affects agriculture through changes in yields and in areas planted. Farmers respond by changing their management practices. The resulting production effects work their way through agricultural markets, affecting prices. Consumers respond by changing consumption patterns. When prices rise, consumption falls and the number of malnourished children rises. Adaptation expenditures on productivity-enhancing investments can offset these impacts of climate change.

The biological effects of climate change are modelled with the Decision Support System for Agrotechnology Transfer (DSSAT) crop modelling program, assessing yield and area effects for five major commodities at 0.5° resolution. The DSSAT model includes a CO_2 fertilization effect of 369 ppm atmospheric concentration, reflecting recent research suggesting that fertilization effects are much weaker in the field than in the laboratory. Using a 532 ppm value reduces the costs of adaptation by less than 10 per cent.

The productivity effects of climate change are aggregated to 32 crops and 281 food production units of the IFPRI's IMPACT model. Growth in crop production in each country is determined by crop and input prices, exogenous rates of productivity growth and area expansion, investment in irrigation, and water availability. Demand is modelled as a function of prices, income and population growth, and has four components: food, feed, biofuels, and other uses. The model links national agricultural markets through international trade. World agricultural commodity prices are determined annually at levels that clear international markets.

Costs of adaptation are measured against the human well-being measure of malnutrition in preschool children, a highly vulnerable group. The number of malnourished children is determined in part by per capita calorie availability, but also by access to clean drinking water and maternal education. Investments in agricultural research, roads and irrigation increase agricultural productivity under climate change, increasing calorie availability and reducing child malnutrition estimates.

The costs of adaptation for agriculture are calculated solely from the perspective of the agriculture sector, so the starting point is investment and asset stocks in the base year (2000). Thus, the estimates of investments in research, irrigation and rural roads do not take account of overlaps in spending on these activities or assets with the baseline growth or of adaptation costs for other sectors, such as infrastructure and water resources management. This is an unavoidable consequence of estimating the cost of adaptation for each sector separately and in parallel. For rural roads, an attempt was made to eliminate overlapping expenditures in compiling the consolidated estimates of the costs of adaptation for developing countries. The baseline provision of rural roads up to 2050 used to estimate costs of adaptation is adjusted to take account of the additional length of rural roads consistent with the baseline projections for road investment. This adjustment reduces the investment in rural roads included in the cost of adaptation for agriculture by about 80–85per cent for the two climate scenarios. The adjustment for these overlaps amounts to US$2.0–2.2 billion a year averaged over the full period.

Fisheries methodology

Climate change is likely to alter ocean conditions, particularly water temperature, ocean currents, upwelling and biogeochemistry, leading to productivity shocks for marine fisheries (IPCC, 2007; Diaz and Rosenberg, 2008). Other studies have documented shifts in species distribution (Perry *et al.*, 2005; Dulvy *et al.*, 2008) and growth rates (Thresher *et al.*, 2007) as a result of changes in ocean temperatures. Climate change may also alter the phenology of marine organisms, creating mismatches between prey availability and predator requirements and leading to coral bleaching and habitat loss for reef-associated fish species (Sumaila and Cheung, 2008).

To account for distributional, productivity and biogeochemical effects, a two-step process is used to establish climate change impacts on fish catches. First, potential losses and gains in fish catches due to the redistribution of fish biomass and changes in primary production are determined under various climate change scenarios for all maritime countries and the high seas. These impacts are then modified by including the potential catch impacts in climate change-vulnerable hotspots, based on knowledge of the locations of different fish species. Potential effects of climate change on these areas include acidification of the oceans from higher carbon dioxide levels, loss of coral reef from ocean warming and acidification, and other changes in ocean biogeochemistry, such as oxygen levels. Second, potential losses and gains in landed catch values or gross revenues and household incomes from global fisheries under different climate change and baseline scenarios are estimated. As a result of data limitations, losses in landed catch values are used as estimates of adaptation costs.

Health sector methodology

Adaptation costs are computed on a disease-specific basis for malaria and diarrhoea for 16 demographic (age and sex) groups in each country at five-year intervals. The adaptation cost for each disease and demographic group in a county is determined by the baseline incidence of disease that would have prevailed in the absence of climate change, the additional risk that climate change poses relative to the baseline, and the unit cost of preventing and treating additional cases of malaria and diarrhoea.

The baseline incidence of diarrhoea and malaria by country for 16 demographic groups for 2004 are available from the World Health Organization (WHO, 2004). WHO has also developed econometric models using panel data on income and health to project cause-specific deaths and disability-adjusted life year

(DALY) rates by demographic group through to 2030. The EACC study extended this baseline to 2050 using the WHO econometric model results (WHO, 2004). The additional risk of incidence for malaria and diarrhoea was estimated from the epidemiological literature. The relative risk for malaria was estimated as the percentage change in population at risk based on Craig *et al.* (1999) and Tanser *et al.* (2003). For diarrhoea, the epidemiological literature is limited, and the estimates are based on the dose–response functions from the WHO global burden of disease study (WHO, 2004).

The relative risks were computed separately for 2010, 2030 and 2050 for the NCAR and CSIRO climate projections. Risks for intermediate years were interpolated. The relative risk was applied to the projected baseline incidence to determine the additional number of cases attributable to climate change and, for malaria, to determine the number of DALYs attributable to climate change.

The total cost of preventing or treating the additional cases is calculated by multiplying the additional cases by the average cost of preventing or treating additional cases. The average cost of averting additional cases of each disease is based on updated treatment costs from the Disease Control Priorities in Developing Countries Project (DCCP2) for the cost-effective methods of treatment. For diarrhoeal diseases, costs are based on breastfeeding promotion; vaccination against rotavirus, cholera, and measles; and improvements in water supply and sanitation. For malaria, costs are based on use of insecticide-treated bed nets; case management with artemisinin-based combination therapy plus insecticide-treated nets; case management with artemisinin-based combination therapy with insecticide-treated nets plus indoor residual spraying; and case management with artemisinin-based combination therapy plus insecticide-treated nets plus indoor residual spraying plus intermittent presumptive treatment in pregnancy.

Extreme weather events methodology

To address the question of how much it would cost to reduce household vulnerability to weather-related disasters by empowering women through improved education, a model of weather-related impact risk is estimated using panel data for 1960–2002. Use of panel data allows for clearer interpretation of results, because it absorbs many sources of potentially misleading cross-sectional correlation into estimated country effects. The need for lengthy time series limits the estimation variables to a sparse set, however.

The study employs fixed effects estimation of risk equations that link losses from floods and droughts to three determinants: weather events that increase potential losses, income per capita, and female education. Separate equations are estimated for the risk of death from floods, the risk of being affected by floods, and the risk of being affected by drought (the data are too sparse to support estimation for death from droughts).

As in the other sector analyses, the analysis combines estimated risk equations with projections of economic growth, population growth and changes in primary and secondary schooling. The same three scenarios are developed: a baseline with socio-economic development but without climate change, and two scenarios with the same baseline development path but with alternative weather paths – a wet (NCAR) scenario and a dry (CSIRO) scenario. For each scenario, the associated changes in the risks of death from floods and being affected by floods or droughts are calculated. Then, using the worst-case risk, the increase in female schooling that would neutralize this additional risk is calculated. The results are multiplied by expenditure per student to estimate the total education investment required to neutralize the additional weather risk posed by climate change.

The approach here is conservative in that it is unlikely to underestimate the required investment and even imparts a strong upward bias. First, the cost assessment is based on general preparedness through increased education, rather than more narrowly targeted investment in emergency preparedness. Second, cost calculations are based on worst-case risk scenarios, which require the greatest increase in schooling to neutralize. (Extreme wet and dry scenarios are both worst-case scenarios for extreme weather, because they generate the greatest number of floods and droughts.) Third, only projected increases in vulnerability are included, not decreases. (An alternative would be a net impact analysis for a wet climate scenario that subtracts lower expected losses from drought from higher expected losses from flooding.) Finally, the results for the two model scenarios are not averaged, which would neutralize their extreme signals.

Notes

1 An additional study looks at the costs of ecosystem adaptation, but results are not included in the totals (Fankhauser, 2010).
2 www.worldbank.org/eacc
3 For a full discussion of the adaptation deficit please refer to Section 2.
4 The one exception is coastal zones, where adaptation costs are defined as the cost of measures to establish the optimal level of protection plus residual damage.
5 Background papers on the methodological approaches used in each sector are available online at: http://beta. worldbank.org/content/adaptation-costs-global-estimate. For a summary of the methodology used for each sector, please refer to the Appendix.
6 GDP projections are based on technical tables from the FUND version published in 2008. FUND growth rates have been interpolated to give indices at five-year intervals, which were then matched to the corresponding countries. The resulting set of indices of income per capita for each country were combined with United Nations medium-fertility population indices and base level of purchasing power parity (PPP) per person. The key assumption here is that all references to growth in income per capita are interpreted as income per person in real terms at PPP.
7 The demand for safety function increases with per capita income and population density and decreases with the cost of dike building, an approach that is posited as the solution to a cost–benefit analysis (Tol, 2006).
8 All new port areas are assumed to include sea-level rise to 2050 in their design, so upgrade costs will be effectively zero.

Bibliography

Acemoglu, D., Johnson, S., Robinson, J.R., 2001, 'The colonial origins of comparative development: an empirical investigation', *American Economic Review* 91, 1369–1401.

Allen, M.R., Frame, D.J., Huntington, C.D., Jones, J.A., Meinshausen, M., Meinshausen, N., 2009, 'Warming caused by cumulative carbon emissions towards the trillionth tonne', *Nature* 458, 1163–1166.

Agrawala, S., Fankhauser, S., 2008, *Economic Aspects of Adaption to Climate Change. Costs, Benefits and Policy Instruments*, Organisation for Economic Co-operation and Development (OECD), Paris.

Anthoff, D., Tol, R.S.J., 2009. 'The impact of climate-change on the balanced growth equivalent: an application of FUND', *Environment and Resource Economics* 43, 351–367.

Burton, I., 2004, 'Climate change and the adaptation deficit', in: A. Fenech, D. MacIver, H. Auld, R. Bing Rong, Y. Yin (eds), *Climate Change: Building the Adaptive Capacity*, Meteorological Service of Canada, Environment Canada, Toronto, 25–33.

Carter, T. R., Parry, M. L., Harasawa, H., Nishioka, S., 1994, *IPCC Technical Guidelines for Assessing Climate Change Impacts and Adaptations,* Department of Geography, University College London, London.

Craig, M.H., Snow, R.W., le Sueur, D., 1999, 'A climate-based distribution model of malaria transmission in sub-Saharan Africa', *Parasitology Today* 15, 105–111.

Dessai, S., Hulme, M., Lempert, R., Pielke, R., 2009, 'Climate prediction: a limit to adaptation?', in: W. N. Adger, I. Lorenzoni, K. O'Brien (eds), *Adapting to Climate Change: Thresholds, Values, Governance*, Cambridge University Press, Cambridge, UK, 64–78.

Diaz, R.J., Rosenberg, R., 2008, 'Spreading dead zones and consequences for marine ecosystems', *Science* 321, 926–929.

Dulvy, N.K., Newson, S.E., Mendes, S., Crick, H.Q.P., Houghton, J.D.R., Mays, G.C., Hutson, A.M., Macleod, C.D., 2008, 'Indicators of the impact of climate change on migratory species', *Journal of Applied Ecology* 45, 1029–1039.

Fankhauser, S., 2010, 'The costs of adaptation', Wiley Interdisciplinary Review *Climate Change* 1, 23–30.

Fankhauser, S., Smith, J.B., Tol, R.S.J., 1999, 'Weather climate change: some simple rules to guide adaptation decisions', *Ecological Economics*, 30, 67–78.

Global Humanitarian Forum, 2009, *Human Impact Report: Climate Change–The Anatomy of a Silent Crisis*, Global Humanitarian Forum, Geneva.

Hope, C., 2006, 'The marginal impact of CO_2 from PAGE2002: an integrated assessment model incorporating the IPCC's five reasons for concern', *Integrated Assessment* 6, 19–56.

IPCC (Intergovernmental Panel on Climate Change), 2007, 'Annex II: Glossary', in: R.K. Pachauri, A. Reisinger (eds), *Climate Change 2007: Synthesis Report*, Contribution of Working Groups I, II and III to the Fourth Assessment Report of the Intergovernmental Panel on Climate Change, IPCC, Geneva, 76–99.

McFadden, L., Nicholls, R.J., Vafeidis, A.T., Tol, R.S.J., 2007, 'A methodology for modeling coastal space for global assessments', *Journal of Coastal Research* 23, 911–920.

McGray, H.A., Hamill, A., Bradley, R., Schipper, E.L., Parry, J.-E., 2007, *Weathering the Storm. Options for Framing Adaptation and Development*, World Resources Institute, Washington, DC.

McKinsey, 2009, *Shaping Climate Resilient Development: a Framework for Decision Making,* Report of the Economics of Adaptation Working Group, Swiss Re and McKinsey Company, 1–164.

Meinshausen, M., Meinshausen, N., Hare, W., Raper, S.C.B., Frieler, K., Knutti, R., Frame, D.J., Allen, M.R., 2009, 'Greenhouse-gas emissions targets for limiting global warming to 2°C', *Nature* 458, 1158–1162.

Nicholls, R.J., Wong, P.P., Burkett, V.R., Codignotto, J., Hay, J.E., McLean, R.F., Ragoonaden, S., Woodroffe, C.D., 2007, 'Coastal systems and low-lying areas', in: M.L. Parry, O.F. Canziani, J.P. Palutikof, P.J. van der Linden, C.E. Hanson (eds), *Climate Change 2007: Impacts, Adaptation and Vulnerability.* Report of Working Group II of the Intergovernmental Panel on Climate Change, Cambridge University Press, Cambridge, UK, 315–357.

Nordhaus, W.D., Boyer, J.G., 2000, *Warming the World: Economic Models of Global Warming*, The MIT Press, Cambridge, MA.

Noy, I., 2009, 'The macro-economic consequences of disaster', *Journal of Development Economics* 88, 221–231.

Ostrom, E., 1990, *Governing the Commons: The Evolution of Institutions for Collective Action*, Cambridge University Press, New York, NY.

Oxfam International, 2007, *Adapting to Climate Change: What's Needed in Poor Countries, and Who Should Pay*, Briefing paper no. 104, Oxfam International, Oxford, 1–47.

Parry, M., Anell, N., Berry, P., Dodman, D., Fankhauser, S., Hope, C., Kovats, S., Nicholls, R., Satterthwaite, D., Tiffin, R., Wheeler, T., 2009, *Assessing the Costs of Adaptation to Climate Change: A Review of the UNFCCC and Other Recent Estimates,* International Institute for Environment and Development and the Grantham Institute for Climate Change, Imperial College, London.

Perry, A.L., Low, P.J., Ellis, J.R., Reynolds, J.D., 2005, 'Climate change and distribution shifts in marine fishes', *Science* 308, 1912–1915.

Project Catalyst, 2009, *Adaptation to Climate Change: Potential Costs and Choices for a Global Agreement*, Climate Works Foundation, San Francisco, CA.

Schelling, T., 1992, 'Some economics of global warming', *American Economic Review* 82, 1–14.

Stern, N., 2006, *Stern Review of the Economics of Climate Change*, Her Majesty's Treasury, London.

Sumaila, U.R., Cheung, W.L., 2008, 'Trade-offs between conservation and socioeconomic objectives in managing a tropical marine ecosystem', *Ecological Economics* 66, 193–210.

Tanser, F.C., Sharp, B., le Sueur, D., 2003, 'Potential effect of climate change on malaria transmission in Africa', *Lancet* 362, 1792–1798.

Thresher, R., Koslow, J.A., Morison, A.K., Smith, D.C., 2007, 'Depth-mediated reversal of the effects of climate change on long-term growth rates of exploited marine fish', *Proceedings of the National Academy of Sciences of the United States of America* 104, 7461–7465.

Tol, R.S.J., 2006, 'Exchange rates and climate change: an application of FUND', *Climate Change* 75, 59–80.

UNDP (United Nations Development Programme), 2008, *Fighting Climate Change. Human Solidarity in a Divided World, Human Development Report 2007/2008*, United Nations Development Programme, New York, NY.

UNFCCC (United Nations Framework Convention on Climate Change), 2007a, *Climate Change: Impacts, Vulnerabilities, and Adaptation in Developing Countries*, United Nations Framework Convention on Climate Change Secretariat, Bonn.

UNFCCC (United Nations Framework Convention on Climate Change), 2007b, *Bali Action Plan*, Decision 1/CP.13, United Nations Framework Convention on Climate Change Secretariat, Bonn.

Vafeidis, A.T., Nicholls, R.J., Boot, G., Cox, J., Grashoff, P.S., Hinkel, J., Maatens, R., McFadden, L., Spencer, T., Tol, R.S.J., 2008, 'A new global costal database for impact and vulnerability analysis to sea-level rise', *Journal of Coastal Research* 24, 917–924.

WHO (World Health Organization), 2004, *Guidelines for Drinking-water Quality*. Vol 1. Recommendations, 3rd edn. World Health Organization, Geneva.

World Bank, 2006, *Clean Energy and Development: Towards an Investment Framework*, World Bank, Washington, DC.

World Bank, 2010, *World Development Report 2010: Development and Climate Change*, World Bank, Washington, DC.

6 Raising climate finance to support developing country action

Some economic considerations

Alex Bowen

6.1 The financing challenge

Arresting human-induced climate change requires global action to reduce greenhouse gas (GHG) emissions sharply. To have a 50 per cent chance of keeping the global mean temperature increase below 2°C, global emissions have to fall by between 2.5 and 3 per cent per year on average between 2010 and 2050 (Bowen and Ranger, 2009). Developing economies[1] now account for well over half of global emissions and their share is growing relative to that of developed economies,[2] so if the 2°C ceiling is not to be exceeded, they will have to start reining in their emissions soon (Clarke *et al.*, 2009). As climate change is likely to hit poorer countries sooner and harder than it will hit developed nations, the former will have to undertake a disproportionate amount of adaptation. A wide range of ethical frameworks suggest that developed countries should finance a significant share of the necessary spending on mitigation and adaptation in developing nations – 100 per cent according to some value systems.[3]

Reflecting this consensus, developed countries have agreed, as part of the United Nations Framework Convention on Climate Change (UNFCCC), to cover the 'agreed full incremental costs' of implementing mitigation measures and to 'assist the developing country Parties that are particularly vulnerable to the adverse effects of climate change in meeting costs of adaptation'. These commitments have been reiterated in the Kyoto Protocol, the Bali Action Plan and the Copenhagen Accord, with the latter setting a goal for developed countries to mobilize jointly US$100 billion a year by 2020 'to address the needs of developing countries'.

This agenda raises several questions considered further below. First, what should the balance be between private and public sources of finance? Second, how can private sources of finance be generated? Third, how should public funds be raised by individual governments and by international collaboration? This chapter discusses the criteria that economic analysis suggests. Fourth, it asks how specific proposals rate according to these criteria and others? The chapter concludes with the hope that governments will act speedily to fulfil the promises of the Copenhagen Accord but without neglecting the principles of public finance in the process.

6.2 Private and public sources of finance

The simple textbook prescription to deal with the GHG externality, a global cap-and-trade system with appropriate allocation of tradable emissions quotas across individuals, countries and time, would entail a reliance on private sources of finance. It would generate a world price for emissions, so that private agents would internalize the externalities they cause. The lump-sum transfers across individuals necessary to correct any adverse distributional impact from the imposition of a price and the residual climate damages would be achieved by appropriate allocation of quotas. The allocation could also be used to compensate those who had to spend proportionally more on adaptation.[4] Private finance flows would be generated entirely in emission reduction markets. Local investments in mitigation and adaptation would be financed by private agents in the developing countries themselves, with the help of their share of revenues from those markets and guided by the changes in relative prices over products and across time induced by the carbon price.

However, this prescription is highly unrealistic. In practice, the problem of GHG externalities is compounded by several other market failures, many of which need to be tackled by public policy. There are also public policy failures, such as the lack of credibility of the policy framework that can arise when governments cannot bind their successors. Where climate change action in developing countries involves these externalities, financial support from developed nations is likely to have to involve public finance. Also, emission reduction markets cannot be relied upon to deliver resources to all those who need to make climate-related investments, particularly those required for adaptation. If projects in developing countries need to raise private finance abroad, they must be able to offer an expectation of an appropriate risk-adjusted return, which in many cases they will be unable to do without public support, given the administrative costs and other obstacles.

One key market failure affects innovation. Many types of knowledge have the characteristics of a public good – one firm using an idea does not prevent another firm from doing so. That tends to lead to under-investment in the creation of knowledge. Hence, public subsidies for such activities are warranted, including for climate-related research and development tailored to the needs of developing countries. The public sector can redirect technological progress by supporting the development of low-carbon technologies that have not benefited from extensive experience. However, the initial costs of adopting a low-carbon development path will be higher, underlining the need for early public intervention to reduce emissions cost effectively over time. There are also numerous problems arising from inadequate and unevenly distributed information, which the public sector may be able to help solve by collecting and disseminating knowledge that would be under-provided by the private sector.

Another important source of market failure is the existence of network externalities: an enterprise joining a network does not take into account the benefits that accrue to others from the expansion of network membership. Without public intervention, the market initially under-invests in expanding the network. Public support is therefore likely to be necessary for the development of network infra-structure in developing countries, notably in energy distribution. It may be easier for the public sector to set up the network rather than to calibrate and apply the appropriate initial subsidies to stimulate private provision.

The malfunctioning of financial intermediation is another obstacle to adequate private flows of finance. Without political stability, regulatory certainty and administrative simplicity, perceived risks can undermine incentives to invest in projects with large up-front costs (as is typical of many mitigation projects[5]). This can make projects that appear to pass cost – benefit tests unattractive in practice. When private-sector financial intermediation is impaired (as it is at the moment) by reduced risk appetite, heightened doubts about counterparty solvency and increased uncertainty about asset valuations, the public sector may be able to act as a financial intermediary of last resort. In some developing countries, financial intermediation is rudimentary or non-existent, partly because of the low levels of income.

A further reason for public-sector support for developing country actions is to demonstrate the commitment of developed-country policy makers to announced policies, thus building credibility and strengthening the impact of incentives to alter private-sector behaviour. Policy commitments that include financial or repu-tational incentives for all participating governments to achieve the announced outcomes can enhance the credibility of the policies and help to align the interests of policy makers more closely with those of private agents. Thus, public support for developing-country actions, especially through multilateral frameworks endorsed collectively by all participating governments, can help to strengthen actions by the private sector.

At present, the credibility of international endeavours to achieve a global deal on climate change is in question, there is increased uncertainty about the global climate policy regime after 2012, firms in developed countries are still being cautious about investing, and private trade and capital flows are impaired. This means that support for developing countries' actions in the short term is likely to have to be much more reliant on public funding than in the future. Also, pervasive market failures, together with an inability to deal with international income distri-bution impacts simply with global quota allocations, justify some public compo-nent continuing in the long term. However, if global carbon markets can be developed further and their long-term credibility underpinned, the contribution from private funding could be much more substantial. Such a contribution might also be less subject to changes in political will and time inconsistency of policy makers, which have led to considerable scepticism about the reliability of developed countries' pledges on development aid.

The sources of finance for adaptation are likely to be somewhat different from those for mitigation. Private economic agents will generally be in a better posi-tion than public authorities to assess most adaptation needs, given their variety and specificity to particular locations (although some infrastructure investment is likely to require more government involvement). Many adaptation investments will be small scale and likely to be financed through conventional private means.

The challenge is to design mechanisms to distribute flows of public finance to support the incomes of those with the greatest adaptation needs and to help them with the costs of private finance.

6.3 Generating private finance

Economists have debated at length the merits of emission reduction markets relative to emissions taxation.[6] The former approach ensures that, once negotiators have agreed on how the markets are to function and how property rights are to be assigned, private flows of funding are generated. Developed-country governments do not have to continue to redress the distributional impacts of climate change mitigation policies, with the danger of reneging when public budgets are under pressure or particular recipients of financial flows become unpopular. Some see this as an advantage of a markets-based approach compared with a 'taxation and transfers' regime under which developed countries make explicit transfers of public tax revenues to developing countries.[7] However, a markets-based approach may be more susceptible to lobbying and capture by special interests. Domestically, firms may lobby for free allocation of quotas, for example, by 'grandfathering' allocations. This can inhibit competition and reduce the tax base of governments, making public transfers to developing countries more difficult to finance. A global cap-and-trade scheme would also be likely to generate more rents for fossil-fuel exporters, whereas coordinated carbon taxes would allow domestic governments to capture the rents from carbon pricing. The impact on international income distribution could undermine developed-country support for the carbon-pricing regime, although it might be a necessary part of binding in fossil-fuel exporters to any global deal on climate change policies.[8]

A key objective of a markets-based approach should be to internalize GHG externality, which entails GHG pricing – 'getting prices right'. In real-world schemes, different carbon instruments (such as quotas within the EU Emissions Trading Scheme (EU ETS), Clean Development Mechanism (CDM) credits or auction prices for assigned amount units (AAUs)) trade at different prices. Some of these differences may reflect other characteristics of the instruments, but policy makers need to consider whether the proliferation of carbon instruments is providing a blurred signal to potential providers of private finance.

Perhaps more important, it is unlikely that the appropriate level and direction of private finance to developing countries will be ensured without domestic emissions prices (implicit or explicit) at levels broadly comparable across countries, both developed and developing. Fossil-fuel subsidies, for example, will discourage private investment in low-carbon technologies, and the absence of emissions pricing can encourage funding for investments that result in 'carbon leakage' from countries that do impose a carbon price.

Private investors are concerned about carbon prices over time. There is a role for policy makers in reducing the uncertainty about future prices facing private agents, not least because it partly reflects uncertainty about policy makers' future behaviour. Thus, private finance flows will be encouraged if the international policy framework and the rules and regulation of carbon markets are settled, clear and credible for the long term. The design of such markets should also discourage price volatility (e.g. by allowing banking – and perhaps borrowing – in emissions trading schemes and ensuring liquidity and competition in carbon markets).

As argued above, public finance may be necessary to leverage private finance. It might include grants, interest-rate subsidies for private-sector project finance, loan guarantees and insurance premia to help manage the risks unique to investments related to climate change. Innovations like the green investment bank proposed in the UK have considerable potential to help unlock private finance flows, as do the project finance vehicles that public bodies such as the international development banks have experience in building. The public sector can also increase the long-term credibility of climate policies by devices such as equity co-investment and the issuance of indexed bonds that pay more when carbon prices fall, hence allowing carbon market participants to hedge their risks more easily. The crucial requirement at this stage in the evolution of the international policy regime, given the economic environment, is for public institutions to help 'de-risk' investment opportunities for the private sector. However, it should also be noted that carbon markets can generate considerable rents from cheap abatement opportunities, which can lead to very generous private returns to compensate for the risks involved.[9]

6.4 Raising public finance

Public finance theory, as articulated in Atkinson and Stiglitz (1980), Musgrave and Musgrave (1989) and Kay (1990), gives guidance as to how public finance for supporting developing countries' actions should be raised.

First, public authorities have a choice between raising taxes (or fees and user charges) and borrowing. The general principle is to tax to finance current spending and borrow to finance public investment; the social return on the investment should be expected to exceed the cost of raising funds (Blanchard and Giavazzi, 2004; Ismihan and Ozkan, 2008). From the perspective of a developed-country government, this suggests that transfers to developing countries should be financed by tax revenue. However, there is some ambiguity if the developing country uses transfers to invest in mitigation and adaptation that will pay off in the future; should the developed country count that as part of its own social return?

If the case for countercyclical deficit financing by governments is accepted, this justifies a greater share of borrowing, but only in the downturn of the business cycle; an 'exit strategy' to substitute other funding sources is necessary if the associated spending is to continue during recovery.[10]

Another justification for more borrowing is if the government is in a better position than banks to act as a financial intermediary, for example because there are risks that can be better assessed and managed in the public sector – one of the arguments in a domestic context for public-sector sponsorship of 'green' investment banks (e.g. Green Investment Bank Commission, 2010).

Second, taxes should be levied on 'bads' such as emissions and congestion (Pigovian taxes; Pigou, 1932) and, where revenue requirements exceed what can be raised by taxing 'bads', 'goods' in more inelastic supply should be taxed more heavily. This suggests the desirability of working out how to tax 'bads' that are currently escaping the fiscal net.[11]

Third, taxes raise questions of equity as well as efficiency. The ultimate incidence of new taxes therefore needs to be considered and, if necessary, the welfare system adjusted to compensate losers. In practice, this is often difficult without changing incentives and thereby affecting economic efficiency. As a result, governments often prefer to finance new obligations by raising tax revenues across the board, so that the incidence of the tax system is unchanged, on the assumption that it already broadly reflects distributional preferences and efficiency considerations.

Fourth, traditional public finance theory frowns on hypothecation of revenues from particular sources to particular uses, except when setting a user charge to cover the marginal costs of a publicly provided good (McCleary, 1991; OECD, 1996). With the latter exception, there is no reason why the revenue generated by the appropriate tax rate on one activity (e.g. global financial transactions) should equal the appropriate spending on another activity (e.g. public support for developing countries' climate policies). Even if tax rates and spending are initially set so as to bring about the equality needed, there is no guarantee that this will remain the case over time.

The same is true with many activities that are apparently related to one another. For example, there is no reason why the revenue from an optimal global carbon tax should equal the optimal spending on adaptation and mitigation at the chosen target level of GHG concentrations in the atmosphere. Indeed, the 'double dividend' literature[12] is predicated on the possibility that revenues from carbon taxation (or quota auctions) could also be used to reduce distortionary taxes, such as payroll taxes, elsewhere in the economy. The efforts to set different carbon prices for intra-marginal mitigation (e.g. by establishing lower carbon prices for avoided deforestation than for electricity generation) suggest that policy makers suspect that uniform carbon pricing could raise revenues well in excess of mitigation needs. The mere fact that two activities are climate-related does not justify earmarking the revenues from taxing one of them for spending on the other.

Some have argued that hypothecation is likely to make it easier to ensure that funds raised are additional to previous commitments by developed countries (Müller, 2008; Oxfam, 2008). However, finding a new source of revenue and then earmarking it does not prevent the earmarked spending from displacing spending financed from other sources of tax revenue on the same objectives. Additionality is not guaranteed by how the funding is raised (Landau, 2003).

Pirttilä (1998) has advanced a more sophisticated argument for hypothecation: hypothecating the revenues from environmental taxation to the provision of public goods that benefit the losers from the environmental policy may improve welfare (compared with lump-sum transfers) if governments do not have enough information to discriminate more carefully among the losers. That provides some justification for allocating the revenues from carbon taxes or quota auctions to public goods benefiting those hit hardest by carbon pricing. However, it does not justify earmarking revenues from non-climate-related sources to climate actions, or revenues from climate-related sources to mitigation that does not primarily benefit those affected most by carbon pricing.

Brett and Keen (2000) offer a more political explanation for hypothecation, showing how a 'green' incumbent government may choose to earmark revenues if the efficiency loss from doing so is outweighed by the value of constraining subsequent and potentially 'non-green' policy makers from diverting the funds raised. Hence, hypothecation can be seen as a device to discourage backsliding. It is a moot point whether policy makers, at present, are likely to be greener than their successors. If so, that does not bode well for the long-term credibility of the international climate-policy framework.

Where specific sources of finance are hypothecated, given the drawbacks of earmarking, it is necessary to consider whether the revenue raised will, over time, meet either a specific financial target (such as the Copenhagen Accord's US$100 billion per year) or, more generally, the equitable share of developing countries' evolving climate action needs.

Fifth, public finance theory flags the importance of administrative costs, including compliance and monitoring costs, so it is helpful to consider whether proposals entail new administrative burdens or use the most efficient existing tax-raising and disbursement channels. Taxes applied to a broad base, but at low rates, are attractive in this respect to keep tax avoidance activities low.

International collaboration between developed-country governments is desirable in delivering public finance flows where these reflect obligations taken on in the context of international negotiations or where economies of scale in monitoring, verification and reporting are important. However, this does not imply that coordination of revenue sources is necessary. Governments may agree about the appropriate uses of funds without agreeing about appropriate sources. The exception to this principle is when new tax instruments are found to be desirable but would have cross-border implications, as with the taxation of, for example, cross-border pollutants, activities outside individual countries' jurisdictions, and cross-border financial transactions. In such cases, the distributional implications of the new tax would have to be considered as well as the modalities of levying it.

6.5 Some specific proposals

There have been many specific proposals on how to help finance developing-country action on climate change mitigation, adaptation and related capacity building, technology transfer and development. This section considers several, briefly, in light of the discussion above. It also offers a preliminary assessment of the recommendations of the United Nations Secretary-General's High-Level Advisory Group on Climate Change Financing (AGF), which reported in November 2010.

Most of the proposals entail raising public finance from particular sources, leading to two key questions. The first is whether hypothecation is warranted in the case in question. One test is to compare the proposed measure with raising finance through a general increase in domestic tax revenues by developed-country governments. The second is whether, collectively, the balance is right between public and private sources of finance.

Other criteria suggested by the discussion above include the following. Is the scale of funds raised appropriate? If so, will it remain so? In other words, is it reliable? Given the likely administrative burdens (e.g. for tax enforcement, record-keeping and monitoring use), is the proposal practical and cost efficient? Is the ultimate incidence of the tax or interest burden appropriate, given the ethical framework(s) invoked to justify the generation of new finance in the first place? Does the proposal assure that the funds raised are additional to obligations to developing countries previously acknowledged by developed countries? And, in the language of the Copenhagen Accord, does the proposal ensure that financial flows take place 'in the context of meaningful mitigation actions and transparency on implementation'?

6.5.1. Expanding the use of carbon markets

Several proposals have involved stimulating climate-related finance flows by extending the scope of carbon markets, primarily by expanding the scope of the CDM; less emphasis has been placed on extending the number of countries using cap-and-trade systems with offsetting. The CDM allows projects in developing countries that achieve emissions reductions (relative to an appropriate baseline) to generate certified emission reductions (CERs) that can be used by Annex 1 countries to meet their national emission caps. Private firms can purchase CERs to satisfy liabilities under domestic emission trading system caps, but governments can also buy CERs to meet their Kyoto Protocol caps or to provide climate finance. According to the United Nations Environment Programme (UNEP), nearly 1 billion CERs will have been issued by the end of 2012.[13] The UNFCCC has suggested that annual flows of US$15–20 billion are possible, while the European Commission suggests €38 billion. As Hepburn (2009) points out, explicit CERs from the CDM (together with joint implementation) have probably leveraged ten times as much in overall investment from the private sector.[14]

The CDM has been criticized regarding bottlenecks and transaction costs. Serious questions have also been raised over assessments of the additionality of proposed emissions reductions. There is also the broader question of whether the lack of explicit carbon pricing in the countries eligible for the CDM has encouraged sufficient 'carbon leakage' to outweigh any contribution to mitigation from the CDM (e.g. by displacing to developing countries the export production of carbon-intensive products that then become eligible for CDM credits). However, it has the merits of helping to set an implicit carbon price in non-Annex I countries (because of the opportunity cost of neglecting emission reduction possibilities), promoting the cost effectiveness of global mitigation efforts (relative to a world in which CDM-eligible countries had no incentive to mitigate) and demonstrating a track record of some success. It also encourages decentralized private finance flows to developing countries.

Proposals have therefore been made to scale up the CDM by increasing its scope beyond individual projects to sectors and emission-reduction programmes in developing countries and by helping more countries participate in the CER markets (China, India, Brazil and Mexico account for a very large share, although not necessarily much out of line with the distribution of incremental investment needs).[15]

The CDM suffers, however, from mounting uncertainty about what international policy regime will prevail after the end of the 2008–2012 Kyoto accounting period. It has also been disadvantaged by the prospect of the price volatility that afflicts any emissions-quantity-based scheme in the face of macro-economic shocks. Also, experience suggests that CDM private finance is more attracted to some project types than others – it does well with renewable energy and non-CO_2 GHG abatement, but not so well with energy efficiency and transportation, probably because of the various additional market failures involved in the latter. Another potential problem is that the extension of the CDM to low-abatement-cost options (e.g. in forestry) could drive down the price of CERs. One possible response would be the introduction of a new type of offset credit not fully fungible with the CERs. However, that would reduce the incentive for developing forest carbon sinks at the margin. If the price of CERs fell too far, that would be a sign that developed-country caps were not tight enough and should be brought down.

Overall, expanding carbon markets in general, and the CDM in particular, looks an attractive option. It stimulates private finance flows, helps to 'get prices right', overcomes administrative problems, and has already been subjected to much useful scrutiny. Monitoring, verification and reporting are already a central concern. Hypothecation is justified if one believes that the level of emission reduction targets assigned to Annex I countries is appropriate given the required reduction in global emissions by 2050 and ethical perspectives on equity across countries. The scale could be big enough at least to address developing countries' mitigation needs. However, the precise size of flows is difficult to predict, depending on, among other factors, emissions prices in developed countries and the offset rules they adopt. National and international climate-policy regimes have to ensure that demand for offsets rises together with their supply or, in other words, that effective carbon prices are kept high enough to match the level of global ambition for climate change mitigation.

6.5.2 *Multilateral proposals: climate-related sources*

6.5.2.1 *International auctioning of emission quotas*

Proposals have been made for the proceeds of auctions of emissions quotas to be earmarked for climate-action funds, thus using another climate-related source of finance. Norway has suggested that some AAUs could be auctioned by an international body (using Kyoto Protocol mechanisms) instead of being issued to individual countries, with funds going to support climate action in developing countries, including support for their nationally appropriate mitigation activities (Center for Clean Air Policy, 2009).

This category of proposals could generate substantial finance flows; a sale of 2 per cent of AAUs could raise US$14–25 billion, depending on the price. As with the CDM, it has the benefit of helping to establish an emissions price. Also, like the CDM, its revenue prospects depend on having a regime ensuring tight emission caps on Annex I countries in the future.

However, under the Norwegian proposal, countries may seek less stringent caps to compensate for some of (or even more than) the AAUs auctioned. This would reduce the environmental benefit and lower the price. Second, private entities would need to be able to buy the AAUs and use them for compliance to create a demand for the AAUs (currently, installations covered by the EU ETS cannot use AAUs). If the Russian and Ukrainian AAUs from 2008 to 2012 were used, that would generate a huge increase in the supply.

6.5.2.2 Offset levies

At present, a levy of 2 per cent is imposed on all CDM transactions to help fund adaptation to climate change through the Adaptation Fund of the UNFCCC. The World Resources Institute (WRI, 2008) describes this levy as the 'iconic but largely untested' example of a truly global financing instrument. It could raise around US$500 million between now and 2012 (Fankhauser and Martin, 2010). The proposals to extend the scale and scope of the CDM, mentioned above, introduce the possibility of raising considerably more through an offset levy of this sort. The possibility of a 3–5 per cent levy and an extension to joint implementation and emission trading are under discussion. Fankhauser and Martin calculate that, with a broader CDM, a 10 per cent levy could raise US$10 billion a year by 2020.[16]

A major problem with the offset levy is that it is a tax on activities that economic analysis of the Kyoto framework suggests should be encouraged for reasons of cost effectiveness and equity. Thus, it is likely to reduce offset transactions and the implicit carbon price facing projects in developing countries. The uncertainty about revenues from the CDM is compounded by the uncertainty about how a higher-rate levy would affect CDM flows. Fankhauser and Martin point out that sellers of offset credits (developing countries) are likely to bear two-thirds of the cost of the levy, unless buyers in developed countries are subject to supplementarity restrictions, that is, limits on the proportion of their emissions that they can offset abroad. With supplementarity limits, the incidence of the levy is likely to be almost entirely on the buyers. Without supplementarity restrictions, the deadweight loss imposed by the levy rises sharply with the tax rate. One reason why its extension is being discussed may lie in the ambivalent attitude of many towards offset mechanisms.

6.5.2.3 Marine and aviation bunker fuel levies

To date, international aviation and shipping have largely escaped coverage by emissions reduction measures (although some air travel fees and taxes have been justified on environmental grounds, such as the UK's air passenger duty). Aviation will be included in the EU ETS from January 2012. Several proposals involving levies on estimated emissions, bunker fuel sales or some other activity measure likely to be correlated with environmental impact have been put forward.[17] Keen and Strand (2007) point out that a fuel tax is more effective in curbing fuel consumption, and thus carbon emissions, but a ticket tax has the potential to raise more revenue for climate policies in general and hence may be more useful for financing actions in developing countries.[18] The main proposals are for uniform international implementation by the international regulatory bodies: the International Civil Aviation Organization (ICAO) and the International Maritime Organization (IMO) for aviation and shipping, probably with exemption from similar domestic regulations. The main problem that remains is compensation for vulnerable island states, which would face increases in their transport costs.

These proposals have the merit of advocating taxes on 'bads' that have largely escaped fiscal authorities because of their inherent cross-border characteristics and international governance. As with other climate-related finance sources, some justification for hypothecation can be offered. However, revenue streams are uncertain, given uncertainty about the price elasticity involved and about the scope for avoidance. There is a danger that the levies would introduce yet more inefficient variation in carbon prices across industry sectors (unless fully integrated with other international carbon markets) and their interaction with domestic cap-and-trade schemes and other emission reduction measures would have to be considered carefully (the airline industry, for example, has argued that if an international scheme is adopted, airlines should be exempt from domestic policies). However, the amounts likely to be raised are far larger than the current or projected spending of the bodies (ICAO and IMO) that would collect the revenue, so they could commit to a steady stream of funding for climate-related purposes and allow any volatility in revenues to fall on rebates to their members.

6.5.3 Multilateral proposals: non-climate-related sources

6.5.3.1 International financial institutions and funds

A simple way of increasing funding for climate action is to increase the resources available to international financial institutions (IFIs), including the World Bank, the other multilateral development banks (MDBs) and the International Monetary Fund (IMF). The World Bank spent nearly US$3.5 billion on energy efficiency and renewable energy financing in the fiscal year 2009, and has pledged capital to the new climate investment funds. The other MDBs have also been ramping up their climate-related project spending, although this has reflected the diversion of existing development assistance rather than additional funding. The European Bank for Reconstruction and Development (EBRD), for example, has specific targets for lending to meet climate policy goals. There are established mechanisms for increasing their capital through contributions by member governments, which can be leveraged to bring in private funds. They also have some experience with developing innovative sources of finance, such as the advanced market commitment for vaccines. IMF staff have proposed a green fund that could raise US$100 billion a year by 2020 for climate-action finance. The green fund's capital could be raised by member countries subscribing some of their special drawing rights (SDRs) quotas, which were recently much expanded in response to the global financial crisis to build up the IMF's ability to lend. This could then leverage private finance through the issue of 'green bonds' guaranteed by members' SDR reserves.[19] However, the IMF's Executive Board has not been enthusiastic about using SDRs in this way. In addition to the IFIs, there are other funds such as the Global Environment Facility and the Adaptation Fund of the UNFCCC (the funding formulae for which could be amended to provide more finance), and new proposals on the horizon, such as the Green Climate Fund proposed in the Copenhagen Accord.

Initiatives along these lines have the advantage of bringing in private finance, either at a 'wholesale' level, with partly private funding of IFI initiatives and multilateral funds, or at a 'retail' level, with IFIs and private finance co-funding specific mitigation and adaptation measures. The approach also (in the case of the development banks) utilizes existing project appraisal skills. Expanding the IFIs' capital bases would not require the hypothecation of new forms of revenue. Funds would be generated at an appropriate scale. However, subscribing countries' contingent liabilities would be increased, as with the SDR proposals. The main questions about such initiatives are more to do with the terms on which funds would be disbursed, such as the extent of concessions, and the funds' governance.

6.5.3.2 Taxes on global 'bads'

Landau (2003) suggests taxing congestion in maritime straits, rights to geostationary orbits and associated radio frequencies and arms sales— activities that generate more clear-cut adverse externalities than do financial transactions. These taxes no doubt have merit on environmental or other social grounds and would probably need to be levied at an international level. However, the arguments against hypothecation apply with some force. A tax raised by a supranational body could still be distributed to member nations according to some rule rather than earmarked to some collective international objective. And the sums that would be raised are very uncertain, given that the issue of the optimal tax rates has not been explored.

6.5.3.3 Financial transactions taxes

Financial transactions taxes have been proposed as a way of reducing financial instruments' price volatility and the excessive allocation of resources to financial market intermediation (e.g. Baker, 2008; Schulmeister *et al.*, 2008; Schulmeister, 2009) and can be seen as attempts to tax a social 'bad'. James Tobin proposed a tax on spot foreign exchange transactions to reduce currency speculation and volatile cross-border capital flows as early as 1972. This could raise significant sums; a tax rate of a mere 1–2 basis points[20] could raise US$15–28 billion (but note that the euro trades against the US dollar with spreads as tight as 1/10th of a basis point). Atkinson (2004) suggested this approach to funding the pursuit of the Millennium Development Goals (MDGs).

Such taxes suffer from three main drawbacks as sources of funding for climate action. First, the drawbacks of hypothecation are particularly relevant, given competing potential uses for international funds of this sort. Second, the amount that could be raised is very uncertain, because the price elasticity of transactions with respect to transactions costs is very uncertain and liable to change according to circumstances (e.g. whether there is a financial panic). Some proposers want to limit the taxed activity, whereas others hope that a very low tax rate would not significantly affect trading volumes. Market liquidity could be impaired, therefore tending to increase volatility. Third, it is not clear that the activities are necessarily bad. Market liquidity and speculation in competitive markets are usually viewed by economists as desirable in helping to update prices quickly in response to new information. Financial transactions taxes are not well designed to correct the underlying market failures that lead to financial crises. Recently, policy makers' attention has therefore focused more on imposing additional liquidity and capital requirements on banks, and possibly taxes on some measure of balance-sheet growth, rather than on banks' financial market transactions.

There has been much empirical and theoretical research on such taxes. The evidence does not give grounds for enthusiasm. Hanke *et al.* (2010) provide a brief up-to-date discussion of the literature. One problem is that financial trans-actions taxes can simply become capitalized in the price of the assets traded, so that those holding the assets when the taxes are introduced bear all the costs (see e.g. Saporta and Kan (1997), on stamp duty and equity prices).

6.5.4 Proposals based on national government contributions

6.5.4.1 National auctions of emissions quotas

Some schemes rely on national auctions of allowances, with the revenues flowing through national budgets and subject to national policy priorities. Germany allocates part of the revenues from auctions of quotas under the EU ETS to its International Climate Initiative. The European Commission proposes extending this practice (European Commission, 2010b). The US Waxman – Markey Act planned to earmark a share of auction revenues from selling US allowances for international use (but probably determined bilaterally with US policy makers, not by international bodies).

The prices for allowance auctions under domestic cap-and-trade schemes would be broadly similar to those of compliance units in the international market unless the domestic scheme restricts imports or exports of compliance units. Intermittent auctions could contribute to price volatility.

6.5.4.2 Carbon taxes

Switzerland has proposed a tax of US$2 per tonne of CO_2 for emissions exceeding 1.5 tonnes per capita, with a share of the proceeds being subscribed to an international climate fund. The United Nations Development Programme (UNDP) calculates that a tax of US$20 per tonne of CO_2 levied by the OECD on its members would raise US$265 billion at current emission levels (Swiss Confederation, 2008). Several countries (e.g. Sweden, Denmark, Norway, Switzerland and Finland) already have carbon taxes on energy consumption, with various exemptions and allowances.

This approach could, with a sufficiently high tax rate, generate a flow of funds on the scale required. The political economy arguments for hypothecation would apply in this case (but the general argument against hypothecation would still have to be considered). As with any 'green' taxes, which are designed to reduce the activity taxed rather than simply to raise revenue, there would be some uncertainty about the revenue flows, which would depend on the scope for decarbonization. One problem is the potential interaction with cap-and-trade schemes. A tax on activities within the scope of such schemes would simply depress the carbon price, so it would not have any additional environmental benefit. A tax on activities outside such schemes would introduce multiple carbon prices, inducing inefficiency in allocation. The political acceptability of earmarking domestically raised taxes for international bodies at a rate determined outside the country is also in question. A carbon tax, or any other hypothecated source, is at the same time a burden-sharing formula for the contributing countries. Whereas agreement was eventually reached about the distribution of AAUs under the Kyoto Protocol, this instrument would re-open the debate about equity across developed countries.

6.5.4.3 Fossil-fuel royalties and subsidies

Earmarking funds raised from fossil-fuel royalties or the removal of fossil-fuel subsidies would also raise national contributions from a broadly climate-related source. Both sources of revenue have some economic justification as sources of general tax revenue. Apart from the objection that, once again, the grounds for hypothecation to action for climate finance are flimsy, this would result in an implicit burden-sharing formula quite different from that agreed under Kyoto and would be likely to run into political opposition. Fossil-fuel-exporting countries stand to lose from carbon pricing and are therefore likely to be unenthusiastic about sacrificing further rents from their dwindling natural resources.

6.5.4.4 Assessed or indicative contributions

Proposals for assessed or indicative contributions start with an explicit burden-sharing formula and then let governments decide how to raise their contribution, whether with a carbon tax, reduced subsidies, higher royalties, other specific revenue sources or general revenue. This avoids the problem of mandating hypothecation, but requires agreement on the overall ambition and the specific formula to be used. In practice, the latter is likely to be very difficult. The USA has been unable to agree to the one implicit in the Kyoto Protocol, perhaps the most obvious candidate. However, the approach has been used, sometimes with special provisions for the USA, in cases where financial flows are much smaller than the expenditure anticipated for climate change – the UN operating budget, the UNEP core budget and the Multilateral Fund of the Montreal Protocol, for example.

6.5.5 *High-level advisory group on climate change financing (AGF)*

This report investigated the feasibility of achieving the Copenhagen pledge of US$100 billion a year in 2020. It provides a careful review, of the scope for raising funds through the types of measures discussed here, at greater length than is practical in this chapter. The AGF groups potential sources of finance into public sources, development bank instruments, carbon market finance and private capital, assessing each against the eight criteria specified in their terms of reference: revenue-raising capability, efficiency, equity, incidence, practicality, reliability, additionality and acceptability. It was concluded that the US$100 billion target is 'challenging but feasible' if a variety of measures are taken to stimulate both public and private financial flows. However, no specific recommendations for action are made. Like the author of this chapter, the AGF stresses that '[i]nstruments based on carbon pricing are particularly attractive because they both raise revenue and provide incentives for mitigation actions'. The economic disadvantages of some proposals are mentioned (e.g. that levies on cap-and-trade offset purchases are effectively a tax on mitigation actions), although the drawbacks of revenue hypothecation are not fully explored.

Two aspects of the report are particularly helpful. First, quantitative estimates of the potential flows from particular measures are compiled on a consistent and transparent basis. Where arbitrary assumptions have to be made, for example about the proportion of new levies that would be earmarked for climate-change finance, they are laid out clearly and are consistent across instruments. Second, a distinction is drawn between gross and net flows. The latter are likely to be considerably lower than the former, particularly for private capital flows, given that private agents expect a competitive risk-adjusted return on their investments. However, the report makes clear that not all members of the AGF agreed about how net flows should be calculated or whether the target should be regarded as a target for net additional flows. There was also disagreement about whether private flows should be included. As a result, the report does not provide an illustrative breakdown of how the target can be reached, although it is possible to piece one together from the assessments of individual measures.

This chapter argues that considerations of equity warrant substantial transfers from developed to developing countries, so that the net basis is the appropriate one to use, notwithstanding the difficulties in estimating net flows. Also, private and public net flows should be considered; private investment can still generate net flows to developing countries because there are intra-marginal rents to be captured from mitigation and adaptation investments after deducting a competitive marginal rate of return.

On this basis, the AGF report suggests that, assuming a carbon price in 2020 of US$20–25 per tonne of CO_2 equivalent, public net flows derived from 10 per cent of domestic carbon taxes or quota auction revenues, new taxes on aviation and maritime emissions and other new levies could amount to US$50 billion per year. Private net investment flows could reach some US$10–20 billion per year and private transactions in carbon markets could generate US$10 billion per year (a relatively modest amount compared with some other estimates in the literature). MDBs could stimulate net flows of US$11 billion per year. That leaves some US$10–20 billion per year to be raised from direct budgetary support – one measure of how challenging the target is. If the carbon price were higher, the financial flows would be higher. The AGF argues that its low and central carbon price assumptions are broadly consistent with the emission reduction pledges made so far under the Copenhagen Accord, while its 'high' carbon price assumption (up to US$50 per tonne) is more consistent with keeping the increase in global temperature to 2°C. Hence if governments collectively take seriously their support for the 2°C limit, the challenge should be somewhat easier to meet.[21]

6.6 Conclusions

There is a reassuring level of agreement among international policy makers that developed countries should help finance climate change actions in developing countries, despite the range of ethical frameworks that are brought to bear in negotiations. The Copenhagen Accord's target of raising US$100 billion dollars a year by 2020 is modest relative to developing countries' probable needs. The report of the UN Secretary-General's AGF plausibly suggests that generating US$100 billion is challenging but feasible, if a variety of measures are taken to stimulate private and public flows of finance. Developing countries' needs must be kept under review as our understanding of the relevant science, economics and ethical considerations improves, as should the contribution to be made by developed countries. However, this chapter has focused on the principles that should guide efforts to raise finance rather than how much should be raised and for what uses.

The main conclusions are as follows:

- There is an important role for private finance. The key incentive is to have pervasive and broadly uniform emissions pricing around the world. Public authorities can stimulate private finance by helping to manage the risks of investing in mitigation, adaptation and technological innovation. Building the credibility of the long-term international climate-policy framework is one of the main challenges in this regard. Private finance will be particularly important for adaptation, as the latter will depend to a greater extent on private decision-makers. Also, within the right framework, it may be less subject to the vagaries of political popularity than public finance flows would be.

- Public finance is warranted by a range of market – and policy – failures associated with climate change and its mitigation. As well as the central environmental externality imposed by GHGs, there are problems in stimu-lating innovation, establishing infrastructure networks, and overcoming barriers to financial intermediation. That is particularly the case while the long-term outlook for climate policy is still unclear to prospective private investors and, because of the world economic slowdown, the short-term outlook for returns on any investment is poorer than usual.

- Raising tax revenues may be preferable to borrowing as a means of raising public finance, although the economics is not clear-cut. The current budget worries of many developed countries tip the balance further (although the pace of fiscal retrenchment necessary is subject to robust debate), but the need to build policy credibility points in the opposite direction. Theory also advocates taxing 'bads', of which a number have escaped the tax base so far. However, it discourages hypothecation of specific revenue streams to particular uses.

- There is a plethora of ideas and proposals for old and new forms of finance for climate action in developing countries. How much could or should be raised is very uncertain in most cases. So is how multiple schemes would interact. Several could have untoward consequences for emissions prices. Hypothecation is a frequent feature, with very little discussion of whether it is warranted. In many cases, it is clearly not warranted.

- Two sets of proposals do particularly well when judged against this analysis: (i) expanding the scale and scope of the CDM and (ii) expanding the use of IFIs' balance sheets, including the use of SDRs. However, in both cases, governance arrangements are subject to controversy. There are a number of other proposals for new taxes that have merit as far as revenue generation is concerned, but the case for earmarking the revenue raised for climate change finance is not wholly compelling, resting as it does on the supposed benefits of pre-commitment by developed-country governments rather than a quanti-tative assessment of developing countries' needs.

It is to be hoped that governments will act speedily to fulfill the promises of the Copenhagen Accord but without neglecting the principles of public finance in the process.

Notes

1 Defined as non-Annex 1 countries under the Kyoto Protocol.
2 Defined as Annex 1 countries under the Kyoto Protocol. The 47 countries in the UNFCCC's category of Least Developed Countries, in contrast, accounted for just over 4 per cent of emissions, and their aggregate emissions had been growing at an

average 1.5 per cent per year – a reminder that developing countries are by no means a homogeneous group as far as emissions are concerned.

3 Different ethical frameworks point to different allocation schemes in global cap-and-trade proposals, as illustrated by Höhne *et al.* (2005). However, virtually all entail large transfers to developing countries. A more general discussion of the interaction of economics, ethics and climate change can be found in Dietz *et al.* (2009).

4 The second fundamental theorem of welfare economics states that, under certain (rather restrictive) conditions, every Pareto-efficient allocation of resources can be achieved by competitive market equilibrium. When it holds, the problems of efficiency and distributional impacts across individuals can be separated (Varian, 2009). If introducing emissions pricing to correct the inefficiency induced by the GHG externality has adverse distributional consequences, these can be corrected by lump-sum transfers, set to ensure that at least someone is better off after the pricing is implemented, while no-one else is made worse off. The point here is not to rehearse the restrictiveness of the assumptions necessary for the theorem to hold (complete markets, perfect competition, etc.), but to emphasize that in this framework lump-sum transfers are necessary for the introduction of emissions pricing to be unambiguously welfare-enhancing.

5 Private finance is therefore likely to be easier to raise for project operation, where revenues and costs are more closely aligned in time, than for capital investment, unless there is public intervention.

6 See, for example, Nordhaus (2007), who makes a trenchant case for carbon taxation in preference to global quotas, and Metcalf (2009).

7 Stern (2009) is an example. Frankel (2009) is another analysis that is sympathetic to the markets-based approach behind Kyoto.

8 I am grateful to an anonymous referee for raising the issue of fossil-fuel exporters. Aggressive mitigation policies are likely to lower the value of their resources and may depress (carbon-price-exclusive) fossil-fuel prices. To avoid Sinn's 'green paradox' according to which climate change policies may accelerate emissions (Sinn, 2008), it is important that they participate in any global deal. What side payments might be required is a moot point.

9 Concern about the size of rents on intra-marginal abatement opportunities has led to various proposals for price discrimination in carbon markets, not least with respect to the treatment of abatement opportunities in forest management.

10 The relationship between environmental policy and business cycles is discussed in Bowen and Stern (2010).

11 Unfortunately, governments are often better at identifying goods that they should subsidize because of the presence of market failures than they are at identifying untaxed 'bads.' However, revenues from environmental taxes are surprisingly low in many countries (European Commission, 2008, 2010a).

12 This literature is extensive and represents perhaps the richest strand of discussion of public finance issues in the climate-change policy arena. See, inter alia, Bovenberg and Goulder (2002) and Schöb (2003).

13 UNEP Risø Centre website, accessed 24 August 2010.

14 Developed-country investors often sign emission reduction purchase agreements that involve payments at an early stage in the CDM project (often before it is registered) but at a price below the market price for CERs. Thus the funding provided differs in timing and amount from the market value of the CERs generated.

15 The CDM has been much debated in the context of the evolution of the international climate policy regime. See, for example, Schneider (2007) and papers from UNEP's Centre for Capacity Development for the Clean Development Mechanism (http://cd4cdm.org/index.htm). The Green Investment Schemes for post-communist Annex I countries may provide a useful model for a more flexible CDM (Tuerk *et al.*, 2010).

16 Haites points out that the CDM levy can be interpreted as being imposed on the CERs issued or the CERs traded internationally, as they will all be used in developed

countries. The base – issued or traded – makes a huge difference when a levy is to be applied to emission reduction units and AAUs. In the case of AAUs, it would be virtually identical to the Norwegian proposal.

17 Some useful references include Müller and Hepburn (2006), Faber *et al.* (2010), IMO (2009), ODI (2008) and McCollum *et al.* (2009).

18 I am indebted to an anonymous referee for alerting me to this argument.

19 The IMF proposals are discussed in IMF (2010). Williamson (2009) reviews the economics of SDRs, which are essentially an international form of fiat money. The opportunity cost of using them for a green fund would be the reduction in their utility as reserve assets for the subscribing countries.

20 A basis point is 1/100 of a percentage point.

21 Of course, more aggressive mitigation and higher carbon prices would also warrant more action by developing countries and more finance from developed nations. It is not clear whether policy makers see the US$100 billion target as consistent with the needs of developing countries in a world that takes the 2°C limit seriously.

References

Advisory Group on Climate Change Financing (AGF), 2010. *Report of the Secretary-General's High-level Advisory Group on Climate Change Financing*. United Nations, New York.

Atkinson, A.B., 2004, *New Sources of Development Finance: Funding the Millennium Development Goals*, Policy Brief No.10, UNU-WIDER, September.

Atkinson, A.B., Stiglitz, J.E., 1980, *Lectures in Public Economics*, McGraw Hill, New York.

Baker, D., 2008, *The Benefits of a Financial Transactions Tax*, Center for Economic and Policy Research, Washington, DC, December.

Blanchard, O.J., Giavazzi, F., 2004, *Improving the SGP Through a Proper Accounting of Public Investment*, CEPR Discussion Paper No. 4220, February.

Bovenberg, L., Goulder, L., 2002, 'Environmental taxation and regulation', in: A. Auerbach, M. Feldstein (eds), *Handbook of Public Economics*, Vol. 3, Chapter 23, Elsevier BV, Amsterdam.

Bowen, A., Ranger, N., 2009, *Mitigating Climate Change Through Reductions in Greenhouse Gas Emissions: The Science and Economics of Future Paths for Global Annual Emissions*, Policy Brief, Grantham Research Institute on Climate Change and the Environment, London School of Economics and Political Science, London, December, 21–34.

Bowen, A., Stern, N., 2010, 'Environmental policy and the economic downturn', *Oxford Review of Economic Policy* 26(2), 137–163.

Brett, C., Keen, M., 2000, 'Political uncertainty and the earmarking of environmental taxes', *Journal of Public Economics* 75(3), 315–340.

Center for Clean Air Policy, 2009, *Norway's Proposal to Auction Assigned Amount Units: Implementation Options*, CCAP, Washington, DC.

Clarke, L., Edmonds, J., Krey, V., Richels, R., Rose, S., Tavoni, M., 2009, 'International climate policy architectures: overview of the EMF 22 international scenarios', *Energy Economics* 31, S64–S81.

Dietz, S., Hepburn, C., Stern, N., 2009, 'Economics, ethics and climate change', in: K. Basu, R. Kanbur (eds), *Arguments for a Better World: Essays in Honour of Amartya Sen*, Volume 2: Society, Institutions and Development, Oxford University Press, Oxford.

European Commission, 2008, *Environment Policy Review 2008*, European Commission, Brussels.

European Commission, 2010a, *Taxation Trends in the European Union 2010*, European Commission, Brussels.

European Commission, 2010b, *International Climate Policy Post-Copenhagen: Acting Now to Reinvigorate Global Action on Climate Change*, Communication from the Commission to the European Parliament, the Council, the European Economic and Social Committee and the Committee of the Regions, Brussels.

Faber, J., Markowska, A., Eyring, V., Cionni, I., Selstad, E., 2010, *A Global Maritime Emissions Trading System*, CE Delft, Delft, January.

Fankhauser, S., Martin, N., 2010, 'The economics of the CDM levy: revenue potential, tax incidence and distortionary effects', *Energy Policy* 38, 357–363.

Frankel, J.A., 2009, *An Elaborated Global Climate Policy Architecture: Specific Formulas and Emission Targets for all Countries in all Decades*, National Bureau of Economic Research (NBER) Working Paper No. 14876, Cambridge, MA, April.

Green Investment Bank Commission, 2010, *Unlocking Investment to Deliver Britain's Low Carbon Future*, GIBC, London.

Hanke, M., Huber, J., Kirchler, M., Sutter, M., 2010, 'The economic consequences of a Tobin tax – an experimental analysis', *Journal of Economic Behavior and Organization* 74, 58–71.

Hepburn, C., 2009, Climates of Change: Sustainability Challenges for Enterprises, Smith School Working Paper, University of Oxford, Oxford, September.

Höhne, N., Phylipsen, D., Ullrich, S., Blok, K., 2005, *Options for the Second Commitment Period of the Kyoto Protocol*, Ecofys for the Federal Environmental Agency, Berlin, February.

IMF, 2010, *Financing the Response to Climate Change*, International Monetary Fund (IMF) Staff Position Note 2010/06, IMF, Washington, DC, March.

IMO, 2009, *The Second IMO GHG Study 2009*, International Maritime Organization, London.

Ismihan, M., Ozkan, G., 2008, *Golden Rule of Public Finance: A Panacea?*, Discussion Paper in Economics No. 2008/19, Department of Economics and Related Studies, University of York, York.

Kay, J.A., 1990, 'Tax policy: a survey', *Economic Journal* 100(399), 18–75.

Keen, M., Strand, J., 2007, 'Indirect taxes on international aviation', *Fiscal Studies* 28, 1–41.

Landau, J.-P., 2003, *The Landau Report* [available at www.cttcampaigns.info/documents/fr/landau_en/Landau1. pdf].

McCleary, W., 1991, 'The earmarking of government revenue: a review of some World Bank experience', *World Bank Research Observer* 6, 81–104.

McCollum, D., Gould, G., Greene, D., 2009, *Greenhouse Gas Emissions from Aviation and Marine Transportation: Mitigation Potential and Policies, Pew Center on Global Climate Change*, Arlington, VA, December.

Metcalf, G.E., 2009, *Cost Containment in Climate Change Policy: Alternative Approaches to Mitigating Price Volatility*, NBER Working Paper No. 15125, Cambridge, MA, July.

Müller, B., 2008, *To Earmark or Not to Earmark?*, EV43, Oxford Institute for Energy Studies, Oxford, November.

Müller, B., Hepburn, C., 2006, *IATAL – An Outline Proposal for an International Air Travel Adaptation* Levy, EV36, Oxford Institute for Energy Studies, Oxford, October.

Musgrave, R.A., Musgrave, P.B., 1989, *Public Finance in Theory and Practice*, McGraw Hill, New York.

Nordhaus, W.D., 2007, 'To tax or not to tax: alternative approaches to slowing global warming', *Review of Environmental Economics and Policy* 1(1), 26–44.

ODI, 2008, *Innovative Carbon-Based Funding for Adaptation,* Overseas Development Institute, London, November.

OECD, 1996, *Implementation Strategies for Environmental Taxes,* OECD, Paris.

Oxfam, 2008, *Turning Carbon into Gold*, Oxfam Briefing Paper No. 123, Oxfam International, December.

Pigou, A., 1932, *The Economics of Welfare*, 4th Edn, MacMillan, London.

Pirttilä, J., 1998, *Earmarking of Environmental Taxes: Efficient, After All*, Bank of Finland Discussion Paper 4/98, Helsinki.

Saporta, V., Kan, K., 1997, *The Effects of Stamp Duty on the Level and Volatility of Equity Prices*, Working Paper No. 71, Bank of England, London, October.

Schneider, L., 2007, *Is the CDM Fulfilling Its Environmental and Sustainable Development Objectives? An Evaluation of the CDM and Options for Improvement*, Report for WWF, Okö -Institut, Berlin, November.

Schöb, R., 2003, *The Double Dividend Hypothesis of Environmental Taxes: A Survey*, CESifo Working Paper No. 946, Munich, May.

Schulmeister, S., 2009, *A General Financial Transaction Tax: A Short Cut of the Pros, the Cons and a Proposal*, CESifo Working Paper No. 344, WIFO, Vienna, October.

Schulmeister, S., Scratzenstaller, M., Picek, O., 2008, *A General Financial Transaction Tax: Motives, Revenues, Feasibility and Effects*, WIFO, Vienna, October.

Sinn, H.-W., 2008, 'Public policies against global warming', *International Tax and Public Finance* 15, 360–394.

Stern, N., 2009, *A Blueprint for a Safer Planet: How to Manage Climate Change and Create a New Era of Progress and Prosperity*, The Bodley Head, London.

Swiss Confederation, 2008, *Funding Scheme for Bali Action Plan: A Swiss Proposal for Global Solidarity in Financing Adaptation*, Berne, May.

Tuerk, A., Frieden, D., Sharmina, M., Schreiber, H., Ürge-Vorsatz, D., 2010, *Green Investment Schemes: First Experiences and Lessons Learned*, Joanneum Research Working Paper, April.

Varian, H., 2009, *Intermediate Microeconomics: A Modern Approach*, 8th edn, W.W. Norton & Co., New York.

Williamson, J., 2009, *Understanding Special Drawing Rights (SDRs)*, Policy Brief 09/11, Peterson Institute for International Economics, June, Washington, DC.

WRI, 2008, *Financing Adaptation: Opportunities for Innovation and Experimentation*, WRI Conference Paper, Washington, DC, November.

7 Sources of finance for climate action

Principles and options for implementation mechanisms in this decade

Mattia Romani and Nicholas Stern

7.1 Introduction

In the Copenhagen Accord of December 2009 developed countries committed

> to a goal of mobilizing jointly US$100 billion dollars a year by 2020 to address the needs of developing countries. This funding will come from a wide variety of sources, public and private, bilateral and multilateral, including alternative sources of finance.[1]

Although the Copenhagen Accord was not adopted it was supported by a large number of countries. The Copenhagen Accord also proposed the creation of a Copenhagen Green Climate Fund to disburse a significant portion of the new multilateral funding for adaptation.[2] A Green Climate Fund was established by the next conference of the parties (COP 16) in Cancun (see Chapter 13). The Accord was a fairly well balanced outcome, with developing countries signing up to it on the back of the financial commitment of developed countries, and developed countries on the back of the pledges made by developing countries. These transfers were interpreted (at least by developing countries) as being linked to equity: without some attention to equity an agreement would have been very difficult.

Shortly after the Copenhagen meeting, the UN Secretary General established a High-Level Advisory Group on Climate Finance (AGF) to study the potential sources of revenue for financing mitigation and adaptation activities in developing countries.[3] The AGF was charged with developing technically and politically feasible proposals that could raise US$100 billion per year by 2020 from public and private sources to finance mitigation and adaptation strategies in developing countries.

The AGF consisted of 20 members including heads of state and governments, ministers of finance, high office holders and experts on public finance, development and related issues serving in their expert capacities.[4] The Group had equal representation of developed and developing countries.

The AGF worked during 2010 to produce a set of proposals on sources of climate change funding. Its report, published in November 2010, concluded that "it is challenging but feasible to reach the goal of mobilising US$100 billion annually for climate actions in developing countries by 2020. Reaching the goal will likely require a mix of sources, both existing and new public sources as well as increased private flows."[5]

The AGF report has been followed by a number of studies that address the challenge of raising finance for climate action in developing countries.[6] These studies have explored some of the potential sources of finance suggested in the AGF report in more detail, assessing their practicality and refining estimates of the amounts they could generate. Most have fallen short, though, of placing at the heart of their analysis the strong set of sound economic principles that is at the core of the AGF report.

As the AGF Report suggests, what is needed is a reliable and principle-based bundle of sources of finance, involving both public and private instruments that can be scaled up according to the adaptation and mitigation financing needs of developing countries, in the context of their development plans and programmes. In fact, while the AGF was tasked with analysing options for raising US$100 billion per annum by 2020, the amount of climate finance required is highly uncertain, very likely much larger. Sources of finance, moreover, should provide incentives for production and consumption around the world consistent with the overall move to the low-carbon economy.

In our view, the AGF report offers the most coherent, well-founded, and developed overview of the package of potential sources now available for generating long-term climate finance. The individuals that worked on the AGF report included a mix of developed and developing countries government high-level officials and experts. To avoid political stalemate they focused on reaching convergence on principles and on the logic and clarity of arguments. This proved to be a good approach and achieved some agreement on the potential package of financial sources. Accordingly in this chapter we set out the logic underlying that package and the principles that can serve as the basis for a robust climate finance system as drawn from the AGF report.

Although the economic crisis has put at risk implementation of the Copenhagen commitment to increase climate finance, we argue that the resources are still needed by developing countries where rapid economic growth continues and that sensible policies to generate climate finance can help developed countries deal with the economic crisis as well.

7.2 Sources of climate finance

7.2.1 The principles

Sound policy around raising new sources of finance should be based on clear principles. The additional resources should take into account both the base for taxation and political acceptability, foster effective and efficient incentives for the transition to a low-carbon economy and involve both private and public sources. In the context of generating significant additional long-term finance to support mitigation and adaptation action in developing countries these principles can be translated into the following:

- *Tax the bad.* Sources should contribute to tackling the problem; taxing greenhouse gas emissions generates revenue and provides an incentive to reduce emissions thus correcting the market failure associated with the GHG externality and promoting efficiency.
- *Additionality as new-ness or innovative finance.* Additionality is often assessed relative to existing financial flows. One cannot say with any confidence what investment or development flows to developing countries would be in 2020 without taking into account climate change. Rather than attempting to assess 'additionality' relative to an inevitably arbitrary reference case, the AGF considered the *new-ness* of each potential source. This corresponds in large measure to the statement in the Copenhagen Accord that funds will come from alternative sources.
- *Incidence on rich countries.* The measures should have no net incidence implications for developing countries if they are to constitute net flow from developed to developing countries. This has two implications: first, sources of finance that have incidence on developed countries only should be preferred (e.g. revenues from carbon taxes or cap-and-trade auctions implemented by developed countries to help meet their emissions limitation commitments); second, if a source has a direct or indirect incidence on developing countries this impacts should be compensated accordingly (e.g. if a tax on international aviation is introduced, flights between developing countries should be either exempt or compensated). The compensation mechanism, while fair, poses possible efficiency issues. Putting a price on or regulating such emissions and providing compensation is more efficient than exempting them.
- *Promoting public and private sources.* While private sources will finance the lion's share of the capital needed for the new energy and industrial investments, public funds will also be required for many activities. These include mitigation investments unlikely to attract sufficient private finance because of associated market failures (e.g. those involving R&D or building networks), risk-sharing instruments to leverage private investments (e.g. debt guarantees and first-loss equity) and those adaptation investments unlikely to attract private finance.
- *Scalability and robustness.* The scale of climate action needed is uncertain. This implies that the financial sources chosen will need to be scalable and thus that the base of taxation should be substantial so that tax rates are not too high. The bundle of sources should be flexible, both to fund strong action and to deliver different combinations of grants and loans depending on the mix of finance required.

7.2.2 Distinguishing between net and gross flows

The distinction between *'net'* and *'gross'* flow is important in understanding the nature of support the flows embody. A private sector loan at market rates for low-carbon investment does not increase the net resources available to a country. The same is true of a public-sector loan at market rates. In contrast grants or contributions, such as aid from public or philanthropic sources, without repayment obligations, which are over and above existing commitments, increase the net resources available to the recipient country. So do concessional loans, which carry a repayment obligation but have a 'grant equivalent' value depending on the nature of their concessionary element.

An increase in the total value of all loans (including private and public, i.e. the gross flow) may not increase the net resources available to a country, but is of interest as a measure of the climate change activities being financed. And the scale of new types of investment carries important information and learning about future opportunities and the overall direction of the economy.

Thus net/gross and public/private amounts of finance are relevant concepts and distinctions, and none should be dismissed. Perhaps unsurprisingly, developing countries focus on the net-public combination of sources when looking at climate finance flows. This derives from the equity argument for a high share of funds that increase the resources available to developing countries in the US$100 billion pledge. Many developing countries can already borrow at reasonable market rates but need additional public resources to fund climate change action on the scale required.

The political acceptability of both the origin and use of the financial flows, from the perspective of both developing and developed countries, could involve a number of issues of public confidence. It will influence their potential size, growth over time, and certainty of the revenue generated.

7.2.3 Sources

The individual sources examined by the AGF are discussed at length in its report and the workstream papers.[7] In summary, the sources examined are:

Public finance

- Revenues from the international auctioning of emission allowances (such as assigned amount units (AAU) under the Kyoto Protocol). This would involve retaining some allowances from developed countries and auctioning them to raise revenue.
- Revenues from the auctioning of emission allowances in domestic emissions trading schemes. This would involve auctioning domestic allowances (as in the European Union Emission Trading Scheme) and allocating part of associated revenue for international climate finance.
- Revenues from offset levies. This would involve withholding a share of the offsets, as is currently done in the Clean Development Mechanism (CDM), and selling them to raise revenue.
- Revenues generated from taxes on international aviation and shipping. This would involve either a levy on maritime bunker/aviation jet fuels for international voyages, or a separate emissions trading scheme for these

activities, or a levy on passenger tickets of international flights. It is inefficient and distortionary to leave the emissions associated with these activities
untaxed.

- Revenues from carbon taxes. This is a tax on greenhouse gas emissions in
developed countries raised on a per-ton-CO_2 equivalent basis, with part of the
revenue going to international climate finance.
- Revenues from a wires charge. This involves a small charge on electricity
generation, either per kWh produced or linked to the CO_2 emissions per kWh
produced. This could lead to double-taxation if applied together with carbon
related taxes.
- Revenues generated by removing fossil energy subsidies in developed countries. This comprises budget commitments freed by the removal of fossil
energy subsidies, part of which can be diverted towards climate finance for
developing countries. Fossil energy subsidies in developing countries amount
to hundreds of billions of dollars annually, wasting precious revenues and
distorting incentives. But these are matters for developing countries to decide.
- Revenues from fossil fuel extraction royalties/licences. These could be
increased and/or allocated in part to international climate finance.
- Revenues from a financial transaction tax. This builds on existing proposals
for a global financial transaction tax (with a focus on foreign exchange transactions). Concerns were raised as such a tax is motivated by the externality
arising from financial market volatility rather than the greenhouse gas externality and is, depending on the design, international in its basis.
- Direct budget contributions. This involves revenues provided through
national budgetary decisions.

International financial institutions (IFIs)

- Resources generated via multilateral development banks using current balance sheet headroom.
- Resources created via potential further replenishments and paid-in capital
contributions by countries to multilateral development banks (i.e. generating
new cash resources for multilateral development banks). These could support
both highly concessional and non-concessional loans;
- Potential contribution to a fund dedicated to climate-related investment
financed on the back of the commitment of existing or new Special Drawing
Rights of the International Monetary Fund.

Private finance sources

- Carbon market finance refers to resource transfers related to developed country purchases of emissions offsets implemented in developing countries.
Carbon markets offer important opportunities to leverage private investment
and finance new technologies in developing countries. Presently, purchases
of project-based offsets by private entities and governments in developed
countries from private entities in developing countries through the Clean

Development Mechanism (CDM) dominate the market. Additional flows could be generated as carbon markets are further developed and deepened. The potential scale of resources generated depends on the stringency of the emissions reduction commitments of developed countries, and thus on carbon-market prices, on carbon market design and on the availability of eligible emissions reductions in developing countries.

- The relevant international private finance flows are those resulting from specific interventions by developed countries. The interventions include the use of risk mitigation or revenue-enhancing instruments that compensate private investors for otherwise lower risk-adjusted required rates of return ("crowding in") as well as capacity-building for adaptation and implementation of climate policies in developing countries. Such flows cannot be committed *ex ante*, since they depend on private choices. However, developed country policy actions, as well as the multilateral and bilateral development banks, can catalyse and foster additional private sector flows.

To estimate the potential gross revenue that could be generated by each source, the AGF considered three scenarios involving carbon prices of US$15, 25 and 50 per ton CO_2 equivalent in 2020. The key assumptions underlying the estimates are described in the appendix. The estimated amounts are presented in Table 7.1.

7.2.4 Bundles or portfolios of choices

Since no single source is able to generate US$100 billion per year, it is inevitable that different sources of finance will need to be combined into portfolios of sources ('bundles') to generate sufficient revenues. The AFG report describes bundles as combinations of sources that are mutually supportive and internally consistent.

Bundles can be built around different governing principles by including public and private sources based on their match to such principles as illustrated in Figure 7.1. For example, a bundle can be built around the principle of promoting 'carbon efficiency', i.e. prioritizing the use of sources that are directly related to carbon and apply a tax to the 'bad', such as revenues from carbon taxes, from auctioning and carbon markets. Alternatively, a bundle can be created following a principle of non-dependence on carbon markets to ensure the reliability of the flows in the absence or weakness of carbon markets. Or a bundle can be based on strong international cooperation, if the political conditions allow it. Such a bundle may include a larger share of revenue generated through an international transport tax, with a substantial share of the funds being channelled through MDBs. Alternatively, one can envisage a domestic-focused bundle that relies on domestic measures, such as revenues from carbon taxes/wire charges, or from auctioning permits.

A bundle approach offers several important advantages:

- a range of sources allows countries flexibility in choosing domestic sources;
- it spreads the risks associated with individual sources not delivering the expected flows and hence makes overall flows more reliable;

Table 7.1 Assessment of gross revenue potential for international climate of individual sources (US$ billion in 2020)

	Low carbon price ($15)	Medium carbon price ($25)	High carbon price ($50)
Public finance sources			
AAU/ETS auctions	$2–8	$8–38 ($25–50)*	$14–70
Offset levies	$0–1	$1–5	$3–15
International transport	$3–8	$6–11 ($7–11)*	$11–25
Carbon tax (other than AAU/ETS auctions)	Approximately $10 for every $1/t of CO_2e		
Wires charge	$5 for a charge of $0.0004/kWh or $1/t of CO_2e		
Removal of fossil subsidies	$3–8 ($4–12)*		
Redirection of fossil royalties	Approximately $10		
Financial transaction tax	$2–27		
Contributions from International Financial Institutions (IFIs)			
IFIs	For each $10 in capital replenishment, ~$30–40 in gross MDB lending		
Private finance sources			
Carbon market offsets	$8–12	$38–50 ($20)*	$150
Private finance	Up to $200 billion, generated with a leverage factor of 2–4 on public flows/carbon market offsets. ($100–200)*		

Note: The figures in this table refer to the flows available for international climate finance using AGF and World Bank assumptions. A substantial amount of revenues, not accounted for in this table, would be retained in national budgets. For example, the AGF assumes that 90% of auction revenues and 50–75% of travel would be retained domestically.

* Estimates in parenthesis are from World Bank 2011.

Source: Compiled by the authors from AGF 2010a and World Bank 2011.

- different sources can reinforce each other. For example, risk-sharing instruments through international financial institutions will be more effective in leveraging investment if carbon-pricing instruments are in place, strengthening arguments for their joint inclusion.

Some sources will overlap with each other, so there would be arguments for a direct choice between them. The overall revenue potential of a bundle, therefore, is not necessarily the sum of its parts.

The dynamic relationship between the sources and the potential for mutual reinforcement in the wider context of a move towards a low-carbon economy is important. The portfolio approach pursued by the AGF Report attempts to move the debate on sources from picking individual sources in isolation to crafting reliable, self-reinforcing bundles of sources that both benefit from and contribute to laying the foundations for the low-carbon economy.

Illustration of potential combinations

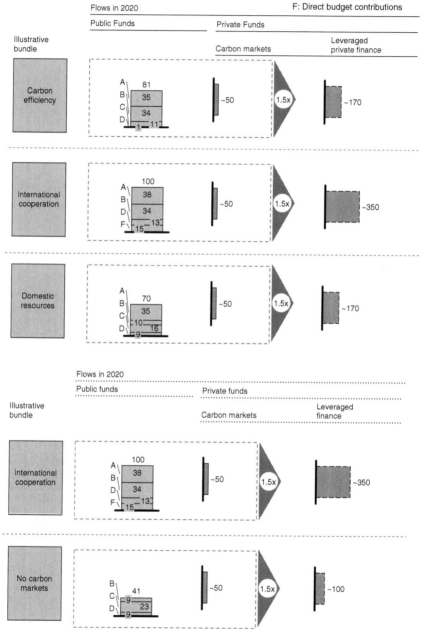

Figure 7.1 Potential combinations of sources (US$ billion per year).

Not all of these bundles have the same potential to raise revenue. In particular bundles based on carbon pricing in a context where there is little appetite for taxing emissions, or for international coordination of carbon markets and taxing international transport, would fall short of meeting the US$100 billion per year commitment.

A bundle of sources built around the principle of carbon efficiency, making use of the revenues generated through carbon markets and taxing emissions, seems to be a particularly attractive option, especially when associated with some international cooperation. The mix of instruments in such a bundle could deliver:

- approximately US$30 billion annually in net public funds from the emissions trading/taxing, depending on the level of ambition and commitment of developed countries;
- approximately US$30 billion per year in net public funds from taxing international transport and removing fossil fuel subsidies;
- approximately US$20 billion per year in gross flows in the form of loans from IFIs by contributing an additional US$5 billion annually to their capital;
- approximately US$200–300 billion per year in gross private flows generated by using the leverage potential of public funds.

Such a bundle would leave US$150–200 billion per year in developed country national treasuries. It would build on the self-reinforcing nature of its different components and contribute to the transition to a more efficient and sustainable low-carbon economy.

Looking at the combined characteristics of different combinations of sources is of great importance in generating reliable and principled financial foundations for climate finance on the scale required. Simple public finance principles, such as the ones used in the AGF to examine the individual sources, – revenue potential, efficiency, incidence, practicality, reliability, additionality, political acceptability – can be used to assess different potential bundles.

7.2.5 *Political will is critical*

It is clear that bundles built on charges for greenhouse gas emissions are preferable both from an efficiency perspective and in terms of potential revenue generation. But they require the political willingness of individual countries to have a carbon market for or a tax on the emissions together with strong emission reduction commitments.

Signals of such political commitment are more and more evident both in developed and in developing countries. The EU continues its commitment to creating a strong carbon market and an emissions trading scheme has just started in Australia. Korea and Brazil are both considering the introduction of a cap-and-trade scheme and several provinces in China are moving to implement markets as an initial step towards a national scheme.

We should recognize that political will is basic to any of the measures. Political will is more likely to exist the greater the recognition of the climate challenge, the greater the recognition of an international sense of community, the greater the recognition of the attractions of a low-carbon path and the greater the conviction resources will be spent wisely.

7.2.6 *Scaling up*

To generate action and to help international agreement sources must begin to be ramped up now to generate US$100 billion per year by 2020. Sources that require coordinated international action take more time to implement than domestic measures. Sources that could potentially deliver resources relatively quickly are public revenues from domestic carbon markets, carbon taxes, carbon market offsets, wire charges and the removal or redeployment of fossil fuel subsidies; contributions from multilateral development banks; direct budget contributions; and public finance that is used to leverage private investments. Sources that might deliver only in the medium to long term are public revenues from international carbon markets, aviation and maritime policy measures, financial transaction taxes, and special drawing rights.

7.3 Current flows of climate finance

At the time of the Copenhagen Accord and the AGF report only fragmented information on current climate finance flows was available. A year after the AGF report was released, the Climate Policy Initiative estimated that climate finance flows to developing countries at US$97 billion per annum (Buchner *et al.*, 2011, Chapter 2).[8] Of the estimated US$97 billion approximately US$55 billion is private finance. Around US$56 billion is in the form of market rate loans and US$13 billion is in the form of concessional loans through bilateral and multilateral institutions. Only US$4 billion of climate finance is provided in the form of grants.

While the current flow of funds to low-carbon activities in the developing world may be close to US$100 billion, this does not mean that the Copenhagen pledge has been met. First, the pledge is for *additional* funds – funds arising from policy action by rich countries – while most of the current flows pre-date the pledge. Second, the current flows are not *incremental*; they represent the full capital investment, rather than the additional cost, of low-carbon infrastructure. Third, they constitute gross flows rather than net contributions. Finally, the current flows include some domestic finance and funds from developing countries so the flows from developed to developing countries are smaller.

Nevertheless, the estimates of the current flows indicate that there already exist significant flows of climate finance to developing countries. They indicate that processes and institutions to generate and deploy significant amounts of climate finance already exist. This infrastructure can be utilized as climate finance is scaled up to deliver the Copenhagen commitment of US$100 billion annually

by 2020. Indeed, as discussed in section 7.5, the US$100 billion pledge consti-
tutes only a small part of what the flows will have to be over the next decades.

7.4 Climate finance and the economic crisis

While the economic crisis was already evident in December 2009, in Copenhagen
many thought that coordinated action would overcome the economic problems
fairly rapidly. The ensuing events have been on the pessimistic ends of expectations at that time. We now recognise that our economic systems are undergoing a
profound and lengthy crisis, involving major macroeconomic structural imbal-
ances, major debt and deficits in some countries and severe strains to the current
financial system. The prospects for growth are fragile. This puts at risk implementation of the commitment to increase climate finance.

Developed country leaders, understandably, are focusing on the economic
crisis. But sensible policies to generate climate finance can help deal with the
economic crisis as well. Sources that put a price on greenhouse gas emissions –
such as auctioned allowances for domestic emissions trading systems, carbon
taxes, and reduced fossil fuel subsidies – have the highest potential in this sense,
both in terms of increasing the efficiency of the economy by addressing market
failures and in terms of potential revenue generation.

A bundle of sources that would generate international climate finance of
US$100 billion per year would generate even more revenue – US$150–200 billion
per year – for developed country national treasuries.[9] Thus, sensible policies to
generate the finance needed to meet the Copenhagen commitment would also
produce significant sums to deal with developed country deficits and debt or
to reduce existing distortionary taxes and so help stimulate economic growth.

A time of economic crisis, it will be argued, is not the appropriate time to
implement policies that raise costs for industry and consumers. Market-based
mitigation policies that generate revenue are among the most attractive policies
available in this sense, as they tend to be countercyclical; emissions and prices are
lower during a recession. So if any new policies are being considered they merit
careful consideration particularly during a period of economic crisis. Since such
policies take a few years to implement, economic conditions may be better when
they take effect.

The need of developing countries for climate finance has continued to grow
despite and because of the economic crisis. Economic growth in developing
countries was interrupted only briefly by the economic crisis. Investment in
renewable energy in developing countries increased, on average, by more than
45 per cent a year between 2004 and 2011, and over 20 per cent per year since
2009.[10] Their need for climate finance continues to grow despite the crisis.

UNEP notes that the sovereign debt crisis in Europe in late 2011 affected the
ability of banks to provide project finance for renewable energy consequently
forcing project developers to focus on alternative sources of investment such as
pension funds and other long-term institutional investors.[11] Thus, the economic
crisis increases the need for climate finance from alternative sources. If the

resources needed to finance low-carbon growth are scarce during this period of crisis and investment is lower, future mitigation and adaptation costs will be higher, making the need to identify and put in place mechanisms to raise sources of finance even more pressing.

7.5 Principle based climate finance

We do not have accurate information on the scale of climate finance that will be required. Available estimates suggest that the financial resources required by developing countries for adaptation and mitigation, on their own, could be larger than the full US$100 billion committed in the Copenhagen Accord.[12] As noted above, this uncertainty concerning the resources needed implies that the financial sources will need to be scalable and that the bundle of sources should be flexible and be able to deliver different combinations of grants and loans depending on the mix of finance required.

Development, mitigation and adaptation are closely intertwined – adaptation is essentially development in a more hostile climate – and all three should be at the heart of developing countries', and indeed global, policies to manage climate change. At the same time, development ambitions such as the Millennium Development Goals and developing countries' long-term objectives were established before the grave dangers of climate change were fully understood. Development is thus more challenging than anticipated when those objectives were set. Hence, it is important that provision of climate finance be over and above the long-standing commitments to development finance; that the climate finance be "additional".

The AGF report identified acceptability as a fundamental principle of sourcing climate finance. This concept should include, from the perspectives of both developed and developing countries, confidence that the monies will be spent wisely in terms of productivity and integrity. From this perspective it should combine the willingness to provide resources and the willingness to receive them on the terms offered. Acceptability also should include appropriate mechanisms to give those developing countries taking climate action a prominent role in shaping spending decisions. And priority for the resources should be accorded to the poorest and most vulnerable.

Developing countries formulating plans for resilient low-carbon growth would be greatly helped by predictability in the potential scale and nature of funding. The relationship between development aid and climate finance is crucial for countries as they plan their strategies around development, adaptation and mitigation. For developing countries this is critical to the efficient and effective use of the funds. Good financial planning – spending the resources provided wisely and effectively – is important for developed countries as well. The governments of both developed and developing countries are accountable for the efficient spending of resources to their taxpayers, citizens and voters.

The world must go through an energy-industrial transformation in the next few decades if it is to manage responsibly the immense risks of climate change.

The absolute level of global emissions of greenhouse gases must be reduced by at least 30 per cent over the next 20 years to give a 50-50 chance of holding to a 2°C increase in global temperatures relative to the nineteenth century.[13] This brutal arithmetic has two consequences. First, the world needs to raise its game from the Copenhagen and Cancun pledges starting now. Second, the rich countries simply cannot deliver enough by emission reductions alone to create the space that the poor countries understandably argue is their right given basic notion of equity and past history of emissions.

That surely tells us that finance and technology support to developing countries is both critical and just. The rich countries are not only wealthier and better equipped technologically than developing countries but they also emitted around 75 per cent of cumulative global GHG emissions since the mid-nineteenth century. The consequences of anthropogenic climate change, which are occurring now and will occur over the next 20 years and are largely the result of these past emissions of rich countries, will also require substantial investment in adaptation.

A majority of the world's growth in the next decade is likely to be in the developing countries, thus shifting investment towards resilient low-carbon growth in those countries is critically important. Multilateral and bilateral institutions can support policies that foster investment and help share and reduce risk. Investors are increasingly realizing that the future of economic growth is in the low-carbon economy and are responding to the strong actions and policies that many developing countries governments are taking to lay the foundations for resilient low-carbon growth in their economies.

7.6 Conclusions

The AGF was charged with developing technically and politically feasible proposals that could raise US$100 billion per year by 2020 from public and private sources to finance mitigation and adaptation strategies in developing countries. To help identify and evaluate potential sources of finance the AGF used the following principles:

- Sources should not only raise money, they should foster the transition to a low-carbon economy. It is important that they create incentives to encourage resource allocation to low-carbon technologies and adaptation activities. Sources that raise revenues from greenhouse gas emissions are a good way of achieving this.
- Sources need to be new and innovative. This is a practical way of interpreting additionality in this context.
- The incidence of the taxes used to mobilize funds should be limited to developed countries. If there is an impact on developing countries, they should be compensated accordingly.
- The private sector is crucial to the transition. Public sources should be combined with private not only to leverage investment as much as possible, but also to structure risk, influence policy, and generate a business environment

that is conducive to private investors. This is a particularly important role for the IFIs.

- Climate finance needs are uncertain and the balance of flows across countries and sources may need to vary over time according to domestic constraints, requirements and economic conditions. This is a good reason to consider bundles of sources. Flexible bundles will increase the reliability of the financial flows. Bundles should be designed with flexibility to scale up resources if and when needed.

Estimates of the potential gross revenue that could be generated by each source under a medium carbon price scenario of US$25 per ton CO_2e in 2020 indicate clearly that no source, on its own, would generate US$100 billion per year. The AGF therefore examined the attractiveness of different bundles of sources. A bundle built around the principle of carbon efficiency, making use of the revenues generated through carbon markets and taxing emissions could deliver:

- Public finance of US$60 billion per year raised from a mix of AAU/ETS auctions and offset levies, taxes on international transport, removal of fossil subsidies and redirection of fossil royalties. Other sources such as other carbon taxes, wires charges, and a financial transactions tax could also contribute.
- Loans of US$20 billion per year from IFIs for each additional US$5 billion contributed annually to their capital.
- Private finance of US$200–300 billion in gross private flows from carbon markets and private investment, leveraged by public funds.

These numbers are calculated on the basis of an assessment of developed countries' commitment to reducing emissions by charging for them. They assume the strengthening of existing carbon markets and the creation of new ones. They assume some willingness to tax international transport and to channel those revenues to climate investment. And they assume willingness to remove fossil fuel subsidies and to use the resources freed for climate finance. These are strong assumptions, which, given the current political conditions, sometimes require taking the long view to seem credible.

Admitting defeat in mobilizing the necessary resources on the basis of short term considerations would be a mistake. Although there is a need to start ramping up resources now to meet the 2020 commitment, some instruments can be mobilized more quickly than others. Revenue from domestic measures could be mobilized relatively quickly. These could be then leveraged through increased lending by multilateral banks. More in general, the strengthening of the IFIs to enable them to increase the scale of investment in sustainable infrastructure seems an urgent requirement given the future needs for infrastructure in developing and emerging markets. Sources that require coordinated international action take more time to implement.

Although the economic crisis has put at risk implementation of the Copenhagen commitment to increase climate finance, the resources are still needed by developing countries where rapid economic growth continues. Some of the sources, especially the ones related to pricing carbon through market mechanisms, are particularly well suited to be put in place during periods of low economic growth. They increase the overall efficiency of the economy by correcting a market failure and are designed to be counter-cyclical hence have a modest impact on prices for industry and consumers during periods of crisis. They would also generate much needed general revenue on top of the required US$100 billion for climate finance: as much as US$150–200 billion per year for developed country national treasuries. The treasuries could use this revenue to help reduce their deficits and debt or to reduce existing distortionary taxes and so help stimulate economic growth.

Funding is crucial to a global agreement, and a global agreement of some kind is crucial for reducing the risks of climate change. The financial resources required by developing countries for adaptation and mitigation, on their own, could be larger than the full US$100 billion committed in the Copenhagen Accord. Generating the financial resources to meet these needs will require a principle based system.

The system must be flexible in terms of the sources yet predictable in terms of the amount of revenue generated. The sources must be additional so as not to compromise developing countries' development ambitions. The sources of funds and their disbursement must be acceptable from the perspectives of both developed and developing countries. Money is unlikely to flow unless there is a clear sense that these funds will be spent wisely.

There is unlikely to be a global agreement without a clear commitment on funding. This is why it is imperative that such commitment is made credible by taking action now. The Durban Platform has created a framework where substantial progress can be made. This could, coupled with technology creating and sharing, chart the way to equitable access to sustainable development. But both the finances and the investment will take time to emerge, thus we must start now, using the recovery from the economic crisis to lay the foundations for the generation of increased climate finance and enhanced low-carbon growth.

Appendix

Overview of assumptions based on AGF analysis (calculation based on a US$25/t carbon price)

International auctioning of emission allowances and auction of allowances in domestic emission trading schemes (AAU/ETS auctions)

- total market size approximated by forecast developed country emissions of 15 Gt CO_2e by 2020;

- assumption that 2–10 per cent of total market size would be auctioned and earmarked for international climate finance.

Carbon price in medium scenario of US$25/t equates to market size of US$375 billion, 2–10 per cent auctioning provides a total of US$8–38 billion in revenues.

Offset levies

- assumes levy of 2–10 per cent on offset market transactions;
- offset market size assumed at 1.5–2 Gt CO_2e in medium scenario, or US$37.5–50 billion at an estimated carbon price of US$25/t
- Total levy amounts to 2–10 per cent of US$37.5–50 billion or US$1–5 billion.

International transport

Maritime

- assumes 0.9–1 Gt CO_2e of emissions, priced at a US$25/t price of carbon (captured through auctions or levies) equivalent to US$22.5–25 billion;
- subtracting developing country incidence estimated at 30 per cent and estimating that of the remainder, 25–50 per cent could be used for international climate finance, leads to total estimate of US$4–9 billion.

Aviation

- assumes total passenger and freight emissions in 2020 of 800 Mt CO_2e of which 250 Mt CO_2e are in scope (excluding intra EU flights and developing country incidence);
- total revenue pool at carbon price of US$25/t on 250 Mt CO_2e equates to US$6 billion;
- assuming 25–50 per cent of these revenues can be earmarked for climate finance delivers estimate of US$2–3 billion.

Carbon-related revenues (other than AAU/ETS auctions)

Carbon tax

- calculates that US$1 of tax on 11–13 Gt CO_2e of energy related emissions translates roughly into US$10 billion of revenues; assumes 100 per cent used for international climate finance.

Wires charge

- calculates that power sector emissions priced at US$1/t tax on CO_2 on 4.7 Gt CO_2e of power generated emissions in OECD countries resulting in total of US$5 billion of revenues; assumes 100 per cent used for climate finance;

- equivalent to wires charge of US$0.0004/kWh on ~12,000 TWh of power generated in OECD countries in 2020.

Removal of fossil subsidies

- fossil fuel subsidies estimated at up to US$8 billion in Annex II countries within G20; assumes 100% used for climate finance.

Financial transaction tax

- assumes US$3000 billion of trading per day through the CLS times 255 trading days results in total trading volume of ~US$756 trillion;
- assumes tax rate of 0.001 to 0.01 per cent and reduction in volume of 3–6 per cent for 0.001 per cent tax, and 21–37 per cent for 0.01 per cent tax rate which translates into revenues of US$7–60 billion;
- assumes 8.5 per cent compensation for developing country incidence based on share of transactions and use of 25–50 per cent of total revenues for climate change which translates into US$2–27 billion.

Contributions from IFIs

- additional replenishment provided by developed countries only, no incidence in developing countries;
- for gross lending, leverage factor of US$3–4 per US$1 of paid in to capital/ replenishment based on existing capital structures

Carbon markets offsets

- assumes offset price of US$25/t on 1.5–2 Gt CO_2e of offset flows, which generates gross revenue of US$38–50 billion. This would require a high level of mitigation ambition in developed countries, with correspondingly tight caps.

Private finance

- generated with a leverage factor of 2–4 on public flows/carbon market offsets.

Notes

1 UNFCCC, 2009, para. 8.
2 UNFCCC, 2009, paras. 8 and 10.
3 AGF, 2010b.
4 AGF, 2010a, p. 4.
5 AGF, 2010a, p. 3.
6 See, for example, Houser and Selfe, 2011 and World Bank, 2011.

7 The eight work-stream papers are available at the same location as the final report (see AGF, 2010a).
8 Data mostly relate to 2009 and 2010.
9 World Bank (2011) estimates a revenue base of US$250 billion/year from carbon pricing, US$22 billion for taxation on international transport, and US$40–60 billion from the removal of fossil fuel subsidies.
10 Calculated from UNEP, 2012, Figure 3.
11 UNEP, 2012, p. 11.
12 See, inter alia, Chapter 4; Fankhauser, 2010; UNDP, 2008 and World Bank, 2010 for adaptation and Chapter 3 for mitigation.
13 Current total global emissions are nearing 50Gt CO_2 equivalent (CO_2e) per annum, with approximately 20Gt CO_2e in the rich world and the remaining 30 Gt CO_2e in the developing world. Taking into account the pledges in the Cancun agreement, total emissions would be in the 48–52Gt CO_2e range by 2020, with rich countries contributing 16–19Gt CO_2e and developing countries 32–33Gt CO_2e. If the rich countries accelerated their actions to reduce emissions they could potentially get to 10Gt CO_2e by 2030. If poor countries held tight to a modest increase in their per capita emissions, they might hold their total emissions to 40Gt CO_2e by 2030. This would mean global emissions of approximately 50Gt CO_2e by 2030. Scientists tell us that to have a medium chance of holding temperature below 2°C global emissions would need to be below 35Gt CO_2e by 2030.

References

Buchner, B., A. Falconer, M. Hervé-Mignucci, C. Trabacchi and M. Brinkman, 2011. *The Climate Finance Landscape*, Climate Policy Initiative, Venice.
Fankhauser, S., 2010. *The Costs of Adaptation*. Wiley Interdisciplinary Reviews: Climate Change, v.1.
High-level Advisory Group of the UN Secretary-General on Climate Change Financing, (AGF) 2010a. *Final Report*. Available at: http://www.un.org/wcm/webdav/site/climatechange/shared/Documents/AGF_reports/AGF%20Report.pdf
High-level Advisory Group of the UN Secretary-General on Climate Change Financing, (AGF) 2010b. *Terms of Reference*. Available at: http://www.un.org/wcm/content/site/climatechange/pages/financeadvisorygroup/tors
Houser, T. and J. Selfe, 2011. *Delivering on US Climate Finance Commitments*, Working Paper 11–19, Peterson Institute for International Economics, Washington, D.C. Available at: http://www.iie.com/publications/interstitial.cfm?ResearchID=1992
United Nations Development Programme (UNDP), 2008. *Human Development Report: Fighting Climate Change*. New York.
United Nations Environment Programme (UNEP), 2012. *Global Trends in Renewable Energy Investment 2012, Frankfurt School – UNEP Collaborating Centre for Climate Change & Sustainable Energy Finance*, Frankfurt. Available at: http://fs-unep-centre.org/sites/default/files/media/globaltrendsreport2012_3.pdf
United Nations Framework Convention on Climate Change (UNFCCC), 2009. *Copenhagen Accord*, FCCC/CP/2009/L.7, Bonn. Available at: http://unfccc.int/resource/docs/2009/cop15/eng/l07.pdf
World Bank, 2010. *EACC Synthesis Report.* Washington, D.C.
World Bank, 2011. *Mobilizing Climate Finance*. Washington, D.C. Available at: http://climatechange.worldbank.org/content/mobilizing-climate-finance

8 Mobilizing climate finance[1]

Milan Brahmbhatt and Andrew Steer

8.1 Introduction

While there is not yet an internationally agreed definition of climate finance, the term generally refers to financial resources that help catalyze climate adaptation and mitigation. Flows of climate finance from developed and developing countries are at the forefront of international climate discussions. The Copenhagen Accord set out a collective commitment by developed countries to provide new and additional resources for adaptation and mitigation activities in developing countries approaching US$30 billion for the period 2010–2012 (so-called Fast-Start Finance) and to mobilize US$100 billion per year by 2020 (from a wide variety of sources, public and private, bilateral and multilateral, including alternative sources).

The rationale for climate-finance flows from developed to developing countries is both economic and ethical. From a global efficiency perspective, climate stabilization requires mitigation in both developed and developing countries. The World Bank's *World Development Report 2010: Development and Climate Change* (World Bank, 2010a) estimates that the global least-cost mitigation pathway would require about 65 per cent of efforts to occur in developing countries by 2030 (compared to a 'Business-As-Usual' baseline). The bulk of climate damage and adaptation needs are also expected to occur in these countries. Developing countries are concerned that shouldering the cost of mitigation and adaptation will hinder rapid economic growth, particularly when they have historically contributed little to the current stock of greenhouse gases. By separating who finances climate action from where it occurs, flows of climate finance from developed to developing countries are a key way to reconcile economic efficiency with equity in dealing with the challenge of climate change and development.

The relative roles of private and public actors have been contentious in climate discussions. Both clearly have major roles to play. The private sector generally accounts for at least two-thirds of overall investment in developing countries, and it will be decisions made by such players – from the small-scale farmer to the largest multinational enterprise – that will decide whether the battle is won or lost. The public sector has a crucial dual role. The first is to establish the incentive needed to catalyze high levels of private investment in mitigation and adaptation.

By creating an appropriate price for carbon, fiscal instruments such as carbon taxes or tradable emission permits help ensure that producers' and consumers' decisions adequately reflect the externality associated with greenhouse gases (GHGs). The second is to invest in public goods needed to complement private investments, whether in the form of physical infrastructure, information and forecasting or R & D in new technologies.

Debate has centred on two questions. First, should private finance for mitigation and adaptation be counted towards the needs for overall climate finance? Some developing countries argue that all additional costs due to climate change should be financed by grants from developed countries and strongly oppose the idea that private and public funds are substitutes. This view has evolved since Copenhagen, partly in recognition that public funding will be much less than hoped, partly because "incremental cost" has proven a less useful practical concept than anticipated, and also because private financial markets have already demonstrated their ability to channel significant funds to climate smart investments (See Section 8.3).

Second, should public funds be channeled to support private investment? Some argue that in light of the modest amounts available, public funding should be reserved for priority public investments. Others argue that the careful injection of public funds into primarily private transactions through guarantees, loans, grants or equity can yield impressive leverage.

The remainder of this chapter discusses some prominent potential public sources of climate finance. Section 8.2 looks at three *carbon-linked* sources of finance: fiscal instruments to price carbon, such as a carbon tax; charges on international aviation and maritime fuel use; and reform of fossil-fuel subsidies in developed countries. Since climate finance need not come only from instruments related to carbon-pricing, this section also briefly discusses other sources of public financing. Section 8.3 – instruments that leverage private and multilateral flows – considers cases where innovative and well-designed policy reforms and public outlays can potentially leverage much larger flows of private or multilateral climate finance. This includes: options for buttressing carbon offset markets, an important vehicle for private cross-border climate finance flows to developing countries; options for developing other innovative instruments for leveraging private finance; and options for expanding flows of climate finance from multilateral development banks, using the range of leverage, risk mitigation and other tools available to these institutions. Section 8.4 concludes.

8.2 Sources of public finance

Climate finance does not necessarily require new financing instruments. It could rely on mobilizing traditional revenue sources, such as taxes on income or consumption. Some new *carbon-linked* sources of public revenue merit serious attention however. These are generally designed to correct for market failures by putting a price on greenhouse gas emissions. Such taxes or other instruments also raise revenues, although this aspect is distinct from their corrective role.

In principle the revenue from these new sources could flow into the national budget pool. The amounts allocated from the budget pool *to* climate finance could be based on factors distinct from the level of carbon-linked revenues. Indeed public finance economists generally do not recommend earmarking the proceeds of particular taxes for particular uses because of the risk of creating inflexible and inappropriate spending patterns. Nonetheless, directing some of the revenue from carbon-linked instruments to climate finance is an option with apparent political salience and appeal.

8.2.1 Carbon pricing policies

Policies to price the carbon content of fossil fuels are widely viewed as a highly promising option. They are more efficient at raising revenue than broader fiscal instruments because they correct for a huge and largely unaddressed market failure – excessive global emissions of greenhouse gases. As the carbon price is reflected in higher prices for fuels, electricity, and so on, consumers and producers have an incentive to exploit all possibilities for reducing energy-related CO_2 emissions across the economy. These opportunities include reducing electricity demand, promoting a shift to cleaner fuels for power generation, reducing demand for transportation fuels, and reducing use of fuels by households and industry. Regulatory measures (e.g. energy efficiency standards or minimum generation shares for renewable fuels) on their own are much less effective at exploiting all emission reduction opportunities: they are a more costly way to achieve any given emissions reduction, because they do not automatically equate the incremental cost of emissions reductions across different sources. Comprehensive carbon pricing also provides incentives across all sectors for the development of the new clean technologies ultimately needed for global climate stabilization. And, not least, by promoting international carbon markets, carbon pricing with appropriate crediting provisions can potentially leverage large private sources of climate finance for developing countries.

The choice between carbon taxes or cap-and-trade systems is less vital than getting right the design features of whichever instrument is chosen and using the revenues generated productively. Important design features include achieving comprehensive coverage of fossil-fuel emissions rather than pricing just one fuel, avoiding excessive tax exemptions, and, in the case of cap-and-trade, auctioning allowances to raise revenues and including provisions like allowance banking and borrowing to limit allowance price volatility. Productive uses of revenue include climate finance, cutting existing taxes that reduce incentives for work effort or capital accumulation, or – an urgent concern in many advanced economies – for fiscal consolidation. A failure to raise revenues or to use revenues productively substantially raises the overall cost of carbon pricing policies.

Roughly speaking, given the difficulties of making such long range projections, a carbon price of US$25 per ton – corresponding to the medium damage scenario studied in the UN Secretary General's High Level Panel on Climate Finance (AGF 2010) – if applied to all CO_2 emissions in developed economies might reduce their emissions on the order of 10 per cent compared to baseline emissions in 2020. The revenue raised at this price would be around US$250 billion in 2020. "Low" and "High" case scenarios with carbon prices of US$15 and 50 per ton are estimated to raise revenues of around US$155 billion and US$450 billion respectively.

Most of this revenue presumably would be retained for domestic purposes, for example to support fiscal consolidation or reduce other taxes. Nonetheless, allocating 10 per cent of US$250 billion for climate finance would meet one-quarter of the funding target of US$100 billion (from public and private sources combined) for 2020. This revenue would be raised with no direct burden on developing countries, while within the developed economies the tax burden (and revenues) would be lower for greener economies (i.e. those with lower emissions intensity).

The overall economic costs of a US$25 per ton carbon pricing policy in developed economies (such as the costs of switching to cleaner but more expensive fuels) are likely to be modest: around 0.03 per cent of GDP for the average developed economy (IMF, 2011). Higher energy prices caused by the pass through of carbon pricing can nonetheless have social and competitiveness effects – though they are relatively small when set against normal volatility in energy prices. Distributional concerns about the impact on low-income families can be addressed through broader fiscal adjustments, for example by expanding earned income tax credits, raising personal income tax thresholds or adjusting social contributions. For vulnerable industries, returning some revenues to these industries to help them adjust might be considered, although there is a risk that compensation will become permanent and come at a high economic cost. Another option is to mitigate competitiveness effects through border tax adjustments applied to the embodied carbon content of imports, though this can be difficult to measure, may run afoul of international trade obligations, can be costly to the country imposing them and yet may have only limited benefits for the competitiveness of energy-intensive industries. A more promising option for dealing with concerns about equity and competitiveness is to offset burdens from carbon pricing by scaling back pre-existing energy taxes that raise prices to consumers but have little effect on emissions, for example excise taxes on electricity or taxes on vehicle ownership.

8.2.2   *Market-based instruments for fuels used in international aviation and shipping*

International aviation and maritime transport are currently taxed relatively lightly from an environmental perspective: unlike domestic transportation fuels, they are not subject to any excise tax that can reflect environmental damages in fuel prices. These sectors also receive favourable treatment from the broader fiscal system. For these reasons market-based instruments (MBIs) for international aviation and maritime fuels – either emissions (fuel) charges or emissions trading schemes – are likely a more cost-effective way to raise finance for climate or other purposes than are broader fiscal instruments: increasing from zero a tax on an activity that causes environmental damage is likely to be a more efficient way to raise revenue than would be increasing a tax (on labour income, for instance) that already causes significant distortion.

A globally implemented carbon charge of US$25 per ton of CO_2 on fuel could raise around US$12 billion from international aviation and around US$25 billion from international maritime transport annually in 2020 while reducing CO_2 emissions from each industry by perhaps 5 per cent, mainly by reducing fuel demand. The burden imposed by a US$25 per ton carbon pricing policy for these sectors is likely to be small, raising average air ticket prices by around 2 to 4 per cent and the price of most seaborne imports by around 0.2 to 0.3 per cent. Nevertheless, compensating developing countries for any economic harm they might suffer from such charges – ensuring that they bear 'no net incidence' – is widely recognized as critical to their acceptability. Such compensation seems unlikely to require more than 40 per cent of global revenues. This would leave about US$22 billion or more for climate finance or other uses (IMF and World Bank, 2011).

Extensive cooperation would be needed to design and implement international transportation fuel charges – especially for maritime transport – to avoid revenue erosion and competitive distortions. If governments set taxes unilaterally, they would be under pressure to set lower rates than in other countries to protect their domestic industries and carriers. Thus, some degree of international coordination is needed. Both the International Civil Aviation Organization (ICAO) and the International Maritime Organization (IMO) are committed to principles of uniform treatment for carriers and nations. A globally applied charge would be consistent with this and could be reconciled with the UNFCCC principle of common but differentiated responsibilities and respective capabilities by a system of clearly identified compensatory transfers to developing countries, which likely would evolve over time as economic circumstances change. More generally, combining a global charge with targeted compensation provides an effective and feasible way to pursue efficiency and equity objectives.

Ensuring 'no net incidence' for developing countries requires careful consideration of the 'real' incidence of these charges. Who it is that ultimately suffers a loss of real income can be quite different from who bears legal responsibility for the payment of the charge. In these sectors the two groups may well reside in different countries. It is the real incidence that matters for potential compensation and this is sensitive to views on demand and supply responses. It will also vary across countries according to their share of trade by sea and air, the importance of tourism, and so on.

The introduction of such charges has been opposed by some counties highly dependent on tourist arrivals by air, and by countries dependent on bulky exports. It will be necessary to demonstrate that compensation measures can be made to work in practice as well as in theory. The design challenge could be relatively modest for aviation, where fully rebating aviation fuel charges for developing countries would be an important start. Indeed most developing countries are likely to be made better off by such an international regime, even without considering the climate finance received. This is because much of the incidence of charges paid on jet fuel disbursed in developing countries (especially tourist destinations) would be borne by passengers from wealthier countries. While this proposal needs further study (for example, to find a way to deal with hubs), it appears to be a reasonably practicable approach.

In contrast, rebating charges on maritime fuel taken up in developing countries is less likely to adequately compensate most developing countries. Unlike airlines, shipping companies cannot be expected to normally tank up when they reach their destination. Some countries – hub ports like Singapore – dispense a disproportionately large amount of maritime fuel relative to their imports, while the converse applies in importing countries that supply little or no bunker fuel, including landlocked countries. Revenues from charges on international maritime fuels could instead be passed to or retained in developing countries in proportions that reflect their share in global trade. While relatively straightforward to administer, further analysis is needed to validate whether this approach would provide adequate compensation, for example for countries that import goods with relatively low value per ton. Much detailed work remains to be done to design compensation schemes, but practicable approaches can surely be found.

Implementing globally coordinated charges on international aviation and maritime fuels would also raise significant governance issues. New frameworks would be needed to determine how and when charges (or emissions levels) are set and changed, to provide appropriate verification of tax paid or permits held, to govern the use of funds raised and to monitor and implement any compensation arrangements. Policies might be administered internationally, nationally with international coordination, or in some combination of the two – with the appropriate institutions for monitoring and verification depending on the approach taken. Thorough consideration of the legal challenges arising in the aviation sector is also needed, given the fact that current fuel tax exemptions are built into multilateral agreements within the ICAO framework and bilateral air service agreements which operate on a basis of reciprocity (ICAO, 2000). Overall, however, while implementation and governance need further study, it is clear that feasible operational proposals for pricing international aviation and maritime emissions can be developed.

8.2.3 Fossil-fuel subsidy reform

Many developed and developing countries have policies that explicitly or implicitly subsidize the production or consumption of fossil fuels. Many of these mechanisms effectively subsidize CO_2 emissions. Reform of these policies would reduce greenhouse gas emissions, improve economic efficiency and free up scarce public resources that could be directed to climate finance and to other public priorities.

A recent OECD inventory of mechanisms that support fossil-fuel production or consumption in 24 OECD countries estimates that the value of such supports in Annex II countries amounted to US$40–60 billion per year in 2005–2010 (OECD, 2011). In 2010 a little over half was estimated to be for petroleum with a little under a quarter each for coal and natural gas. About two-thirds of the total in 2010 was estimated to be for consumer support, with a little over 20 percent being producer support and just over 10 per cent general services support.[2]

Several caveats are in order. Systems for fossil-fuel support in developed coun-tries are extraordinarily complex, using diverse instruments. Over 250 individual producer or consumer support mechanisms are identified in the inventory. Not all of these are inefficient or wasteful and governments may wish to maintain some. Moreover, given interactions among support mechanisms and the potential effect on fossil fuel demand of removing support, the exact revenues from removing supports might be lower than the total of the individual measures. Most of the support mechanisms are tax expenditures, which are measured with reference to a benchmark tax treatment that is generally specific to a given country, so the estimates are not comparable across countries.

Noting these caveats, if for illustration reforms are assumed to redirect 10 to 20 per cent of the current estimated support of US$40–60 billion in Annex II coun-tries to public climate finance, that would yield about US$4–12 billion per year.

Experience shows that subsidy reforms are often difficult, given political sensi-tivity to the distributional consequences and concerns about affected industries and workers. A number of developed and developing countries have made progress in reforming fossil fuel subsidies in recent years. Governments need to consider the distributional implications of reform and the need for well targeted "safety-net" programs to protect the poor and vulnerable in addition to transparency about the expected impacts and incidence of the reform. Countries such as Indonesia and Iran have managed to implement significant reductions in subsidies without economic or social disruption through special schemes, mainly cash transfers, to offset the burden on the poor. Governments may also consider assistance for affected firms, for example to restructure operations, exit the industry or adopt alternative tech-nologies, as well as initiatives for worker retraining or relocation. In general, it is important that assistance for economic restructuring or industry adjustment in response to subsidy reform be well-targeted, transparent and time-bound.

Efforts to use major international meetings to make progress on fossil fuel subsidies have largely failed. The Rio+ 20 Declaration in June 2012 gave only weak support in principle. But in the same month the G20 meeting in Los Cabos, Mexico provided a modest indication that the tide may be turning by reaffirming the group's commitment to phase out inefficient fossil fuel subsidies while providing targeted support for the poorest, with Finance Ministers required to report back on progress made and to explore options for a peer review process.

8.3 Policies and instruments to leverage private and multilateral flows

This section begins by looking at some of the critical barriers that hamper private investment in climate mitigation and, to a lesser extent, climate adaptation before looking at approaches to address such barriers.

The absence of policy to internalize the global climate externality is one of the most important factors depressing private returns on climate-friendly investment: in the absence of a robust carbon pricing regime, firms and consumers suffer little of the damage caused by their carbon emissions and, conversely, are able to internalize few of the potential social gains from mitigating emissions. Policy distortions such as fossil fuel subsidies aggravate the problem by rewarding investment in high emission activities. Private returns are also affected by the public good externality associated with knowledge, which hampers private investment in climate-related innovation and – more relevant for most developing countries – in the adaptation to local conditions and transfer of existing climate technologies. Risk perceptions for climate-related investments are often high because of uncertainties about future global and domestic climate policy frameworks, technological uncertainties, uncertainties about future climate outcomes, and project risks.

And even where risk-adjusted private returns are high – for example in many energy efficiency projects – investment is restrained by lack of awareness and information, agency problems and status quo bias. Information failures and other problems affecting financial markets can contribute to lack of access to finance (especially for the long term), excessive volatility, contagion, sudden stops in capital flows, mispricing of risks and incomplete availability of commercial insurance and other risk management instruments. Finally, both risk-adjusted returns and access to finance will be greatly influenced by the broader factors that affect all private investment, such as the domestic investment climate, institutional capacity and the enabling policy environment.

8.3.1 Carbon markets

The Kyoto Protocol offers industrialized countries three ways to meet mitigation commitments. They can take domestic actions to reduce emissions. They can trade emission allowances with other industrialized country signatories. Or they can purchase emission reductions ("carbon offsets") generated by low-emission projects in developing countries (the Clean Development Mechanism, CDM) or in industrialized countries (Joint Implementation, JI). Such projects must be certified as generating emission reductions that are "additional", which would not have occurred without the incentive provided by the offset market. In principle carbon offset revenues provide an additional revenue stream that enhances the overall financial viability of low-emission projects in developing countries, as illustrated in Figure 8.1.

Over 4,800 CDM projects, involving a total investment of between US$90 and 175 billion, have been registered.[3] Revenue from the sale of carbon offset credits generated by these projects amounted to at least US$9.5 billion through 2011. The value of transactions in the primary CDM market – the largest offset market by far – totaled around US$27 billion during 2002–2011. But carbon offset markets – and carbon markets generally – now face major challenges due to uncertainties about future mitigation targets and the role of market mechanisms after 2012. A number of other factors are further constraining the potential of carbon finance, including market fragmentation in the absence of a global agreement, transaction costs associated with complex mechanisms, low capacity in many countries, lack of upfront finance, weaknesses in the current "project by project"

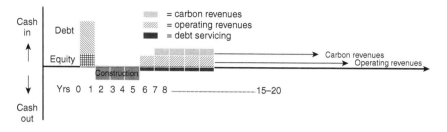

Figure 8.1 Impact of carbon payments on mitigation project finance

approach and non-inclusion of some sectors with significant abatement potential (e.g. agriculture).

Despite the slowdown in market activity, a number of recent developments show continued interest in advancing carbon market solutions. The 2010 United Nations Climate Change Conference in Cancun adopted reforms to enhance the efficiency of the CDM. The Conference recognized developing countries' Nationally Appropriate Mitigation Actions (NAMAs), some of which plan the use of market mechanisms. It also recognized the contribution of forest-related activities in efforts to tackle climate change, making not only projects but also developing countries and sub-national regions within them eligible for incentives.[4] New market initiatives are also underway in both developed and developing countries despite the uncertainties about the international regulatory environment, including in Brazil, China, Chile, Colombia, Costa Rica, Indonesia, Korea, Mexico, Turkey, and Ukraine.

What will it take to scale up carbon market flows to developing countries? The most important determinant of such flows is clearly the level of international mitigation targets: the more ambitious the targets the greater the scope for such flows. Ambrosi *et al.* (2011) develop several scenarios that illustrate this point. In a scenario where mitigation initiatives in the developed world are essentially limited only to the EU, carbon offset flows are estimated to reach only US$1 to 2 billion per year in 2020, the same as in 2009 and 2010. At the other extreme, with strong mitigation initiatives designed to limit global warming to 2°C offset flows could surpass US$100 billion per year.

Flows of this scale could play a major role in driving down the cost of mitigation, in addition to bringing financial resources and technology to developing countries. Such scale would require a shift towards new programmatic approaches, which would help overcome the high costs and lengthy procedures of current project-by-project approaches. It could also be facilitated by an increase in supplementarity limits, the proportion of mitigation targets that can be met by purchases from developing countries. Innovative steps to broaden the scope, scale, and reach of carbon markets should also be considered. Potential new sectors include REDD+ activities and agricultural soil carbon. The sequestration of carbon in soils is currently a neglected part of the climate solution, yet the carbon market could provide incentives for sustainable land management programs that deliver a triple win: improved yields, enhanced resilience to climate change, and global mitigation. Measurement and verification issues are a challenge, but are by no means insurmountable.

Difficulties in securing sufficient up-front long-term financing have proven a constraint in advancing carbon finance projects. Several institutions including multilateral development banks (MDBs) are now developing a range of solutions, such as frontloading mechanisms that turn anticipated carbon revenues into upfront finance, risk mitigation tools that enhance the confidence of financiers in the value and predictability of future carbon credits, revolving funds where accruing revenues can support a next tranche of investments, and structured finance with innovative use and combination of instruments, each addressing specific barriers and needs.[5] Finally, given the possibility that the carbon market will develop in a fragmented way, through numerous regional and national initiatives, there would be a significant payoff from greater harmonization of rules across regimes to ensure minimum fungibility of carbon assets.

8.3.2 *Other instruments to engage private finance*

Total investment in low carbon energy, low carbon transport and energy efficiency (public and private, foreign and domestic) in developing countries is estimated at around US$200 billion in 2010 with about 60 per cent of that occurring in just the top five countries – China, Brazil, India, Mexico, and Turkey. Investment in renewable energy in developing countries experienced a dramatic nineteenfold increase in just six years from 2004 to 2010. Growth slowed in 2009 with the global financial crisis but rebounded in 2010 with a strong 29 per cent increase, led by sharply higher renewable investment in China (Patel, 2011). Information on the private versus public share or the foreign versus domestic shares of such investments is very sketchy. Improving the quality of information to measure, report and verify (MRV) flows of climate finance is an important priority.[6]

Public finance and policies can leverage private resources at different levels. At the *retail* level leverage refers to the ability of a public financial commitment to mobilize some larger multiple of private capital for investment in a specific project or undertaking. Broadly speaking, experience from the lending portfolio of the MDBs suggests that leverage factors are in the range of 3 to 6 for non-concessional lending, although they can be significantly higher in projects for power sector energy efficiency with well-established private players and relatively few technological surprises. Leverage ratios can be higher where the public finance component is in the form of concessional lending, grants or equity, running at 8 to 10 or even higher.

At a broader *wholesale* level leverage refers to the potential for public investments or policy initiatives to encourage more widespread climate-friendly changes in behavior by private firms across the whole economy – rather than only those involved in specific climate-related projects – typically by addressing economy-wide market failures or barriers to investment.

Leveraging private resources in either the wholesale or retail sense is best accomplished through some combination of policy reforms that change incentives for private investment and address key market failures combined with public financial interventions or investments. Such public resources can come from multilateral development banks (MDBs), bilateral or domestic public sources or pooled financing arrangements. Pooled financing is a relatively new class of structured vehicle that mobilizes concessional resources from a variety of public and private sources. Examples include the Global Environment Facility and the two Climate Investment Funds (CIFs). Resources from these pooled sources can leverage private investment through a range of instruments, for example grants, concessional and/or non-concessional lending and equity investments, often through MDB private sector windows, technical assistance and a range of loan guarantee and other risk mitigation instruments.

The discussion of policies and instruments to leverage private finance can be usefully organized according to the key barriers to climate investment they help address, although there is no one-to-one mapping between instruments and barriers as some instruments can be useful in addressing more than one type of problem.

Leveraging private finance by tackling the global climate externality: Interventions to address the climate externality and improve returns on climate friendly investment through some form of carbon pricing are likely to be among those actions with the highest leverage at the wholesale or economy-wide level. Robust carbon pricing in developed countries provides incentives for significant private flows to developing countries through carbon offset markets. But there is also considerable scope for stronger carbon pricing in developing countries. The most obvious opportunity relates to 'no-regret' reforms to reduce or eliminate fossil-fuel subsidies. More broadly, some 22 developing economies have now set economy-wide mitigation targets according to information provided under the Copenhagen Accord. Advance market commitments such as feed-in tariffs to subsidize renewable energy sources are also being considered in some economies, although they are less efficient than carbon pricing and can have significant fiscal implications. Interest is also increasing in regulation to improve energy efficiency, for example through economy-wide efficiency standards and codes or power sector reforms.

Addressing knowledge externalities: Carefully designed public investments in demonstration projects to pilot and debug new technologies and institutions can have a major impact in promoting learning and the diffusion of new ideas. Such investments also generate valuable new project and sector information and reduce policy risks by establishing safeguards and other standards. Monitoring and evaluation of lessons from learning investments are low-cost public goods that can accelerate the flow of private finance and new technologies. Experience with such projects shows that a blend of grant, concessional, non-concessional and carbon-offset financing can be used to provide an effective mixture of financial incentives and technical assistance that encourages firms to invest in new clean energy technologies, stimulating learning-by-doing and knowledge diffusion for the economy at large. Examples include the *China Renewable Energy Development*

Project (supported by an IBRD loan and a Global Environment Facility grant) to encourage manufacturing of small scale solar home systems, and the EBRD's *Sustainable Energy Initiative*, which supports both energy efficiency and renewable energy projects with a strong emphasis on transfer of skills and learning.

Access to finance and risk mitigation: Development lenders are also gaining experience in how to address lack of access and missing insurance markets in climate finance. Public lenders provide an element of stability through their ability to undertake large-scale, long-duration, non-concessional lending for climate action, especially during periods of high volatility in global capital markets, such as the recent financial crisis. They are able to provide core or anchor financing that, creatively blended with concessional finance, grants, risk mitigation and learning, can leverage increased climate lending by domestic commercial banks and other private lenders. An example might be the *India Solar Power Guarantee Facility* (US$150 million) by the ADB, which aims to reduce the overall cost of financing and lengthen loan tenors for solar projects.

Subordinated or mezzanine debt – financing with a lower payment priority than senior loans – can also be a useful way for the public lender to take on more risk, strengthen a project's equity profile and encourage additional commercial lenders to provide senior debt financing. A variety of other risk sharing instruments can further help address the risk-return tradeoff, including tools such as policy and loan guarantees, insurance products and hedging instruments. Increasing access to risk-sharing instruments is an important strand of comprehensive adaptation strategies, given the likelihood of more frequent extreme events as a result of climate change. There have already been some promising applications of innovative mechanisms such as index-linked insurance and weather derivatives – for example, the Caribbean Catastrophe Risk Insurance Facility, which combines index insurance with risk pooling.

All told, both AGF (2010) and World Bank and others (2011) develop scenarios suggesting that a package of public sources, MDB flows and carbon offset flows could be used to leverage around US$100 to 200 billion in additional international private climate finance flows to developing countries together with an equivalent amount of domestic private resources.

8.3.3 *Multilateral development bank leverage*

It is helpful to recognize that multilateral development banks (MDBs) are, among other things, an institutional device to mobilize private savings for development purposes, leveraging investments several times the size of their share capital by their ability to borrow in private capital markets.

Like all banks, MDBs provide economic services such as risk sharing and asset transformation which allow them to serve as financial intermediaries. But MDBs also have specific features which allow them to address problems that otherwise hinder private capital flows to developing countries. In particular, the multilateral shareholding structure and preferred creditor status of MDBs serves as a commitment device to better deal with the problem of a lack of institutions to enforce contracts in cross-border lending to sovereign governments. These features also give MDBs a comparative advantage in collection and dissemination of information about the investment environment in developing countries, something that the private sector may under-provide because of the public good nature of such knowledge. Finally, MDBs also serve as mechanisms for reallocating subsidies – that is, resources that they derive from their preferred creditor status and access to a subsidized shareholder capital base, which they are able to use for development objectives, for example through concessional lending.[7]

These features enable MDBs to address some of the problems that inhibit private investment in low carbon and climate resilient development. Annual MDB investment in mitigation activities in developing countries was about US$19 billion in 2010 (Basu *et al.*, 2011). Consider first the ability of MDBs to provide additional climate finance by leveraging their existing share capital or, in the longer term, through additional climate-related capital increases. A useful rule of thumb for the current mix of non-concessional loans on MDB balance sheets is that every US$ 1 billion of paid in capital leverages US$3 to 4 billion of lending. World Bank and others (2011) conclude however that, on the whole, MDBs have little head room for significant additional climate finance with their existing capital. The capital replenishments accorded to MDBs in the wake of the global financial crisis were calibrated, in most cases, to the relatively modest aim of meeting existing post-crisis lending needs rather than creating room for newly identified needs such as climate finance. Developing countries are also concerned that efforts to expand MDB climate finance under existing headroom will crowd out more traditional lending, such as for infrastructure, health care and education.

In principle, future MDB capital increases could be more readily directed to expanding lending for climate finance, although this could lead to an increase in the relative voting power of developed countries, a change contrary to the spirit of recent 'Voice and Representation' reforms. World Bank and others (2011) discuss several options for addressing this problem.

A somewhat different concern is that a climate finance focused capital increase would tend to increase the lending capacity of the non-concessional arms of MDBs, the bulk of whose operations are directed to creditworthy middle income countries, while shareholders may want to focus more on concessional financing for low income countries. Other solutions may be more appropriate to fund climate finance in low income countries, for example so-called "pooled" financing arrangements which allow MDBs to mobilize and channel concessional flows through structured vehicles for climate finance.

These vehicles allow MDBs to mobilize off-balance- sheet resources from multiple sources, including traditional sovereign donors as well as non-traditional sources such as private foundations and emerging sovereigns. They allow new ways for donors to contribute (beyond traditional grants), for example through long-term concessional loans. Pooled arrangements can be structured in ways that accommodate the different risk-return appetites of donors, while also allowing great flexibility in providing instruments tailored to the needs of a wide variety of recipients.

A number of types of pooled financing arrangements have evolved in recent years, for example climate-specific financial intermediary funds, of which there are now six, with the World Bank acting as trustee, and with more than US$10 billion in cumulative pledges and contributions and approved outlays for projects of US$6.7 billion. Targeted investment vehicles provide another option, enabling donors and investors to focus resources on specific sectors often by providing complementary tranches that each have different risk and return profiles. An example of this approach is the *Global Climate Partnership Fund (GCPF)* developed by the IFC as a debt investment vehicle (proposed for up to US$500 million) that will provide financing mainly for on-lending through financial institutions for renewable energy and energy efficiency projects by small- and medium-sized enterprises and households in developing countries.

8.4 Concluding comments

It is important to determine which options for increased climate financing are most promising for prioritization in the near term and which for development over the medium term. This chapter provides an overview of the range of options available to countries, the selection and combination of which they will need to consider in the light of their national circumstances. The task is made more challenging by the present difficult economic conditions in the developed world – the most severe in over 70 years – and by growing fiscal pressures in many developed countries.

In this environment reform of fossil fuel subsidies in developed countries is an important short-term option because of its potential to improve economic efficiency and raise revenue in addition to environmental benefits. Carbon pricing shares these advantages by placing a price on a negative externality and improving efficiency while also generating substantial domestic revenues for fiscal consolidation, reduction in less efficient taxes and other desirable policy objectives. Efforts to lay the technical foundation for implementation of market based instruments for fuels used in international aviation and shipping would complement these policies.

Two important principles have emerged in the recent debate over climate finance, and are central to this paper. First, the ability to raise adequate funds for mitigation and adaptation investment in developing countries will depend crucially on the level of ambition and credibility of mitigation plans, especially in developed countries. Only a strong commitment to reduce emissions will drive a meaningful carbon price, in turn enabling higher carbon-linked revenues and larger scale carbon markets. Negotiations over mitigation and finance are thus intrinsically linked. Second, how climate funds are spent will influence the total funds available. Specifically, allocating funds carefully to help de-risk private investment decisions, and in the right kinds of public goods, can have a powerful catalytic effect on total climate investments. These issues must lie at the heart of the detailed design of the Green Climate Fund. Finally all of these initiatives will benefit from improved monitoring and tracking of flows given the relatively limited data currently available on adaptation and private flows. Building the political consensus for implementation of these and other major policy options discussed in the chapter will be critical.

Notes

1 This chapter draws on the findings of the November 2011 report "Mobilizing Climate Finance: A paper prepared at the request of the G-20 Finance Ministers" (World Bank and others, 2011).Work on the paper was coordinated by the World Bank Group, in close partnership with the IMF, the OECD and the Regional Development Banks (RDBs, which include the African Development Bank, the Asian Development Bank, the European Bank for Reconstruction and Development, the European Investment Bank and the Inter-American Development Bank) with comments and information supplied by the International Civil Aviation Organization (ICAO) and the International Maritime Organization (IMO). The report drew on and aimed to update and extend the work carried out by UN Secretary General's High Level Advisory Group on Climate Change Financing (AGF 2010) in conformity with the mandate received.
2 There is also considerable scope for such reforms in developing and emerging economies. The benefits of such reforms would include improvements in economic efficiency, real income gains, reduced greenhouse gas emissions and increased government revenues available for development purposes. From the perspective of climate finance, they would also improve the overall policy environment and incentive structure for encouraging private climate finance flows from developed to developing countries.
3 Over US$90 billion has been invested in registered projects that are known to be operational (have submitted a monitoring report) while the investment for registered projects whose operational status is unknown is estimated at over US$80 billion. Some projects in the latter category may not be implemented.
4 REDD+ refers to all activities that reduce emissions from deforestation and forest degradation, contribute to conservation and sustainable management of forests, and enhance of forest carbon stocks.
5 MDBs are supporting the development of the carbon market, including through 21 carbon funds and facilities with US$4.2 billion in capital, some of which are targeting segments not yet tapped by carbon finance, bringing continuity by purchasing credits beyond 2012, and providing upfront financing and risk-management products.
6 There is currently no formal definition of private climate finance, nor are there dedicated systems to track such flows. The Cancun Agreements under the UNFCCC call for significant improvements on the MRV of climate finance including the frequency and coverage of reporting. In support of collective action to develop a comprehensive system to MRV climate finance the World Bank is introducing a system that will measure the share of investments that provide adaptation and mitigation co-benefits in each new project in its portfolio down to the project sub-component level. This is considered a promising start and a step towards building on the "Rio markers" currently in use by OECD DAC countries. The World Bank is cooperating closely with other multilateral development banks and the OECD DAC secretariat with a view to harmonizing the methodologies across these systems so that climate finance data will be comparable across the multilateral banks and bilateral donors.
7 For further discussion of these points see for example Buiter and Fries (2002), Hagen (2009) and Rodrik (1995).

References

Advisory Group on Climate Change Financing (AGF), 2010. *Report of the Secretary-General's High-level Advisory Group on Climate Change Financing,* United Nations, New York.

Ambrosi, Philippe, Klaus Opperman, Philippe Benoit, Chandra Shekhar Sinha, Lasse Ringius, Maria Netto, Lu Xuedu and OECD Secretariat, 2011. *How to Keep Up Momentum in Carbon Markets?* World Bank. OECD Secretariat staff providing inputs to this background paper include Jan Corfee-Morlot, Robertus Dellink and Andrew Prag. Background paper for World Bank and others, 2011.

Basu, Priya, Lisa Finneran, Veronique Bishop and Trichur Sundararaman, 2011. *The Scope for MDB Leverage and Innovation in Climate Finance*, World Bank. Background paper for World Bank and others, 2011.

Buiter, Willem and Stephen Fries, 2002. *What should the multilateral development banks do?* EBRD Working Paper No. 47.

Hagen, Rune Jansen, 2009. "Basic Analytics of Multilateral Lending and Surveillance," *Journal of International Economics*, 79(1), pp 126–136.

International Civil Aviation Organization (ICAO), 2000. *ICAO's Policies on Taxation in the Field of International Air Transport; Third Edition-2000*, International Civil Aviation Organization, Montreal.

International Monetary Fund (IMF), 2011. *Promising Domestic Fiscal Instruments for Climate Finance, International Monetary Fund*. Background paper for World Bank and others, 2011.

International Monetary Fund and World Bank, 2011. *Market-based Instruments for International Aviation and Shipping as a Source of Climate Finance*, International Monetary Fund/World Bank. Background paper for World Bank and others, 2011.

OECD, 2011. *Fossil-fuel Support*, OECD, Paris.

Patel, Shilpa, 2011. *Climate Finance: Engaging the Private Sector*, International Finance Corporation. With inputs by Josue Tanaka, EBRD. Background paper for World Bank and others, 2011.

Rodrik, Dani, 1995. *Why is there Multilateral Lending?* NBER Working Paper No. 5160, Washington, D.C.

World Bank, 2010a. *World Development Report 2010: Development and Climate Change*. World Bank, Washington D.C.

World Bank, 2010b. *10 Years of Experience in Carbon Finance: Insights from Working with the Kyoto Mechanisms*. World Bank, Washington, D.C.

World Bank, International Monetary Fund, Organization for Economic Cooperation and Development, African Development Bank, Asian Development Bank, European Bank for Reconstruction and Development, European Investment Bank, and Inter-American Development Bank, 2011. *Mobilizing Climate Finance*, Paper prepared at the request of G-20 Finance Ministers. Available (together with background papers) at http:// climatechange.worldbank.org/content/mobilizing-climate-finance

9 International climate finance from border carbon cost levelling

Michael Grubb

9.1 Introduction

The Copenhagen deal on finance – including its objective to reach US$100 billion per year of international finance by 2020 – was hailed as the key breakthrough of the Copenhagen Accord, codified at Cancun. It could also prove to be the Achilles' heel of these agreements, and of prospects for a more substantive international action. The massive debt accumulated by most OECD (Organisation for Economic Co-operation and Development) countries over the past decade, greatly amplified by expenditures under the 'stimulus packages' designed to prevent collapse of the international financial system, means that the OECD faces a decade of budget cuts and belt-tightening. Securing US$100 billion per year through normal public sector channels looks, to say the least, problematic.

Recognizing the difficulties, the UN Secretary General's High-Level Advisory Group on Climate Change Financing (AGF) considered a range of sources, including unconventional sources, of international finance. It had a tough time. It seems increasingly implausible that OECD governments will make meaningful, individually binding long-term commitments on the scale required, from their domestic budgets alone. The USA states that it is constitutionally impossible to make such commitment. Indeed, most national treasuries are already struggling to cut expenditure. There is no strong domestic political mandate in OECD countries to provide public funds for climate change actions in developing countries, especially in China and India. There are a limited number of potential 'new' financing sources, and each faces opposition from those who would pay, legal and/or jurisdictional complications, and/or competition from treasuries who might seek to secure the funds for domestic public expenditures.

Ideally, new options for international finance would have the following characteristics:

- they would be outside the scope of existing sources of national finance, and preferably would not fall naturally under any specific national jurisdiction, thereby weakening the potential claim of national Treasuries to have unique control over the revenue;
- they would be visibly connected with climate change, and would preferably contribute directly to the mitigation of climate change;

- they would carry mutual incentives that could facilitate all sides agreeing to use it as a funding source.

This chapter discusses an option that could meet all these criteria, but which has received little attention from the AGF: extending carbon-pricing systems to include a measure of carbon embodied in carbon-intensive imports, and returning the revenue raised at the border to support low-carbon development and/or adaptation in developing countries. The specific proposal considered here is for World Trade Organization (WTO)-compatible 'border carbon cost levelling' in regions that adopt cap-and-trade or equivalent carbon pricing. This would require key carbon-intensive commodities, such as steel and cement, to pay for emissions, whether they are produced domestically or imported. The prime aim is to prevent carbon-intensive producers moving abroad to avoid carbon costs – 'carbon leakage' – by ensuring that consumers in the EU Emissions Trading System (EU ETS) regions pay for the carbon, regardless of where the commodities are produced. WTO compatibility is most easily assured by auctioning allowances domestically and setting a fixed requirement for importers to purchase allowances equivalent to the best available technology (BAT), to ensure that the measure does not preferentially treat domestic producers. This inevitably raises revenue from importers (as well as domestic producers), and the key proposition is that these revenues should be returned to international funds or to the country of production.

9.2 Rationales

The underlying proposal is located at the interface of two existing policy debates – the divergence between production and consumption views of accountability for climate change, and the competitiveness and leakage impacts of developed-country mitigation policies.

Many developing-country analysts and politicians have stressed that greenhouse gas (GHG) emissions are driven ultimately by consumption – most notably, affluent Western consumption (e.g. Sunwal, 2009). The shift in production patterns over the past two decades and the associated rapid growth of international trade has increased the gap between the emissions associated with consumption in OECD countries and the actual emissions in those countries. The 'carbon footprint' of OECD countries' consumption in aggregate exceeds their domestic production emissions by about 20 per cent. This is matched by a corresponding debit from developing-country emissions. Much of the analysis has concentrated on China, where, for example, Wang and Watson (2008), in common with some other sources they cite, estimate that almost one-quarter of Chinese emissions arise from the production of goods for export.

These authors note that attribution is in fact complex:

> This has led to calls for consumption-based national emission accounts instead of (or alongside) the production-based accounts ... this is believed to have several advantages ... on the other hand, it may not be entirely fair for

countries that produce goods for export – and enjoy the gains from this economic activity – to take no responsibility for the associated emissions.

In other words, responsibility between producer and consumer is ambiguous – and a reasonable topic of negotiation.

The other debate concerns the impacts on competitiveness of unilateral carbon policies, such as the EU ETS, in particular the risk of carbon leakage, if industrial production migrates to escape the carbon policies, with products being imported instead. The idea that industrialized countries should 'protect their industries' through generalized border protection is anathema, but there are two underlying issues that do deserve attention.

First, industrialized countries are taking action to avoid carbon leakage: it is politically impossible for governments to inflict significant economic loss with no environmental gain (or, even, a worsened environmental impact), which is what carbon leakage implies. The main action they have taken is to largely exempt major industries from carbon pricing, mostly by giving them emission allowances for free. This is a common feature of all emission trading schemes to date, and the EU now has an extensive list of sectors receiving free allowances for precisely this reason. The sectors so treated globally account for most manufacturing emissions. To start the journey towards deep emission reductions by exempting sectors that account for about one-third of global emissions is not a very promising way to solve the climate problem.

The second issue is moral: there is no ethical or reasonable basis on which to expect governments trying to charge for carbon emissions, or their consumers, to actively discriminate against their own producers by paying for carbon on domestically produced goods while giving an exemption to imports.

Note that this is a very different perspective from the general argument about 'border adjustments' vis-à-vis other countries, as has been suggested by some European political leaders and, more prominently, in early versions of proposed US legislation. These proposals put the emphasis on assessing 'adequate' action by other countries. The proposition here is entirely non-discriminatory and more modest: policies that seek, as far as practicable, to equalize the price of carbon paid on a product consumed within a region, whether it is produced at home or abroad.

9.3 Specific proposition

Climate policy can only realistically move forward if both of the above concerns – the role of consumption and the need to facilitate a level playing field in a world of unequal carbon pricing – are acknowledged and considered. Moreover, although consumption is seen to be a 'southern' preoccupation, and carbon leakage a 'northern' concern, they are two sides of the same coin; a consumption-based perspective implies that consumers should pay for the full carbon consequences of their consumption, wherever goods are produced. In short, to move forward on climate policy, we will need to find some middle ground between the production and consumption views of the world. This implies that internationally traded goods should pay a charge to reflect the carbon emitted in making them, if they are consumed in regions implementing a carbon price. Key questions relate to how this could be done and what might happen to the revenues.

The question of 'how it could be done' is considered by various analyses. One relatively early proposition (Mueller and Sharma, 2005) was that developing countries should levy carbon charges on their exports of carbon-intensive goods. This indeed could be desirable, but it comes with the difficulty that the exporters themselves face a problem of 'carbon leakage': unless the charge is applied in a fully multilateral way, with all producers participating, production would tend to shift to those countries not levying such export charges. It is potentially a goal, but not a starting point, of the probable evolution of border-related measures.

Others have considered actions by countries that seek to impose a carbon price. Droege *et al.* (2009) have reviewed the principles and estimate carbon impacts, and Monjon and Quirion (2010) have looked at EU design. Lockwood and Whalley (2008), meanwhile, point to the many parallels with VAT, now adopted by around 130 countries. Khrebtukova (2010) has explored and developed the argument that border adjustment is an essential and legitimate part of developing healthy regulatory competition in carbon control. The Carbon Trust (2010)[1] emphasizes the need for sector-specific treatment, a theme developed in Grubb *et al.* (2011) to emphasize that policy should develop incrementally, on the basis of scale, exposure and simplicity.

Any border-related measure, including a requirement to purchase allowances for the emissions associated with the production of a good, would be subject to WTO rules unless explicitly exempt. GATT (General Agreement on Tariffs and Trade) compatibility can be most simply assured by requiring importers to buy allowances at a fixed rate reflecting the BAT. Any costs levied on imports should be in conjunction with an actual price levied on domestic products (e.g. through auctions), and the domestic carbon cost cannot then be less than that charged on imports. For example, EU cement importers would have to buy a fixed number of allowances per tonne upon import, the rate (CO_2 per tonne of cement) being similar to that of the best plants in the EU. This ensures that the measure is intrinsically non-discriminatory and also cannot preferentially treat domestic producers that pay for their actual emissions. The Carbon Trust (2010) study concludes that cement is the simplest sector; the complexities of the steel sector suggest that several years would be required to develop a workable scheme. Other commodities might require different approaches due to their indirect (e.g. electricity-related) emissions. The BAT approach does have limitations in terms of economic incentives (e.g. Ismer and Neuhoff, 2007), but it is much simpler as a starting point than most other proposals.

For exports, the Subsidies and Countervailing Measures (SCM) agreement could allow for carbon charges incurred in domestic production to be reimbursed upon export (Lockwood and Whalley, 2008; Droege *et al.*, 2009; Khrebtukova, 2010).

Since the focus is on levelling carbon costs between consumption and production at the border, I use the distinct term 'border carbon-cost levelling'. The BAT approach adopted here is quite distinct from more ambitious proposals to charge for actual embodied carbon in imports (e.g. Gros and Egenhofer, 2010), and all variants of 'border levelling' differ fundamentally from broader and more political proposals to use border adjustments as a lever to discriminate between different countries on the basis of their domestic climate policies.

Although not the main motivation, such measures would clearly have revenue implications. First and foremost, they would enable domestic regulations like the EU ETS to move towards auctioning, rather than free allocation, raising domestic revenue. In regions still debating options, such border levelling would also remove one of the most potent arguments against carbon taxation. Import and export adjustments would have different revenue implications, as well as different legal bases. Export carbon cost reimbursements would reduce the net revenue to Treasuries from domestic auctioning, for the sake of ensuring that exports were not placed at an unfair competitive disadvantage. The central argument of this chapter is that import levelling would generate revenues that should be made available for developing-country climate-related expenditures.

9.4 Overall revenue implications

Given the complexities of negotiating and implementing such a system, it is useful to consider scenarios some years hence, say in 2020, focusing on just the most exposed big sectors. The Carbon Trust (2010) study proposes starting with the simplest and most carbon-intensive commodity, cement, and moving to other big direct emitters, notably steel, not later than 2020. Cement and steel production activities each account for about 6 per cent of global CO_2 emissions (far exceeding the emissions from international bunker fuels, for example). As shown in Figure 9.1, together they account for about one-third of total global industrial CO_2 emissions.

Moreover, emissions from cement manufacturing and flat steel production from blast furnaces (which accounts for most of the steel trade) are almost entirely direct (as opposed to electricity-related). Indeed, these two sectors alone account for more than half of all industrial direct emissions. This hugely simplifies the process: their 'border benchmark' can ignore any electricity-related component (which is equivalent to a BAT assumption of electricity from renewables or nuclear).[2]

Table 9.1 examines possible revenue implications associated with just these two sectors paying for the direct carbon emitted domestically, and also in the production of imported goods. It presents numbers based on recent data for just two illustrative regions – Europe (the EU ETS region) and the OECD. Estimates are shown for carbon prices of €15/tCO_2 and €30/tCO_2, roughly the range seen to date in the EU ETS and within range of 2020 projections. For simplicity, production and imports are converted at approximately the BAT emission rate, in part to allow for continuing improvements in performance under the influence of carbon pricing, and also for comparability with a fixed rate for border levelling (current average performance is far short of that used in the table).

Emissions

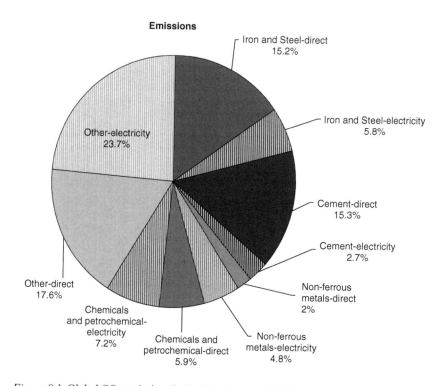

Figure 9.1 Global CO_2 emissions by industrial sector, 2005.

Source: *International* Energy Agency (IEA), World Energy Balances, plus process emissions ESDS International (Mimas, University of Manchester), as compiled in Grubb *et al.* (2011).

Both production and import volumes would be changed by carbon pricing (for some estimates see the calculations in Droege *et al.*, 2009), but given the intrinsic projection uncertainties, this is ignored in the table, which aims to give a sense of overall orders of magnitude only.

If domestic EU producers had to pay €15–30/tCO₂ for all their emissions, the cement and steel sectors combined would have to pay €5–10 billion annually in domestic auctions, with steel being the slightly larger component. Cement trade is relatively small, and the revenues associated with the carbon embodied in imports to Europe – even if these were at roughly the highest level seen in recent years (a volume driven partly by the construction boom in southern Europe) – would be under €0.5–1 billion per year. Steel is another matter; it has a much higher trade intensity already, which is expected to grow further. If Europe imported 70 Mt of steel, the revenue raised at the border would be around €2–4 billion per year.

If a wider area, such as the OECD as a whole, were engaged in carbon pricing, each € (or US$) per tonne of CO_2 paid would raise about €1 billion (or US$)

Table 9.1 Indicative carbon revenues from cement and steel production and trade

	EU		OECD	
	Production[a]	*Imports*	*Production[a]*	*Imports*
Annual volume (Mt)[b]	250	35	560	70
Carbon emissions benchmarked at 0.7 tCO$_2$/tonne cement	175	24.5	392	49
Approx. revenue if paid at €15/tCO$_2$[a]	2,625	367.5	5,880	735
Approx revenue if paid at €30/tCO$_2$[a]	5,250	735	11,760	1,470
Annual volume (Mt)[c]	120	70	250	130
Carbon emissions benchmarked at 1.8 tCO$_2$/tonne steel	216	126	450	234
Approx revenue if paid at €15/tCO$_2$[a]	3,240	1,890	6,750	3,510
Approx revenue if paid at €30/tCO$_2$[a]	6,480	3,780	13,500	7,020

Notes:
a Note that reimbursement of carbon costs upon export would offset against the production revenues. The EU and OECD export virtually no cement, but the EU is a significant steel exporter. However, this is mostly to other OECD countries, has been quite volatile, and is expected to decline. As the focus of this chapter is upon international finance, no attempt at such adjustment is made here.
b Cement including clinker imports, roughly at 2006–2007 levels. Data from Cook (2009) and the Cement Sustainability Initiative (www.wbcsdcement.org).
c Blast furnace (production), gross commodity steel European imports into EU ETS and linked countries, roughly as at 2007 levels but with a modest increase over time reflecting trends for OECD. data from World Steel Association (2009).

per year from cement and steel combined. Total OECD auction revenues would be €15–30 billion per year for prices in the range €15–30/tCO$_2$, although the higher end of this range seems less plausible across the OECD by 2020. With the cement trade static and some growth in steel imports, the revenues associated with border levelling at a carbon price of €15/tCO$_2$ could be around €3.5 billion per year, perhaps about US$5 billion, primarily from steel.

Clearly, these estimates are rough and are reliant on the assumptions made, but they are sufficient to give a sense of scale. Extending the coverage to other products would, of course, increase the revenue accordingly. In the context of the US$100 billion per year sought, making the revenues from border levelling available to international climate expenditures would be a modest, but – after allowing for exchange rates and other sectors – far from trivial contribution.

9.5 Border levelling as an international resource

It is, of course, simplistic to identify a source of revenue and assume it could be available for international purposes. In the international arena, policy has more to do with the economic interests of individual countries and finding approaches that provide mutual benefit. Why might countries agree?

Countries pursuing emission reductions through cap-and-trade (or other carbon pricing) have two reasons to consider the option. Today, even regions making strenuous efforts to price carbon are having to give almost all the energy-intensive trade sectors free emission allowances; the fear of 'carbon leakage' is too potent and pervasive to ignore. Border levelling would enable the reduction or elimination of free allocation to internationally traded sectors. Even if claims to the revenues from border levelling were given up, there is a huge leverage incentive. In cement, for example, for each euro paid for imports, EU countries would raise around ten times as much by being able to auction allowances to domestic cement producers as well, without fear of carbon leakage.

The other reason is that the same fears impede strengthening of the system. The EU ETS rules for Phase III allow free allowances in proportion to a sector's share of the overall EU cap. Moving from a 20–30 per cent emission reduction by 2020 would both reduce these free allowances and drive up the carbon price, and the resulting increased risk of carbon leakage is a major reason why the EU is politically unable to strengthen its position. The lack of border levelling means that ETS regions both forego revenues (associated with domestic auctioning) and are trapped into a weaker climate change policy than would otherwise be possible.

The underlying research demonstrates that the simplest form of border levelling – domestic auctioning combined with a requirement for importers to purchase allowances at a rate per tonne of product close to a BAT benchmark – would be WTO-compatible (Droege *et al.*, 2009). In theory, this suggests that countries could implement this basic measure unilaterally. For multiple reasons, it would, however, be desirable to gain international acceptance.

Is this likely? Other countries would benefit from the ability of these countries to strengthen their climate action; no region benefits from ETS countries having to exempt large swathes of industrial production from paying a carbon price. To see the potential benefits of border levelling, they need only acknowledge the truth that no politician is going to impose a carbon price on a sector that can make a politically credible threat to migrate.

However, this may carry limited weight in international trade and financial circles. As indicated, the revenues associated with border levelling would not only be a new source of revenue, but one specifically associated with international exchanges. As noted in the quotation by Wang and Watson in Section 9.2, it is a matter of open debate who is really responsible for the associated emissions – the producer or the consumer. This introduces an additional factor in gaining international acceptance; countries could negotiate not just about the revenues, but also about the underlying attribution of associated emissions between producer and consumer, addressing a point made by key developing countries, including China, for many years.

Of course, the first preference of key developing-country producers might be to capture the revenues directly themselves, through a charge on their exports (Mueller and Sharma, 2005). However, as noted, attempting this unilaterally would put their own producers at a disadvantage in export markets vis-à-vis other producers. The best approach again is to negotiate border levelling – including the use of revenues – at a multilateral level. This, ultimately, is why all parties have an incentive to consider the option seriously.

9.6 Who really pays?

A key question will be who really pays? Most directly, the answer is the consumer in the carbon-pricing region, who now cannot escape any domestically imposed carbon cost through imports. Of course the full effects can be more complex.

As compared to the default case (carbon-intensive production escaping carbon costs), a carbon price on a commodity consumed in any given region will reduce demand. Assuming that domestic and imported 'embodied' carbon is charged at the same rate – most simply by requiring importers to purchase emission allowances from the same market as domestic production – their relative costs (including carbon) will influence the impact. If the border levelling is a fixed benchmark based on BAT, then imports may gain a slight relative advantage, to the extent that domestic production on average falls short of the best technology.

Economic principles related to the elasticity (price-sensitivity) of demand dictate the exact response, but in general the demand for basic commodities is not very price-sensitive, and producers pass on most of the costs. The net result is that the final consumer would indeed pay the great majority of costs associated with border levelling. Moreover, a significant proportion of revenues would arise from trade flows between Annex I Parties. If the money is used for expenditure in developing countries, therefore, it easily satisfies the basic principle behind 'common but differentiated' responsibilities.

Moreover, any direct effects would, to a degree, be offset by equilibrating effects in the rest of the economy. A simple equilibrium model by Whalley (2010) suggests that the net effect of a US$25 border levelling charge by the EU would be an impact on China of around 0.001 per cent of GDP even if none of the money came back to China – equivalent to less than one foregone hour of Chinese economic growth.

9.7 Revenue collection and disbursement

Border levelling could be implemented in various ways. The crudest would be for Customs and Excise in ETS countries to require importers to hold domestic emission allowances (e.g. EU ETS allowances) upon import.

Alternatively, requiring importers to hold Clean Development Mechanism (CDM) certified emission allowances (excluded from the kind of 'supplementarity' constraints the EU currently imposes) would be the simplest way of ensuring the revenue is recycled back to developing-country projects in a neutral way. At the opposite extreme, money raised could be returned directly to the country of export, but perhaps governed to ensure the money is spent on Nationally Appropriate Mitigation Actions (NAMAs) or other forms of recognized low-carbon development plans.

If the finance were to be placed firmly in the context of the new fund proposed under the Copenhagen Accord, other avenues might need to be considered. These could include, for example, negotiating a special form of allowance to be auctioned under the authority of the Conference of the Parties (COP), which all signatories would agree to recognize as qualifying for border levelling compliance.

This would have the advantage – from a multilateral and trade perspective – of placing the terms of international auctions (e.g. the 'benchmark' level of assumed best-practice emissions) in the multilateral arena, further insulating the process from protectionist pressures. The decision on such terms would presumably have to be decided jointly between the COP and WTO. Intermediate approaches, less onerous in international governance, are also possible.[3]

9.8 Conclusions

Border levelling has two major benefits. It can facilitate stronger climate policy action by countries pricing carbon, and can raise revenue that is intrinsically well suited as a source for international expenditures (with revenues, as illustrated in this chapter, that are far from trivial even from just two industrial commodities). The world is currently struggling on both fronts.

Developed countries need to abandon rhetoric about using trade protection to force other countries to do more, and focus instead on legitimate goals associated with ensuring that their own policies do not create unreasonable disadvantage. Within this they need to accept shared responsibility for emissions associated with their consumption patterns, and pursue the obvious consequence that imports should also pay for their embodied emissions.

Developing countries do not benefit in any way from the current situation, in which countries adopting carbon prices have to exempt large swathes of industrial production from paying it, for fear of carbon leakage. To see the potential benefits of border levelling, they need only acknowledge the truth that no politician is going to impose a carbon price on a sector that can make a politically credible threat to migrate. For trade purposes, this needs to be non-discriminatory; concepts of 'common but differentiated responsibilities' can be addressed through the use of the revenues, which could be devoted to international climate finance in a multilateral setting.

If industrialized countries are keen to price carbon properly, and if developing countries are serious about a more consumption-oriented approach, then it makes sense that border levelling and the use of associated revenues should be on the table of international negotiations. It is time to shake off prejudices and rhetoric, and take a close look at the potential mutual benefits.

Notes

1 The author was Chief Economist at the Carbon Trust at the time, and lead author of the report, as well as Chair of Climate Strategies, the organization that commissioned the underlying academic analysis led by Droege *et al.* (2009).
2 Indirect (electricity-related) emissions add hugely to the complexity of any border-related measures because they require emissions to be measured at source, and also require the assignment of electricity producer emissions to specific industrial consumers, which is fraught with difficulty.
3 Another option would be to require importers to purchase and surrender special import permits for the carbon embodied in the imported products, measured in accordance with

best-practice calculations. This is different from requiring importers to buy allowances on the domestic market, which may be politically unpalatable because it would cut into the domestic cap, reducing the allowances available to domestic producers and thus driving up domestic allowance price.

Bibliography

Carbon Trust, 2010, *Tackling Carbon Leakage: Sector-Specific Solutions in a World of Unequal Carbon Prices*, February 2010 [available at www.carbontrust.co.uk].

Cook, G., 2009, *Climate Change and the Cement Industry*, Climate Strategies, Cambridge, UK [available at www. climatestrategies.org].

Droege, S., 2009, *Tackling Leakage in a World of Unequal Carbon Prices*, Climate Strategies Synthesis Report [available at www.climatestrategies.org].

Gros, D., Egenhofer, C., 2010, *Taxing Carbon at the Border?,* Centre for European Policy Studies (CEPS), Brussels.

Grubb, M., Hourcade, J.C., Neuhoff, K., 2011, *The Carbon Connection: Climate Change Solutions for our Energy, Economic and Geopolitical Challenges*, Earthscan, London.

Ismer, R., Neuhoff, K., 2007, 'Border tax adjustment: a feasible way to address stringent emission trading', *European Journal of Law and Economics,* 24, 137–164.

Khrebtukova, A., 2010, 'Using national border climate adjustment schemes to facilitate global greenhouse gas management in industrial production', *Washington and Lee Journal of Energy, Climate, and the Environment,* 1(1), 95.

Lockwood, B., Whalley, J., 2008, *Carbon Motivated Border Tax Adjustments: Old Wine in Green Bottles?*, NBER Working Paper No. 14025 [available at www.nber/org/ papers/ w14025].

Monjon, S., Quirion, P., 2010, 'How to design a border adjustment system for the European Union Emissions Trading System?', *Energy Policy*, 38(9), 5199–5207.

Mueller, B., Sharma, A., 2005, *Trade Tactic Could Unlock Climate Negotiations*, ScienceDevelopment.net, 23 June 2005 [available at www.scidev.net/Opinions/index.cfm?fuseaction=readOpinions&itemid=399&lan guage=1].

Sunwal, M., 2009, 'Reflection on the climate negotiations: a southern perspective', *Climate Policy,* 9(3), 330–333.

Wang, T., Watson, J., 2008, 'China's carbon emissions in international trade: implications for post-2012 policy', *Climate Policy,* 8(6), 577–587.

Whalley, J., 2010, *The Impact of Carbon Motivated Border Tax Adjustments*, presentation to seminar at Cambridge University, 28 August 2010.

World Steel Association, 2009, *World Steel in Figures, 2009*, World Steel Association, Brussels and Beijing.

10 Sources of long-term climate change finance

Erik Haites and Carol Mwape

10.1 Introduction

This chapter provides an overview of possible sources of finance to fund climate change adaptation and mitigation in developing countries. Possible sources of international climate change finance have been analysed by the UNFCCC,[1] the High-level Advisory Group on Climate Change Financing (AGF),[2] the G20 finance ministers[3] and other studies. This chapter groups the sources into five categories based on how the funds would be raised and channelled to adaptation and mitigation activities in developing countries. As well, estimates of the amount that could be generated by each source are tabulated.

It is useful to group the possible sources of climate change finance into the following five categories based on how the funds would raised and channelled to developing countries:

1. funds provided by developed-country governments from national budgets;
2. sources that contribute to national budgets, dependent on national decisions;
3. sources that contribute to national budgets, dependent on international agreements;
4. funds collected internationally pursuant to an international agreement; and
5. leveraged private sector funds.

Each of these categories is discussed in turn. For each category possible sources and how the funds would be applied to adaptation and mitigation actions in developing countries are described. A table that compares estimates of the amount that could be generated by each source is found in section 10.7.

10.2 Funds provided by developed-country governments from national budgets

Developing countries argue that developed-country governments should be the main source of international climate change finance because those governments committed, in Article 4 of the Convention, to provide new and additional financial resources for adaptation, mitigation and other actions by developing countries.

These funds flow through developed country national budgets and hence usually depend on the annual budgetary process of each country. Once the budget has been approved, the funds are disbursed through bilateral (typically the country's aid agency) and multilateral (climate funds under the Convention, such as the Least Developed Countries Fund and, when operational, the Green Climate Fund, and outside the Convention, such as the Climate Investment Funds) channels.

Provision of funds by national governments often is subject to explicit or implicit burden sharing criteria.

- Assessed contributions are a form of explicit burden sharing. The core budget of United Nations Environment Programme (UNEP) and replenishment of the Multilateral Fund of the Montreal Protocol are funded through assessed contributions.[4] Both of these processes include assessed contributions for developing countries. The United States objects to the principle of assessed contributions and is not formally part of either process.[5]
- The amount that parties pledge for replenishment of the Global Environment Facility (GEF) depends, in part, on the amounts other parties commit. In short, the burden sharing formula is implicit; each party contributes what it considers its fair share given the pledges by other parties. The fifth replenishment of the GEF includes pledges by almost all Annex II Parties plus a number of other Annex I and non-Annex I Parties.
- Contributions to other multilateral climate funds under the Convention – the Least Developed Countries Fund, Special Climate Change Fund and Adaptation Fund – and outside the Convention – the Climate Investment Funds, Congo Basin Forest Fund, and UN REDD Programme for example – are voluntary. Each country decides whether and how much to contribute.

In practice the options are assessed contributions or voluntary contributions where the latter may involve implicit burden sharing.

The assessed amount could be a country's total contribution to international climate finance through all bilateral and multilateral channels or only its contribution to a specified fund or funds, such as the Green Climate Fund or all funds under the Convention. Allocation of the contribution among adaptation, mitigation and other purposes (technology and capacity building) could be specified. Developing countries have proposed that each Annex I country contribute the percentage of its GDP needed to meet developing country needs.[6] The AGF estimated that contributions of 0.5 to 1 per cent of Annex I GDP would generate US$200 to 400 billion by 2020.

At present developed-country contributions to international climate finance are voluntary. Each country chooses how much to contribute and how the funds are disbursed. Most funds are disbursed bilaterally. Contributions to multilateral funds are spread among many funds under and outside the Convention. Most of the funds target mitigation. Government contributions currently amount to at least US$ 21 billion per year.[7] Development assistance is a useful indicator of the maximum amount that might be generated by voluntary contributions. In 2010 Annex II parties committed almost US$128 billion of official development assistance (ODA) to developing countries; about 0.32 per cent of their gross national income (GNI).[8] The contributions ranged from 0.15 per cent of GNI (Italy) to 1.10 per cent of GNI (Norway).

Assessed contributions are likely to be much more difficult to agree than voluntary contributions. But a fair arrangement for funding the international climate change finance needs of developing countries is likely to be important for contributions by developed country governments. Then each country's budget request can be presented as its fair share of the total need.

The contributions – assessed or voluntary – would come from developed country budgets and be funded from general revenue. Every developed country government currently has a budget deficit and is attempting to reduce expenditures. Hence, commitments to provide substantial new and additional funding to developing countries to address climate change are likely to be difficult to agree.

The next two sections review sources that could generate additional revenue for developed-country governments to fund their climate finance contributions.

The full amount generated by a source is unlikely to be allocated to international climate finance for several reasons:

- In some countries the revenue generated by a source is divided between different levels of government so the national government, which has the climate finance commitment, does not receive the full amount. In some countries fossil fuel subsidies, for example, are provided by national and state/provincial governments, so only part of the revenue saved by phasing out the subsidies accrues to the national government.
- The amounts received by national governments from a given source would not be considered a fair distribution of climate finance commitments. Using additional fossil fuel royalty revenue for climate finance, for example, would mean that developed countries with no fossil fuel production would not contribute to international climate finance. Although this is an extreme example, it is unlikely that the revenue generated by any source, or combination of sources, would be considered a fair distribution of climate finance commitments as reflected in assessed or voluntary contributions.
- Finance departments traditionally oppose "earmarking" revenues – dedicating the revenue raised from a particular source for a specific purpose. The revenue generated is unlikely to precisely match the specific need over time. Thus finance departments will resist earmarking the revenue raised from the potential sources identified for climate finance.
- As noted above, every developed country government currently has a budget deficit and is attempting to reduce expenditures so each government will want to retain some of the additional revenue.

Rather the sources discussed should be considered options that could generate additional revenue for developed country governments to fund their climate finance contributions where those contributions are determined by international negotiations related to the amount of climate finance needed and a fair distribution of voluntary or assessed contributions to meet those needs. Some, perhaps most, of the revenue raised from these potential sources is likely to be retained for domestic purposes.

10.3 Sources that contribute to developed country national budgets, dependent on national decisions

The AGF and G20 reports assessed several sources that developed-country governments could implement to generate additional revenue. Some or all of this additional revenue could then be used to finance climate change actions in developing countries. The sources reviewed by those reports are:

- *Revenue from a domestic carbon tax or sale of allowances for a domestic emissions trading scheme*
  With a carbon price of US$20–$25 per ton of CO_2 equivalent, the AGF estimates that auctions of emission allowances or carbon taxes in developed countries could generate about US$300 billion annually in 2020. Allocating 10 per cent of the revenue for international climate action could mobilize around US$ 30 billion annually. The G20 report estimates that a carbon price of US$25 per ton of CO_2 equivalent in Annex II economies could raise around US$250 billion in 2020. Allocating 10 per cent for climate finance could yield US$25 billion per year.
- *Phase out of fossil fuel subsidies in Annex II countries*
  The G20 report states that fossil fuel subsidies in Annex II countries currently amount to US$40–60 billion per year.[9] Reducing the subsidies and allocating 20 per cent of the current amount for climate finance in developing countries could generate up to US$10 billion per year.[10] The AGF estimated the potential revenue from this source at up to US$8 billion per year.
- *A share of fossil-fuel royalties*
  The AGF report identified fossil fuel royalties as a possible source of funds for developed-country contributions to international climate finance. The report did not estimate the amount that might be raised. To generate additional revenue for developed countries the royalties would need to be increased.[11] Only 5 Annex II countries collect royalties from fossil-fuel production.
- *A "wires charge" on electricity generated or CO_2 emissions due to electricity generation*
  A charge of US$1 per ton of CO_2 on electricity emissions in OECD countries would raise about US$5 billion per year according to the AGF report. A country may hesitate to implement such a charge if it has a carbon tax or emissions trading scheme that also covers emissions by electricity generators.

The assumed share of each source that might be used for international climate finance – 10 per cent of the tax/auction revenue and 20 per cent of the reduced subsidy payments – is unlikely to be accurate for each country. It is much more likely that Annex II governments agree on a burden sharing approach, such as assessed contributions or pledges by country, and that each country then raises its share of the funds in the manner it chooses.

The percentages assume that most of the revenue raised from these potential sources would be retained for domestic purposes. The potential sources identified by the AGF and G20 reports could raise US$290 to US$360 billion per year of which US$35 to US$40 billion is assumed to be used to meet their commitment to fund the climate change finance needs of developing countries and about US$250 to US$325 billion is retained by developed countries for domestic purposes.

10.4 Sources that contribute to national budgets, dependent on international agreements

The AGF and G20 reports also identified potential sources whose implementation is best coordinated internationally, but which have no international bodies with an appropriate mandate. Thus, they would be implemented by national governments in accordance with international agreements. The revenue would be collected by each developed country national government and some or all of the revenue could be used by each country to help meet its commitment to fund the climate change finance needs of developing countries.

Two possible sources fall into this category – an international financial transactions tax (FTT) and border levies on GHG-intensive products imported by Annex I Parties.

- *International financial transactions tax*
  A small tax in international financial transactions was proposed by James Tobin in the 1980s as a means to discourage currency speculation. The UNFCCC estimated that such a tax could generate US$15 to US$20 billion per year. The AGF estimate is US$7 to US$16 billion per year. The report of Bill Gates to the G20 is reported to show that between US$9 billion and US$48 billion per year could be raised if such a tax were applied to major European countries or to the G20 respectively. A legislative proposal by the European Commission for an EU-wide FTT indicates that €57 billion per year could be raised.

An FTT is best implemented through an international agreement because many transactions can easily be moved to a different jurisdiction, so the tax can be avoided by moving transactions to a non-tax jurisdiction. An international agreement is likely to involve only countries with significant financial centres. The revenue is likely to accrue to the national governments and be treated as general revenue. Annex II governments could use the revenue they collect to help meet their assessed contributions or voluntary pledges.

The EU has announced that it proposes to implement such a tax beginning 2014. The United States has steadfastly opposed such a tax since it was first proposed.

When Annex I Parties implement policies to limit greenhouse gas emissions they attempt to minimize production shifts to countries that do not have such policies ("carbon leakage"). Production shifts to countries without emissions limitation policies undermine both the emissions reduction goal and the economic activity of the Annex I Party.

An Annex I Party can minimize carbon leakage through the design of its mitigation policy; for example, implementing an emissions trading scheme, giving free allowances to vulnerable firms, and accepting CERs for compliance. Policy designs that reduce leakage have a cost; distributing free allowances for example, reduces the revenue from auctioned allowances. Border levies on GHG-intensive imports by an Annex I Party discourage carbon leakage and so permit adoption of more efficient domestic policies.

Developing countries strongly oppose unilateral imposition of border taxes on imports of GHG-intensive products. But an internationally negotiated agreement on border levies could benefit both developing and developed countries. Two options for internationally negotiated border levies have been proposed.

- *Border carbon cost levelling*[12]
  Developed countries with a carbon tax or emissions trading scheme would collect an internationally agreed levy on imports of GHG-intensive products from countries without such a policy.[13] Participating developed countries would impose the same levies on the same products regardless of the origin of the product. The levy for each product would be based on the emissions associated with best available production technology, so it does not protect inefficient industries. The levy revenue would be transferred to an international fund, such as the Green Climate Fund.
- *A carbon exports optimization tax*
  The AGF evaluated an export fee levied by developing countries on exports of GHG-intensive products to developed countries with a carbon tax or emissions trading scheme. This serves the same purpose as the developed country border levies but is administratively more complex. The AGF estimated that such a tax could raise as much as US$9 to US$31 billion per year.

Developing countries benefit because additional revenue is generated to finance climate change action in their countries. They benefit further if the reduced risk of carbon leakage induces developed countries to adopt more stringent emission reduction commitments.

Developed countries are able to implement more efficient domestic policies due to the reduced risk of carbon leakage. In particular, they are able to auction more of the allowances thus generating more domestic revenue even though all of the revenue from border levies goes to an international fund.

Such a system of border levies would best implemented through an international agreement, perhaps under the UNFCCC but currently is not under serious consideration.[14]

10.5 Funds collected internationally pursuant to an international agreement

Funds also can be raised internationally pursuant to an international agreement. The share of proceeds – the 2 per cent share of certified emission reductions (CERs) issued for most clean development mechanism (CDM) projects that is the main source of funds for the Adaptation Fund is the best example of such a source. To date over US$170 million has been raised through the sale of 10.4 million CERs.

The CDM is an international market mechanism established by the Kyoto Protocol. The CERs can be used by Annex I Parties to help meet their emissions limitation commitments under the Protocol. So they are purchased by Annex I governments and entities in Annex I countries that can use them for compliance with domestic policies, such as installations subject to the EU emissions trading scheme (EU ETS).[15] A 2 per cent share of proceeds is levied on the CERs issued for most CDM projects.[16] These CERs are transferred to the Adaptation Fund and are sold to finance the activities of the Fund.

Additional funds could be generated from international market mechanisms. Specific proposals include:

- *Extension of share of proceeds*
  While a 2 per cent share of proceeds is levied on the CERs issued for most CDM projects, joint implementation (JI) and international trading of assigned amount units (AAUs) are not subject to a share of proceeds levy. The AGF estimates that a share of proceeds of 2 to 5 per cent applied to all offsets – CDM, JI and any new mechanism – could raise US$1 to US$3 billion per year.
- *Auction a share of the AAUs*
  Norway proposed that a share of the AAUs corresponding to future commitments of Annex I Parties by auctioned internationally. The balance would be allocated free of charge to the Annex I Parties as in the Kyoto Protocol. The AGF estimates that auctioning 2 to 5 per cent of AAUs could generate US$5 to US$12 billion per year.

The second option requires that developed-country emissions reduction commitments be expressed in AAUs. Commitments that are not part of a second commitment period under the Kyoto Protocol are less likely to be expressed in AAUs. The amount that could be generated also depends on the stringency of the commitments adopted by Annex I Parties.

The first option depends on a continued market for developing country offsets in Annex I countries. That, in turn, depends in part on how the commitments are expressed – in AAUs or not – and the mechanisms that can be used for compliance. Use of developing country offsets for compliance is less likely if Annex I commitments are not expressed in AAUs.

Funds to finance climate change actions in developing countries could also be generated through international regulation of emissions from international aviation and shipping. The high and rising CO_2 emissions by these sources could be regulated by an emissions – or fuel – levy or an emissions trading scheme with auctioned allowances that could generate revenue for climate change actions in developing countries.

- *Regulation of international aviation emissions by the International Civil Aviation Organization (ICAO)*
  The UNFCCC estimated that a levy or allowance price of US$23.60 per ton of CO_2 could generate US$10 to US$25 billion per year. The G20 report estimates that a globally implemented carbon charge of US$25 per ton of CO_2 on fuel used for international aviation could raise around US$13 billion in 2020. The AGF assumes that part of the revenue is used to compensate developing countries and that 25 to 50 per cent of the remaining revenue is used for measures to reduce emissions from international aviation. That leaves US$1 to US$3 billion per year for climate change actions in developing countries.
- *Regulation of international shipping emissions by the International Maritime Organization (IMO)*
  The UNFCCC estimated that a levy or allowance price of US$23.60 per ton of CO_2 could generate US$10 to US$15 billion per year. The G20 report estimates that a globally implemented carbon charge of US$25 per ton of CO_2 on fuel used for international shipping could raise around US$26 billion in 2020. It estimates that 40 per cent of the revenue be used to compensate developing countries, leaving up to US$ 15 billion per year for climate finance. The AGF assumes that part of the revenue is used to compensate developing countries and that 25 to 50 per cent of the remaining revenue is used for measures to reduce emissions from international shipping, leaving US$3 to US$9 billion per year for climate change actions in developing countries.

Some developing countries oppose regulation of international aviation and shipping emissions by ICAO and IMO because the regulations adopted by those organizations apply to all parties. They argue that developed countries should bear the burden of reducing these emissions in accordance with the principle of common but differentiated responsibility. The principle of common but differentiated responsibilities applies to Parties, so it is not evident that it applies to airlines and shipping companies or to emissions beyond national borders. The principle also does not mean there can be no burden at all on developing countries.

Nevertheless, the principle of common but differentiated responsibilities can be addressed through compensation to developing countries. Each developing country would receive compensation equal to, for example, its share of global trade multiplied by the revenue collected.[17] That would leave net revenue equal to the revenue collected multiplied by the developed country share of global trade.[18] A portion of the net revenue, the AGF assumed 25 to 50 per cent, likely would be used to help finance emission reductions by the sector. The remainder could be transferred to a fund, such as the Green Climate Fund, to provide financial assistance for climate change actions in developing countries.

In the case of international aviation emissions, it may be possible to exempt some routes or countries without distorting competition in lieu of paying compensation. But exemptions also reduce the funds generated for climate finance. The revenue foregone through exemptions is, in effect, another formula for determining the compensation to each developing country.

With a compensation arrangement each developing country would receive two financial flows – compensation based on the agreed formula and a share of the revenue generated to finance climate change action in developing countries. Some countries might receive more assistance if no compensation was provided and all of the revenue generated was used to provide financial assistance for climate change actions in developing countries. If compensation is based on a developing country's share of international trade, a developing country with a small share of global trade but substantial adaptation needs might get more money if no compensation were paid and all of the funds were used to support climate change actions in developing countries.

While ICAO has studied options for regulating CO_2 emissions from international aviation, it has taken virtually no action to regulate those emissions. This prompted the European Union to pass legislation that includes the emissions of all flights that arrive at or depart from an EU airport in the EU ETS effective 1 January 2012. Several countries and airlines oppose this initiative. Legal challenges to this requirement by non-EU airlines have been unsuccessful. Various forms of retaliation have been mooted but, to date, have not been implemented.

Most allowances are distributed free to airlines. They may find, as other industries covered by the EU ETS have, that participation may be profitable. That might reduce the opposition by airlines to regulation of international aviation emissions by the EU or ICAO.

The governments of EU member states will collect revenue from the sale of allowances to airlines from around the world for the emissions of flights to and from the EU. The EU has indicated that it is prepared to exempt the emissions of flights covered by equivalent policies implemented by other countries or an international organization. Thus other countries and ICAO have an incentive to implement equivalent policies so they can collect a share of the revenue.

If other countries, rather than ICAO, implement equivalent policies, the revenue will accrue to national governments. The extent to which some of that revenue is available to provide financial support for climate-change actions in developing countries then would be a decision of each government subject to its national budgetary process as discussed in section 10.2. Only if ICAO implements a levy or emissions trading scheme would revenue be collected internationally to finance climate change actions in developing countries.

An alternative to regulation of international aviation emissions is an international air transport levy.[19] A charge reflecting the associated emissions is levied on the price of international passenger tickets. Such charges have been introduced by several countries to raise fund to fight HIV/Aids and other pandemics. Müller and Hepburn suggest an average levy of €5 per passenger per flight and estimate that it would raise about €10 billion (US$13 billion) annually. The UNFCCC estimated that such a levy could raise US$10 to US$15 billion per year. An air transport levy is more likely to be implemented by national governments than by ICAO so the revenue would flow through national budgets as discussed in section 10.2.

More progress has been made in IMO, which implemented a regulatory measure setting minimum energy efficiency standards for the design of new ships in June 2011. It has also studied market-based measures to further reduce emissions and potentially generate finance for climate action in developing countries, including those assessed in the AGF and G20 reports that provide compensation to developing countries to ensure they face no net cost as a result of the measure.[20]

The EU is committed to studying how to include international shipping emissions in its EU ETS as well, and to taking a regional approach if there is no progress on a global deal. That could leads to a similar choice – implementation of policies and collection of revenue by national governments in the EU or regulation by IMO with revenue generated internationally, and used both to compensate developing countries for their incidence under the scheme and to help finance climate change actions in developing countries.

In summary additional revenue could be generated internationally from international market mechanisms and regulation of international aviation and shipping emissions. The ability to generate revenue from the market mechanisms (AAUs, CDM, JI, etc) depends critically on the nature of future developed country commitments and changes to the mechanisms. The ability to generate revenue from regulation of international aviation and shipping emissions depends on whether the emissions are regulated by ICAO and IMO or by national governments. Only if they are regulated by ICAO and IMO will there be a possibility of compensation for developing countries and a predictable flow of revenue to help finance climate change actions in developing countries. The amount of revenue generated for climate finance depends on whether the design includes compensation for the economic impacts on developing countries.

10.6 Leveraged private sector funds

Private resources can best be leveraged through a combination of policy reforms that change incentives for private investment and public financial resources from international and domestic sources. International sources include multilateral development banks, bilateral support and carbon market finance.

Multilateral development banks (MDBs) borrow funds from capital markets at lower rates than those available to many developing countries, based on the strength of their paid-in capital and guarantees of their member countries. The AGF and G20 reports note that the MDBs could borrow additional funds based on their existing paid-in capital contributions and guarantees.[21] Further replenishments and paid-in capital contributions would enable them to borrow more money still. The G20 report estimates that US$10 billion of additional paid-in capital allows a development bank to raise US$30 to US$40 billion that could be devoted to climate change actions in developing countries.

The MDBs lend money to developing countries on concessional and non-concessional terms.[22] Since the banks need to repay the money they have borrowed, they provide loans rather than grants. Loans are better suited to mitigation actions than adaptation measures. Since changes to paid-in capital are decided only periodically, neither the AGF nor the G20 report estimates a corresponding annual financial flow.

An International Monetary Fund (IMF) analysis indicates that an initial endowment of US$120 billion of assets by developed countries would enable a fund to borrow US$1 trillion over 30 years and use that money to fund US$100 billion of climate change actions per year in developing countries.[23] To provide grants and highly concessional loans to developing countries would require subsidy resources – donations – from developed countries. The IMF indicated it would not create, finance, or manage the fund.

A World Bank paper finds that a fund with US$68 billion of paid-in capital from Annex I countries could borrow at favourable terms while making loans to mitigation projects in developing countries.[24] Over a decade retained earnings would increase the paid-in capital to US$80 billion and loans to developing countries would rise to US$100 billion per year generating a portfolio of US$1 trillion.

Ultimately financial resources from these institutions depend on contributions by developed countries. The institutions can borrow additional funds commercially. The larger the share of grants and highly concessional loans provided to developing countries, the lower the amount of commercial borrowing that can be supported.

Developing-country policies can increase the incentive for domestic and foreign sources to invest in mitigation measures. Such policies include reduction of fossil fuel subsidies, feed-in tariffs for renewables, and energy efficiency regulations. Developed countries, bilaterally and through multilateral institutions, can leverage domestic and foreign private investment using tools such as export credits, risk-sharing, policy and loan guarantees, insurance products, and green bonds.

The AGF estimated that public climate finance from developed countries, MDB finance and carbon offset flow could leverage in the range of US$ 100–200 billion of gross private climate finance flows to developing countries. The G20 report estimates that the same mechanisms could yield international private financing for mitigation measures in developing countries of around US$150 billion per year.

Sales of offset credits (CERs) generated by the Clean Development Mechanism have resulted in revenues to developing countries of at least US$9.5 billion through 2011 while stimulating investments of over US$100 billion in mitigation projects.

As noted in section 10.5 above, the future of the international carbon market requires a demand for developing country credits in Annex I countries. That depends in part on how the Annex I commitments are expressed and the mechanisms that can be used for compliance. The G20 estimates that offset market flows could range from US$5 to US$40 billion per year in 2020.

Foreign direct investment (FDI) in developing country emitting sectors by developed country entities was between US$37 and US$200 billion in 2008.[25]

The G20 report states that investment (public and private, foreign and domestic) in developing countries in low carbon energy, low carbon transport and energy efficiency totaled around US$200 billion in 2010, with about 60 per cent in China, Brazil, India, Mexico, and Turkey. Current foreign equity investment in mitigation measures in developing countries is estimated at US$16 billion.[26] FDI flows vary with economic conditions, so future flows are difficult to predict.

10.7 Summary

Many potential sources of revenue that could generate funds for adaptation and mitigation action in developing countries have been identified. They are listed in Table 10.1 in the categories used in this chapter. The table lists estimates of the amount each source could generate, whether the funds would be directed to adaptation or mitigation, consistency of the source with the principle of common but differentiated responsibility (CBDR) and the political acceptability of the source.

Table 10.1 Summary of potential sources of climate finance

	Amount (US$ bn/yr)	*Mitigation or adaptation*	*Consistent with CBDR*	*Political acceptability*
1. Funds provided by developed country governments from national budgets				
Assessed contributions	Could be needs-based (e.g. 1.5% of GDP)	A requirement for thematic balance could be set	Strong	Low
Voluntary contributions	Likely to be well below 0.7% of GDP	Likely to tend towards mitigation	Moderate	High
2. Sources that contribute to developed country national budgets, dependent on national decisions				
Domestic carbon taxes	AGF: $30 G20: $25	Depends on whether contributions are assessed or voluntary (see 1 above)	Depends on whether contributions are assessed or voluntary (see 1 above)	Moderate
Phase out of fossil fuel subsidies	AGF: $8 G20: $10			Moderate
Increase fossil fuel royalties	No estimates			Low
Wires charge on electricity generation	AGF: $5			Low

(Continued)

Table 10.1 (Continued)

	Amount (US$ bn/yr)	Mitigation or adaptation	Consistent with CBDR	Political acceptability
3. Sources that contribute to national budgets, dependent on international agreements				
Financial transactions tax	UNFCCC: $15–20 AGF: $7–16 Gates: $9–48 EC: €57	Depends on whether contributions are assessed or voluntary (see 1 above)	Depends on whether contributions are assessed or voluntary (see 1 above)	Moderate
Border carbon cost levelling	Grubb: $5			Low
Carbon exports optimization tax	AGF: $9–31			Low
4. Funds collected internationally pursuant to an international agreement				
Extension of the "share of proceeds"	AGF: $1–3	Either	Weak	Low
Auctioning a portion of AAUs	AGF: $5–12	Either	Strong	Low
Carbon pricing for international aviation	UNFCCC: $10–25 AGF: $1–3 G20: $13	Either	Strong (with a compensation mechanism)	High
Carbon pricing for international shipping	UNFCCC: $10–15 AGF: $3–9 G20: $15	Either	Strong (with a compensation mechanism)	High
5. Leveraged private sector funds				
MDB capital increases	G20: $30–40 for every extra $10 of paid-in capital	Mitigation	Weak	High
Private flows leveraged by public policies and instruments	AGF: $100–200 G20: $150	Mitigation	Mixed (depends on instrument)	High
Carbon market finance	G20: $5–40	Mitigation	Weak	Moderate

Estimates of the potential revenue that could be generated by a source vary widely in some cases. The amounts that could be generated by different sources range from US$1 billion to over US$100 billion per year in the case of private flows. To meet developed country commitments to provide financial support for adaptation and mitigation actions in developing countries is likely to require funds from several of the potential sources.

Funds generated by many of the sources identified will flow into national treasuries. Then the amounts to be provided for climate finance in developing countries and the channels through which the funds are delivered will be subject to national budgetary processes. It is likely that most of the revenue raised will be retained by developed countries for domestic purposes. This may make them attractive to developed countries, but is unlikely to meet the climate finance needs of developing countries.

Significant amounts of revenue could be raised internationally through regulation of international aviation and shipping emissions by ICAO and IMO. The amount generated for climate finance will depend on whether developing countries are compensated for the economic impacts. That is a distributional issue for developing countries; is the revenue used only for climate finance or for climate finance and economic compensation. If these emissions are not regulated by ICAO and IMO they likely will be regulated by national governments and any associated revenue will flow into national treasuries, which is likely to significantly reduce the amount provided for climate finance.

Acknowledgements

This chapter is based on a concept note prepared for ecbi – The European Capacity Building Initiative. The authors wish to express their appreciation for the financial support provided for the preparation of the concept note and for permission to use the material for this chapter. The authors also wish to express their thanks to Tim Gore for helpful comments on the ecbi concept note and a draft of the summary table.

Notes

1 UNFCCC (2007) Table IX-66 (p. 186) and Annex IV.
2 AGF, 2010. *See also* Chapter 7 and Sterk *et al.* 2011.
3 World Bank Group, 2011. *See also* Chapter 8.
4 The total amount needed for a two or three year period is agreed by the relevant body of parties. The assessed contribution specifies the percentage of the total, and hence the amount, to be paid by each party.
5 The United States often makes bilateral and multilateral contributions roughly equal to the amount it would contribute under the formula used to calculate the assessed contributions.
6 For example, if the amount needed by developing countries is equal to 0.83 per cent of the total GDP of Annex I Parties, the contribution expected of each Annex I Party would be 0.83 per cent of its GDP.
7 Buchner *et al.* 2011.

8 OECD development assistance committee (DAC). Korea has been excluded. Available at: http://www.oecd.org/dataoecd/54/41/47515917.pdf
9 The cost of fossil-fuel subsidies in developing countries is estimated to be much higher. Whether fossil fuel subsidies will affect the level of financial support for mitigation actions in developing countries has not yet been decided.
10 Reducing fossil fuel subsidies should help developed countries meet their emission reduction targets.
11 Depending on the royalty structure, increases in fossil fuel prices might generate additional royalty revenue. Ambitious climate mitigation policies could reduce fossil fuel prices, which might lower royalty revenue.
12 Grubb, 2011. See also Chapter 9.
13 Developing countries would not impose the border levies, so their imports are not affected.
14 The agreement would address the principles – criteria to determine the products affected, how to set the levy for each product, how often levies are adjusted, which countries impose the levies, which fund(s) receive the revenue collected – and create a body to calculate the levies for the affected products.
15 To comply with the domestic policy, the entity transfers CERs to the national government and the government can then use them to meet its Kyoto Protocol commitment.
16 Some people claim that the share of proceeds is a tax on the developing country entities that own CDM projects. No estimates of how the cost of the levy is actually shared between CER buyers and sellers are available. All of the revenue goes to the Adaptation Fund which benefits developing countries.
17 For example, if the total revenue collected during 2020 was US$10 billion, a developing country whose share of global trade (measured as total exports, total imports or the average of exports and imports) was 0.45 per cent would receive compensation of US$45 million. The share of each developing country also could be calculated using other data such as the revenue ton kilometers of arriving (departing) flights.
18 Since all developing countries receive compensation, the amount remaining after compensation would be the developed country share of total trade (about 70 per cent) multiplied by the total revenue collected (US$10 billion), about US$7 billion.
19 Müller and Hepburn, 2006.
20 A number of countries are now supporting a global approach with a compensation mechanism for developing countries.
21 The amount of additional borrowing possible is called "headroom".
22 The AGF called the amount of the loans the gross contribution and the grant equivalent value of concessional loans the net contribution.
23 Bredenkamp and Pattillo, 2010. Assets provided by developing countries could include special drawing rights (SDRs).
24 de Gouvello *et al.*, 2010.
25 Buchner *et al.*, 2011, Figure 1, p. 15.
26 Buchner *et al.*, 2011, Figure 1, p. 15.

Bibliography

Advisory Group on Climate Change Financing (AGF), 2010. *Report of the Secretary-General's High-level Advisory Group on Climate Change Financing*, United Nations, New York.

Bredenkamp, H., and C. Pattillo, 2010. *Financing the Response to Climate Change*, International Monetary Fund, Washington, D.C.

Buchner, B., A. Falconer, M. Hervé-Mignucci, C. Trabacchi, and M. Brinkman, 2011. *The Climate Finance Landscape*, Climate Policy Initiative, Venice.

de Gouvello, C., I. Zelenko and P. Ambrosi, 2010. *A Financing Facility for Low Carbon Development*, Working paper 203, World Bank, Washington, D.C.

Grubb, M., 2011. "International Climate Finance from border cost leveling," *Climate Policy*, 11, pp. 1050–1057.

Müller, B. and C. Hepburn, 2006. *IATAL – an outline proposal for an International Air Travel Adaptation Levy*, Oxford Institute for Energy Studies, Oxford.

Sterk, W., H-J. Luhmann and F. Mersmann, 2011. *How Much is 100 Billion US Dollars?* Friedrich-Ebert-Stiftung, Berlin.

UNFCCC, 2007. *Investment and Financial Flows to Address Climate Change*. UNFCCC, Bonn.

World Bank Group, IMF, OECD, and regional development banks (G20), 2011. *Mobilizing Climate Finance*, Paper prepared at the request of G20 Finance Ministers, World Bank, Washington, D.C.

11 Spending adaptation money wisely

Samuel Fankhauser and Ian Burton

11.1 Introduction

The debate about climate change finance has so far been as much about trust (or, more accurately, about the lack of trust) as it has been about finance. The protracted UN Framework Convention on Climate Change (hereafter referred to as the Convention) negotiations under the Bali Action Plan (agreed in December 2007) have devoted much time and energy to the discussion of process: how funds should be raised, through which channels they should be disbursed, how spending decisions should be governed and how activities are to be monitored, reported and verified. This preoccupation with monitoring and governance is a direct reflection of the low and apparently declining level of trust among and between the Parties to the Convention. To what extent this decline in trust has been reversed by the Cancun Agreements remains to be seen, but there appear to be grounds for some cautious optimism. Among other factors, the origins of this lack of trust can be traced back to a string of donor promises of financial support that have not been fully met or were long delayed, and to a lack of confidence among donors in the reliability of some developing countries in managing funds.

The process questions are important. Adaptation to climate change will require substantial amounts of money (UNFCCC, 2007; Fankhauser, 2010; World Bank, 2010a; Narain *et al.*, 2011), and funding is beginning to become available. The World Bank reckons that between US$2.2 billion and US$2.5 billion in adaptation finance has so far been committed (World Bank, 2010b). This could be topped up with a portion of the US$30 billion in fast-start funding pledged in Copenhagen at the end of 2009 and a share of the annual $100 billion in climate finance promised by 2020 (AGF, 2010). In light of these magnitudes, getting the process right is critical.

The decision at COP-16 to establish the Green Climate Fund under the guidance of the Conference of the Parties (COP) is generally seen as a step in the right direction. The Board has 12 members from developed countries and 12 from developing countries, the latter group including seats for the least developed countries and small-island developing states. A Transitional Committee with a developing country majority will design the Green Climate Fund during 2011. The World Bank will act as interim trustee, subject to review three years after the operationalization of the Fund. These encouraging developments leave open many questions about how the Fund, as well as other channels of investment in adaptation, will work to ensure successful adaptation.

There is a danger that, instead of getting on with the urgent tasks of adaptation, the Parties will become increasingly embroiled in debates about governance, monitoring and additionality. It will be unfortunate and counterproductive if these concerns are allowed to overwhelm equally or more important questions relating to the efficient, effective and equitable use of funds. To a large extent, the decision on adaptation priorities belongs to national governments. However, nothing is likely to undermine progress on adaptation in the developing countries more than evidence, or even suspicion, that the funds are being diverted or used wastefully, and are not reaching those most in need of assistance.

In this chapter, the focus of the debate is moved away from process issues and back towards the substance of adaptation. We try to answer the question of what 'good adaptation' in developing countries might look like, and what kind of adaptation measures should therefore be financed as a priority.

Stern (2008, 2009) defines 'good' adaptation as meeting three criteria. First, it is efficient in the sense that it achieves results at the lowest possible cost. Second, it is effective in keeping down the negative impacts of climate change. Third, it is equitable, targeting the countries and population groups most worthy of assistance.[1] Bird and Brown (2010) highlight the criteria of timeliness, appropriateness, national ownership, and focus on the most vulnerable.

It is hard to disagree with these high-level criteria, and indeed they are not unique to adaptation spending. For example, similar criteria also form the core principles for the allocation of concessional development assistance. Development agencies such as the World Bank use them to ensure that scarce grant resources are spent wisely and fairly (e.g. IDA, 2007).[2]

However, in practice, the need for efficiency, effectiveness and equity poses some quite complex operational challenges that adaptation institutions may find difficult to address. This chapter reviews the most important of these. In concrete terms, they are concerned with the integration of adaptation and development, the identification of adaptation priorities in the face of uncertainty, and the balance between 'hard' structural adaptation and 'soft' behavioural measures. Aggravating them all is the sheer scale and scope of the adaptation problem.

The question of whether the adaptation regime that is emerging post-Cancun is able to address these challenges and is, in this sense, fit for purpose is not addressed here. Other authors have written extensively about the design of adaptation institutions (e.g. Müller and Gomez-Echeverri, 2009; Müller, 2010), but have not directly answered this particular question either. It is not easy to predict, with confidence, the shape of the future regime and to assess how fit for purpose it will be in the face of multiple forces and stresses.

It is noted, however, that the track record of existing adaptation institutions is not without blemish[3], and the emerging adaptation regime appears to be the result of institutional turf battles as much as thoughtful design. It is clear, therefore, that the delivery arrangements for adaptation will be further developed and revised and that these developments should be continually debated and scrutinized both within and outside the Convention process. This chapter is a contribution to such debate and scrutiny. It is hoped that the characterization of 'good adaptation' provided in this chapter, and of the operational challenges that follow from it, will be helpful in informing the process.

The chapter starts, in Section 11.2, with an exploration of generic priorities for 'wise' adaptation. Setting adaptation priorities has mainly been seen as a location-specific exercise that requires detailed knowledge of local circumstances and place-to-place variations in climate risk. Nevertheless, as will be seen in Section 11.2, the literature on adaptation economics, decision-making under uncertainty, and adaptation and development can offer some broad pointers on adaptation priorities and measures that are likely to be important, 'independent of local circumstances. There has been a move away from a strictly place-based view of adaptation towards the recognition of the need for more programmatic, strategic and even 'transformational' approaches.

In Section 11.3, it is asked what operational challenges adaptation institutions may face in delivering on those generic priorities. Section 11.4 concludes with suggestions about what this might mean for the emerging adaptation regime.

11.2 Adaptation priorities

How to spend adaptation money wisely is at its core a classic economic problem of resource allocation. There are well-established techniques that can be brought to bear on such problems, such as cost–benefit analysis, cost-effectiveness analysis and multi-criteria analysis. However, adaptation to climate change is a much more complex issue than the typical resource allocation problem and requires different approaches to the standard appraisal techniques.

Adaptation is a complex problem for many reasons, but three features in particular stand out (Fankhauser *et al.*, 1999; Ranger *et al.*, 2010):

1   The intricate link between adaptation and other socio-economic trends, such as economic growth and development (e.g. there is much debate about the difference between adaptation to climate change and adaptation to multiple stressors).
2   The pervasiveness and temporal complexity of adaptation decisions (e.g. the need to harmonize or integrate adaptation across spatial and temporal scales).
3   The high level of uncertainty about local climate outcomes (e.g. the uncertainty about the balance between increased temperature and increased rainfall in terms of potential evapotranspiration in specific localities).

The reasons why adaptation is complex contain lessons about what the immediate adaptation priorities should be. These are considered in the rest of this section, with a focus on identifying generic priority projects and programmes, while bearing in mind the localized nature of many adaptation decisions (for country priorities, see Barr *et al.*, 2010).

11.2.1 Adaptation and development

Adapting to climate conditions is one of the oldest challenges of mankind (Lamb, 1988), and human populations and societies have been remarkably successful in coping and adapting to the climate over many generations. Globally speaking, climate varies more over space than over time. Human populations have been able to live successfully in a wide variety and range of climates. However, adaptation is not and never has been perfect. Fluctuations in climate variables cause billions of US dollars of damages each year, and cost countless lives. Some of these losses are the result of a deliberate economic calculus; residual risks are accepted because they are too expensive to avoid. In other cases, however, losses are the consequence of insufficient adaptation or maladaptation.

Cases of maladaptation can be found in many circumstances, but insufficient adaptation – or an 'adaptation deficit' (Burton, 2009) – is often linked to underdevelopment and to deficiencies in choices (Burton, 2010). There is both empirical and anecdotal evidence that the effects of climate events are particularly severe on poor people. Empirical work on climate variation by Dell and colleagues (2008) identified a raft of negative climate effects in low-income countries; annual temperature spikes are associated with lower rates of economic growth, lower industrial and agricultural output, lower investment and greater political instability. However, they found no such effects in high-income countries. Raddatz (2009) found that the gross domestic product (GDP) effect of a given climate disaster is twice as high in low-income countries as in middle-income ones, which in turn suffer twice as much as high-income countries.

The link between climate and economic development has been further unravelled by Noy (2009), who related the adverse effects of climate disasters to basic development indicators such as income per capita, literacy, the quality of institutions, trade openness and the depth of financial markets. Others (Brooks *et al.*, 2005; Barr *et al.*, 2010) have used a similar set of indicators to measure adaptive capacity, which is a determining factor of vulnerability.

Development, or lack thereof, is thus a critical aspect of vulnerability to climate change, and therefore of adaptation. However, we know little about how these various development indicators combine to affect vulnerability. Tol and Yohe (2007) suggest that climate impacts are determined by the aspect of adaptive capacity that is least developed or, as they call it, 'the weakest link'. In other words, weakness in one area (e.g. poor institutions) cannot be fully compensated by strength in another (e.g. good climate information). This suggests that adaptation to climate change cannot be considered just one policy issue, but many. It must also account for the development context and for gaps in existing capacity (e.g. in terms of developing planning, location and relocation issues, insurance, infrastructure codes and standards and their enforcement, agriculture policies and practices, water and public health management).

McGray and colleagues (2007) identified a sequence of measures, both developmental and adaptation, which together would reduce vulnerability to climate change (also Klein and Persson, 2008). They were grouped into four categories:

1   measures that reduce vulnerability to stress more broadly (whether climate-related or not), including fundamental development objectives such as health, sanitation and poverty eradication;
2   creation of 'response capacity', such as resource management practices, planning systems and effective public institutions;
3   management of current climate risks, including flood and drought prevention, and disaster risk reduction and management;
4   policies specifically addressing anthropogenic climate change, such as accelerated sea-level rise and an increased incidence of extreme weather events.

In light of these considerations, it seems reasonable to promote basic development and growth policies such as health, sanitation, primary education and institutional development as a priority for adaptation. Indeed, Vivid Economics (2010) suggests that most of the policies that development agencies have adopted to promote economic growth do, in fact, reduce vulnerability to climate change. There are important exceptions, however, such as accelerated development in high-risk areas and excessive reliance on vulnerable products, such as water-intensive crops. Similarly, developing countries have huge infrastructure needs and these investments should be adapted to climate change from the outset.

The type of development being promoted therefore clearly matters, but, in general, economic development of the right kind seems a good way of starting to reduce vulnerability to climate change; a claim made earlier by Schelling (1992, 1997).

11.2.2 *Timing and scope*

Even if society were perfectly adapted to today's climate, preparing for climate change would still be a major challenge. Responding to prevailing climate conditions is ingrained in most areas of human activity, and the majority of activities will require some degree of adjustment, including agricultural practices, building codes, location decisions and the design of infrastructure and changes in the demand for energy and water. The adjustments required even for modest climate change are therefore wide-ranging and potentially substantial.

Not all adaptation decisions have to be made at once. Adaptation is a long-term process. However, some measures do have to be taken now. Getting the adaptation timing right is a major challenge (Fankhauser *et al.*, 1999; Hallegatte, 2009).

Fankhauser *et al.* (1999) analysed adaptation timing in a simple economic model that compares the net benefits of adaptation now or later (also Agrawala and Fankhauser, 2008). The comparison of the two cost–benefit streams reveals three main differences between early and late adaptation.

First, early action brings forward the cost of adaptation. This normally imposes a cost penalty, as future costs can be discounted. However, early adaptation is sometimes sufficiently cheaper to offset the discounting effect, and early action, therefore, makes sense. One example of this is a long-lived project that is hard to reverse. Building adaptation into the design of such investments will often be cheaper than a costly retrofit.

Second, early action brings forward the benefits of adaptation. This is particularly attractive if these early benefits are very high, for example, if a measure yields strong development benefits, or if the benefits would otherwise kick in too late (as in the case of projects that take a long time to bear fruit).

Third, the long-term benefits of early action may differ from those of delayed adaptation. A delay may result in damages that are impossible to reverse later. For example, sensitive ecosystems like coral reefs may be irretrievably damaged (Carpenter *et al.*, 2008).

The conclusion from Fankhauser *et al.* (1999) and Hallegatte (2009) is that adaptation policy should give precedence to measures that:

- help to prevent costly retrofits later (perhaps the main areas where this will be the case are projects with long lifetimes, such as planning decisions and infrastructure investments);
- have long lead times and therefore require an early start (research into new medicines and crops is a good example);
- yield early benefits, such as those that deal with current climate risks, including extreme events, or address current development;
- prevent irreversible loss, such as the protection of fragile ecosystems.

Note that many of the urgent adaptations identified in Section 11.2 also feature on this list of priorities. Efforts to build adaptive capacity in developing countries, which are highlighted in the adaptation and development literature, require a considerable lead time and will yield immediate development benefits regardless of the level and rate of climate change. They are therefore also a priority from the point of view of optimal timing. Similarly, spatial planning and economic development plans have the potential (in fact the aim) to create lasting economic structures that may be difficult to reverse later on. It is therefore important that they take climate change into account from the outset.

11.2.3 Uncertainty

The one factor that, above any others, makes adaptation difficult is the high level of uncertainty about the exact nature and extent of climate change (Dessai *et al.*, 2009; Hallegatte, 2009; Ranger *et al.*, 2010). There is a high level of confidence in the scientific community about the basic geophysical processes that link emissions to warming; far more than some of the public discussions on climate change would suggest (Solomon *et al.*, 2007). However, a lot less is known about how warming will manifest itself at the local level, not just as a change in mean temperature, but also in terms of factors like precipitation, runoff, seasonal patterns, wind speeds and climate extremes. This is the sort of information local decision-makers need in order to fine-tune their adaptation strategies.

Some of this information can be obtained from the downscaling of general circulation models, but this is coarse and the levels of uncertainty are high, particularly for precipitation and other variables. As a consequence, the accuracy and usefulness of even the most advanced climate models for adaptation decisions has been questioned (Stainforth *et al.*, 2007a, 2007b). Adaptation requires decision-making under much uncertainty.

Dealing with uncertainty is nothing new for decision-makers in other fields, such as finance, and there is a considerable body of literature on the subject (e.g. Gollier, 2001). The tools of the decision-making trade are increasingly being applied to adaptation, and some important insights are emerging. These have been summarized by Ranger *et al.* (2010), Hallegatte (2009) and Lempert and Collins (2007):

- at its most basic level, uncertainty means that the benefits of adaptation have to be expressed in expected value terms; that is, the probability-weighted mean over the range of possible outcomes;
- if decision-makers are risk-averse they may put extra weight on negative outcomes; that is, use an expected utility approach and perhaps adopt the precautionary principle;
- if there is a risk of being locked into an undesirable path, decision-makers may apply the tools of finance, such as option theory, and put a premium on measures that maintain or increase the flexibility to respond when the true state of nature is revealed;
- alternatively, they may react to uncertainty by emphasizing robustness; that is, adopt designs that function under a wide range of climatic conditions;
- one set of adaptation measures that is attractive in the face of uncertainty comprises no-regrets measures – adaptations that are justifiable over a range of climate outcomes.

The above list suggests that uncertainty may alter some of the adaptation priorities identified earlier. The need for robustness and flexibility will affect the adaptation strategy for long-lived investments, certainly in terms of adaptation design and perhaps also in terms of adaptation timing.[4] However, the essential requirement to factor climate change into long-lived decisions is unaffected.

Elsewhere, climate uncertainty reinforces the priorities identified earlier. Given their win-win nature, the capacity-building and hybrid development – adaptation measures emphasized before would fall into this category. The same may be true for many environmental and institutional measures. Agrawala and Fankhauser (2008) note that the call for increased flexibility and robustness not only applies to physical capital, but to natural and social systems as well. They mention the sustainable management of natural systems as a way to increase the resilience of ecosystems to a changing climate. Institutionally, Agrawala and

Fankhauser argue for regulatory frameworks that encourage individual adaptability and, as such, increase the flexibility and robustness of economic systems. Both examples are consistent with the indicative priorities identified previously.

In summary, the three strands of literature considered here (adaptation–development links, optimal timing, and climate uncertainty) result in a fairly consistent set of adaptation priorities, even though they approach the issue from different analytical directions. We next ask what these priorities imply for adaptation institutions.

11.3 Challenges for the emerging adaptation regime

A look at the current adaptation landscape shows that many of the principles set out in Section 11.2 are in fact reflected in current adaptation decisions. However, this is probably due to pragmatism as much as to strategic choice. In the absence of substantial adaptation finance, institutions have been limited to providing technical assistance and projects that can be justified by existing development mandates. There is also a certain amount of positioning to secure a role in the emerging adaptation business.

The question is whether the approach to adaptation will change as it is scaled up and finance begins to flow. We see at least two reasons for concern, institutional challenges, which, if left unaddressed, could compromise adaptation decisions:

1 an inherent preference by adaptation institutions for 'hard' structural adaptations, which are more visible and easier to identify than 'soft' behavioural or regulatory measures;
2 the difficulty of integrating adaptation and development in an environment where the additionality of adaptation finance has to be unambiguously ascertained.

The two challenges are made more difficult by the massive scope of adaptation. The concept of adaptation covers many things, and the limitation of adaptation only to climate change does not, in practice, reduce the scope very much. 'Adaptation' as a stand-alone idea can be used to mean so much that it tends to lose any specific meaning. To talk about 'an adaptation regime' as if it could be some specific reality will increasingly seem fanciful. Economic decision-making, planning and development will become increasingly inseparable from adaptation, and vice versa.

11.3.1 The current adaptation landscape

Adaptation is ramping up. Development institutions have begun to integrate adaptation into official development assistance (ODA) and are providing the sort of assistance that will build adaptive capacity, as argued above. In addition, some institutions are preparing themselves to play a role in the management of the additional adaptation financing that has been promised under the Convention, in the Copenhagen Accord and in the Cancun Agreements.

These institutions include the various financial mechanisms related to the Convention, including the Global Environment Facility (GEF) and the Adaptation Fund under the Kyoto Protocol. Although the Adaptation Fund has only just become operational, the GEF has, through various windows, committed over US$300 million for adaptation measures already (World Bank, 2010b). Most of the 170 GEF projects deal with capacity-building and the preparation for adaptation.[5] Crucially, this includes the preparation of 45 National Adaptation Programmes of Action (NAPAs) for least-developed countries. More recently the COP-16 decisions in Cancun, including the decision to create the Green Climate Fund, have added to the expected capacity to facilitate adaptation through international mechanisms.

The focus on planning is consistent with the guidance from the UNFCCC, which has restricted the scope for full-blown adaptation projects until now. It is also broadly in line with the priorities identified in Section 11.2, although they would probably justify a more accelerated ramp up of adaptation. The NAPAs themselves also emphasize capacity-building and measures with immediate benefits, particularly for agriculture (Osman-Elasha and Downing, 2007; Agrawala and Fankhauser, 2008).[6] However, very few NAPA measures have been financed and implemented to date.

It is unclear to what extent future adaptation funds will be allocated through the existing and proposed Convention channels. They have not inspired enough confidence from either donor countries or (in the case of GEF) recipient countries. This does not mean that such funds will be abandoned. They will probably be supported, perhaps even at an increased level, but they are unlikely to be the only delivery channel.

Another set of players is the multilateral development banks, specifically the World Bank Group and the regional development banks. They signalled their wish to play a larger role in managing adaptation funds by setting up the Pilot Programme for Climate Resilience (PPCR).[7] One of the strengths of the PPCR is the close integration of adaptation into existing development planning. The small handful of PPCR adaptation strategies that have so far been prepared again emphasize capacity-building and win – win measures with early environmental or development benefits (e.g. in terms of agriculture and water management). However, they also envisage the climate-proofing of strategic infrastructure assets (Climate Investment Funds, 2010a, 2010b, 2010c). It is not clear to what extent these long-term, structural adaptations will account for uncertainty in the way that Ranger *et al.* (2010) and others prescribe (see Section 11.2.3).

Donors seem to be willing to allocate a significant share of their new adaptation commitments through the multilateral development banks if potential skill and capacity constraints can be overcome.[8] Relying on existing development institutions like the multilateral banks is the simplest way of integrating adaptation into development, but donor countries also favour it because it affords them more control over spending decisions. The fact remains that development assistance serves the interests of the donors as well as those receiving assistance. Development assistance, whether for adaptation to climate change or other activities, can be linked to the trade, diplomatic and strategic interests of the donor countries.

There is yet another modality for development assistance – through NGOs and the growing number of civil society organizations that are entering the field of climate-related development. Linking adaptation with community-based development, they have been responsible for some of the most interesting adaptation initiatives to date (Berrang-Ford *et al.*, 2010).

11.3.2 Hard and soft adaptation

There is a well-known and long-observed practice in adaptation studies to prefer hard or 'concrete' adaptation measures such as sea walls, dams, irrigation projects and other infrastructure over soft adaptation, which includes changes in planning and practices, and behavioural changes that are not so visible.

This is partly because the incremental component in hard adaptation is more readily identified and measured as additional, but also because hard responses are easier to identify and appraise analytically. Attempts to estimate adaptation costs typically only consider a few alternatives in each sector in order to simplify the estimation of costs, and the emphasis is on hard structural measures (e.g. Swiss Re, 2009; World Bank, 2010a). [9]

However, there is a widely shared view, corroborated by the analysis in Section 11.2, that much effective adaptation can be achieved by relatively low-cost changes in practices. Even when hard adaptation is cost-effective, it may have to be complemented by soft design or regulatory measures either to minimize costs or avoid moral hazard. Apparently sensible adaptation measures such as dams, dykes, seawalls and flood protection infrastructure of various kinds can have the perverse effect of encouraging development in hazardous areas. Regulatory safeguards may be required to prevent this. There is a history of unintended consequences and perverse outcomes that is not unique to climate change adaptation.

As we have seen, funding constraints have ensured that dedicated adaptation support to date has mostly been of a preparatory nature – building capacity, identifying priorities, raising awareness – or, in other words, soft adaptation. The question is whether the bias towards hard measures manifest in adaptation analysis will carry over into international adaptation support, once adaptation begins to be funded in earnest. The current adaptation portfolio does not provide conclusive evidence, but the suspicion is that it will, unless some specific steps or provisions are made in the 'emerging adaptation regime'.

It is conceivable that in institutions with volume pressure, such as the multilateral development banks, the bias towards hard adaptation may persist, despite the long track record and extensive experience of multilateral banks with technical assistance, policy dialogue and sector reform. Hard adaptation may also be favoured as larger amounts of funds become available. There are significant transaction costs in project design and loan arrangements. Transaction costs as a proportion of total costs can be more easily reduced when projects are larger, thus favouring large-scale construction projects.

This is clearly a danger under the emerging adaptation regime, although one that can be partially offset by allocation of some funds through different organizations and NGOs. Institutions specializing in capacity-building or community-based adaptation, such as NGOs, are more likely to emphasize softer, and often more cost-effective, adaptation. Such 'grass-roots' projects may also be more equitable in the sense that there may be more direct access to the poorer and more vulnerable populations.

11.3.3 *Dealing with additionality*

If there is one feature that defines the current approach to adaptation, it is concern with additionality. There is a strong demand from the developing countries for adaptation to be supported over and above mainstream ODA. Developed countries, in turn, want to ensure that additional finance is used specifically to reduce vulnerability to climate change, and for no other purposes.

Additionality concerns are more likely to be met through a dedicated adaptation institution, like the Adaptation Fund under the Kyoto Protocol, where the funds come mainly from the 2 per cent levy on emission reductions achieved by the Clean Development Mechanism.[10] The demands for additionality seem less likely to be met if funding is channelled through existing (bilateral or multilateral) development institutions, where it is often difficult to draw a line between adaptation funding for climate change and other development activities.

However, using existing development channels would make it easier for adaptation to be integrated into development. We have seen in Section 11.2 that the boundary between adaptation and development is blurred and that the best way to reduce vulnerability to (current and future) climate events is often through basic development. Indeed, the desired direction is to mainstream or integrate adaptation to climate change into development so that all development investments are 'climate-resilient'. Similarly, using a programmatic approach to adaptation (akin perhaps to the PPCR) might be more effective than the project-by-project approach that until very recently has dominated adaptation support.

The desire for additionality is understandable. Developing countries need to be reassured that promises of contributions to the costs of adaptation are in fact kept and that they are additional to ODA. For their part, developed countries want reassurance that the funds are indeed used for adaptation to climate change. However, the need to have additionality ingrained in adaptation institutions may create barriers to this ambition. Overcoming the fixation with additionality is, perhaps surprisingly, one of the biggest challenges for wise adaptation.

11.4 Conclusions

This chapter has outlined some high-level criteria to guide adaptation decisions and ensure that adaptation financing is spent wisely. The general philosophy underlying our recommendations is one of adaptation as development or, in the words of Stern (2009), of 'adaptation as development under an adverse climate'. Basic development indicators like literacy and good institutions are associated with lower vulnerability and higher adaptive capacity. A minimum level of adaptive and administrative capacity in all countries is also needed for deeper adaptations to build on. Among these subsequent steps are measures to increase response capacity to stress events in general, and the ability to deal with current climate extremes.

Many of these measures are not adaptation in the traditional sense. Some, like reversing the spread of malaria, are Millennium Development Goals. However, they are classic win-win options that target the world's poor and offer immediate benefits, independent of eventual climate changes.

Priority measures also predominantly fall under the rubric of soft adaptation, that is, institutional, regulatory or behavioural responses to climate change, which are more flexible and often more cost-effective than capital investment.

The need for a climate-resilient infrastructure is one area where hard adaptation may be warranted. Developing countries have massive investment needs for energy, water, transport and other infrastructure demands over the coming decades (UNFCCC, 2007). Ensuring that these investments are resilient to climate change is another adaptation priority, given their multi-decade lifetimes.[11] However, even here, the need for expensive structural measures can often be reduced through smart planning and design, as the example of the Thames Estuary shows (see note 4).

Another priority area where decisions taken early can have wide-ranging long-term benefits is planning, understood broadly to include urban planning, land use planning and coastal zone management, but also agricultural and industrial development. These are areas where countries otherwise risk locking themselves into a vulnerable development path. The answer is to build adaptation systematically into development plans, including national-level growth and development strategies. In doing so, adaptation is linked to poverty alleviation, which safeguards an equitable outcome.

Development organizations are doing many of these things already. Much of the current adaptation work on the ground follows the same principles, and local groups and NGOs are starting to bring adaptation to communities. However, the emerging adaptation regime may discriminate against some aspects of this programme, because the proposed measures are less visible, less well-defined and less obviously additional than hard adaptation or independent adaptation programmes.

Similarly, existing development institutions have yet to demonstrate an 'adaptation mindset' that sees climate change as an integrated part of development, rather than an environmental bolt-on. They have to prove that they have the expertise, strength in depth and credibility (with both developed and developing countries as partners) to take on adaptation.

Wise adaptation also requires a more thorough and systematic approach to knowledge management. The Nairobi Work Programme of the UNFCCC is an important first step in this direction, but much more learning and information sharing will be required to build up a global knowledge base. There is a need to develop a community of practice on adaptation or, more precisely, many communities of practice for regions, different climate risks and different sectors, supported by Web-based information, and facilitated through periodic meetings and conferences including at the global level. The biennial world conference on HIV–AIDS might be taken as a partial model.

Within the Convention process, there is a need to synthesize knowledge and advise the Parties on all aspects of adaptation within the Convention and on coordination with activities outside its scope. The Adaptation Committee established by the Cancun Agreements could perform these functions. The Cancun Adaptation Framework, also established by those Agreements, could build upon the activities of the Nairobi Work Programme and develop it much further. The work of the Adaptation Committee would be predicated on the existence and growing strength of a global network of international centres on climate change adaptation. The Consultative Group on International Agricultural Research, with modifications, might be considered a possible model.

With these or similar structures in place, there would be at least a better chance that the adaptation finance promised in Copenhagen (COP-15) and as elaborated in Cancun (COP-16) will be spent wisely.

Acknowledgements

We are grateful to Alex Bowen, Thea Dickinson, Su-Lin Garbett-Shiels, Erik Haites, Kirk Hamilton, Ian Rowlands, Guido Schmidt-Traub, Joel Smith and John Ward for their comments and suggestions. Fankhauser also acknowledges financial support by the Grantham Foundation for the Protection of the Environment, as well as the Centre for Climate Change Economics and Policy, which is funded by the UK Economic and Social Research Council and Munich Re.

Notes

1 See Adger *et al.* (2006) for a more detailed discussion of equity issues in adaptation.
2 Mirroring the IDA process, Barr *et al.* (2010) and World Bank (2010b) propose efficiency, equity and transparency as the main criteria of the allocation process. Note, however, that they refer to the process of fund allocation, which is different from the adaptation outcomes about which Stern is concerned.
3 See, for instance, Anderson *et al.* (2009), Klein and Möhner (2009) and Osman-Elasha and Downing (2007).
4 An instructive example in this respect is the Thames Estuary (TE) 2100 plan in the UK, which concluded that with suitable alternative measures in place, investment into a new flood barrier can be delayed until more is known about climate risk. See www.environment-agency.gov.uk/research/library/consultations/106100.aspx
5 For a full list see www.gefweb.org or www.climatechangefundsupdate.org
6 The full list of NAPAs can be found on http://unfccc.int/cooperation_support/least_developed_countries_portal/submitted_napas/items/4585.php

7 The PPCR is part of a US$6.2 billion set of Climate Investment Funds. It provides programmatic adaptation support worth US$600 million to nine countries and two multi-country regions (see www.climateinvestmentfunds.org/cif/ppcr).

8 About one-quarter of existing adaptation commitments is channelled through multi-lateral initiatives (World Bank, 2010b), primarily the PPCR.

9 A notable exception is agriculture, where most adaptations concern autonomous farm-level adjustments (Agrawala and Fankhauser, 2008).

10 For an analysis of the CDM adaptation levy see Fankhauser and Martin (2010).

11 Hallegatte (2009) reports timescales of 30–200 years for transport and water infrastructure, 20–70 years for energy investments and 30–150 years for buildings.

Bibliography

Adger, W.N., Paavola, J., Huq, S., Mace, M.J. (eds), 2006, *Fairness in Adaptation to Climate Change*, MIT Press, Cambridge, MA.

AGF, 2010, *Report of the Secretary General's High-Level Advisory Group on Climate Change Financing*, November [available at www.un.org/wcm/content/site/climatechange/pages/financeadvisorygroup/pid/13300].

Agrawala, S., Fankhauser, S., 2008, *Economic Aspects of Adaptation to Climate Change: Costs, Benefits and Policy Instruments*, OECD, Paris.

Anderson, S., Hansen, D.S., Jensen, L.G., Burton, I., 2009, *Evaluation of the Operation of the Least Developed Countries Fund for Adaptation to Climate Change*, Joint External Evaluation, COWI Group and International Institute for Environment and Development, Kongens Lyngby and London, September.

Barr, R., Fankhauser, S., Hamilton, K., 2010, 'Adaptation investments: a resource allocation framework', *Mitigation and Adaptation Strategies for Global Change* 15(8), 843–858.

Berrang-Ford, L., Ford, J., Paterson, J., 2010, 'Are we adapting to climate change', *Global Environmental Change* 21(1), 25–33.

Bird, N., Brown, J., 2010, *International Climate Finance: Principles for European Support to Developing Countries*, Working Paper No. 6, European Development Cooperation to 2020 [available at www.edc2020.eu/82.0.html].

Brooks, N., Adger, N., Kelly, M., 2005, 'The determinants of vulnerability and adaptive capacity at the national level and the implications for adaptation', *Global Environmental Change* 15, 151–163.

Burton, I., 2009, 'Climate change and the adaptation deficit', in: E.L.F. Schipper, I. Burton (eds), *The Earthscan Reader on Adaptation to Climate Change*, Earthscan, London.

Burton, I., 2010, 'Forensic disaster investigations in depth', *Environment Magazine* 52(5), 36–41.

Carpenter, K., Abrar, M., Aeby, G., Aronson, R., Banks, S., Bruckner, A., Chiriboga, A., Cortés, J., Delbeek, J.C., DeVantier, L., Edgar, G., Edwards, A., Fenner, D., Guzmán, H., Hoeksema, B., Hodgson, G.G., Johan, V., Licuanan, W., Livingstone, S., Lovell, E., Moore, J., Obura, D., Ochavillo, D., Polidoro, B., Precht, W., Quibilan, M., Reboton, C., Richards, Z., Rogers, A., Sanciangco, J., Sheppard, A., Sheppard, C., Smith, J., Stuart, S., Turak, E., Veron, J., Wallace, C., Weil, E., Wood, E., 2008, 'One-third of reef-building corals face elevated extinction risk from climate change and local impacts', *Science* 321(5888), 560–563.

Climate Investment Funds, 2010a, *Bangladesh: Strategic Programme for Climate Resilience*, Document PPCR SC.7/5, World Bank, Washington, DC.

Climate Investment Funds, 2010b, *Niger: Strategic Programme for Climate Resilience*, Document PPCR SC.7/6, World Bank, Washington, DC.

Climate Investment Funds, 2010c, *Tajikistan: Strategic Programme for Climate Resilience*, Document PPCR SC.7/7, World Bank, Washington, DC.

Dell, M., Jones, B.F., Olken, B.A., 2008, *Climate Change and Economic Growth: Evidence from the Last Half Century*, NBER Working Papers Series, No. 14132, National Bureau of Economic Research, Cambridge, MA.

Dessai, S., Hulme, M., Lempert, R., Pielke, R., 2009, 'Climate prediction: a limit to adaptation?', in: W.N. Adger, I. Lorenzoni, K. O'Brien (eds), *Adapting to Climate Change: Thresholds, Values, Governance*, Cambridge University Press, Cambridge, UK.

Fankhauser, S., 2010, 'The costs of adaptation', Wiley Interdisciplinary Review: *Climate Change* 1(1), 23–30.

Fankhauser, S., Martin, N., 2010, 'The economics of the CDM levy: revenue potential, tax incidence and distortionary effects', *Energy Policy*, 38(1), 357–363.

Fankhauser, S., Smith, J.B., Tol, R., 1999, 'Weathering climate change: some simple rules to guide adaptation investments', *Ecological Economics* 30(1), 67–78.

Gollier, C., 2001, *The Economics of Risk and Time*, MIT Press, Cambridge, MA.

Hallegatte, S., 2009, 'Strategies to adapt to an uncertain climate change', *Global Environmental Change* 19(2), 240–247.

International Development Association, 2007, *IDA's Performance Based Allocation Systems: Options for Simplifying the Formula and Reducing Volatility*, The World Bank, Washington, DC [available at http://siteresources.worldbank.org/IDA/Resources/Seminar%20PDFs/73449-1172525976405/3492866-1172527584498/PBAformula.pdf].

Klein, R., Möhner, A., 2009, 'Governance limits to effective global financial support for adaptation', in: W.N. Adger, I. Lorenzoni, K. O'Brien (eds), *Adapting to Climate Change: Thresholds, Values, Governance*, Cambridge University Press, Cambridge, UK.

Klein, R., Persson, A., 2008, *Financing Adaptation to Climate Change: Issues and Priorities*, ECP Report No. 8, European Climate Platform, Stockholm.

Lamb, H.H., 1988, *Weather, Climate and Human Affairs*, Routledge, London.

Lempert, R., Collins, M., 2007, 'Managing the risk of uncertain threshold responses: comparison of robust, optimum, and precautionary approaches', *Risk Analysis* 27(4), 1009–1026.

McGray, H., Hamill, A., Bradley, R., Schipper, E.L., Parry, J.-O., 2007, *Weathering the Storm: Options for Framing Adaptation and Development*, World Resources Institute, Washington, DC.

Müller, B., 2010, *The Reformed Financial Mechanism of the UNFCCC*. Part II. The Question of Oversight, Oxford Institute of Energy Studies, Oxford, EV 52, April.

Müller, B., Gomez-Echeverri, L., 2009, *The Reformed Financial Mechanism of the UNFCCC*, Part I: Architecture and Governance, EV 45, Oxford Institute of Energy Studies, Oxford, April.

Narain, U., Margulis, S., Essam, T., 2011, 'Estimating costs of adaptation to climate change', *Climate Policy* 11(3), 1001–1019.

Noy, I., 2009, 'The macroeconomic consequences of disasters', *Journal of Development Economics* 88, 221–231.

Osman-Elasha, B., Downing, T., 2007, *Lessons Learned in Preparing National Adaptation Programmes of Action in Eastern and Southern Africa*, European Capacity Building Initiative (ECBI), Oxford.

Raddatz, C., 2009, *The Wrath of God: Macroeconomic Consequences of Natural Disasters*, World Bank Policy Research Working Paper No. 5039, World Bank, Washington, DC.

Ranger, N., Milner, A., Dietz, S., Fankhauser, S., Lopez, A., Ruta, G., 2010, *Adaptation in the UK: A Decision Making Process*, Grantham Research Institute on Climate Change and Centre for Climate Change Economics and Policy, London School of Economics, London.

Schelling, T., 1992, 'Some economics of global warming', *American Economic Review* 82(1), 1–14.

Schelling, T., 1997, 'The cost of combating global warming: facing the tradeoffs', *Foreign Affairs* 76(6), 8–14.

Solomon, S., Qin, D., Manning, M., Marquis, M., Averyt, K., Tignor, M., Miller, H.L., Chen, Z. (eds), 2007, *Climate Change 2007: The Physical Science Basis*. Contribution of Working Group I to the Fourth Assessment Report of the Inter-governmental Panel on Climate Change, Cambridge University Press, Cambridge, UK.

Stainforth, D., Allen, M., Tredger, E., Smith, L., 2007a, 'Confidence, uncertainty and decision-support relevance in climate predictions', *Philosophical Transactions of the Royal Society A: Mathematical, Physical and Engineering Sciences* 365, 2145–2161.

Stainforth, D., Downing, T., Washington, R., Lopez, A., New, M., 2007b, 'Issues in the interpretation of climate model ensembles to inform decisions', *Philosophical Transactions of the Royal Society A: Mathematical, Physical and Engineering Sciences* 365, 2163–2177.

Stern, N., 2008, 'The economics of climate change', *American Economic Review* 98(2), 1–37.

Stern, N., 2009, *A Blueprint for a Greener Planet*, Bodley Head, London.

Swiss Re, 2009, *Economics of Adaptation to Climate Change: A Framework for Decision Making*, Swiss Re, Zurich [available at www.swissre.com/rethinking/climate/].

Tol, R.S.J., Yohe, G.W., 2007, 'The weakest link hypothesis for adaptive capacity: an empirical test', *Global Environmental Change* 17, 218–227.

UNFCCC, 2007, *Investment and Financial Flows to Address Climate Change*, United Nations Framework Convention on Climate Change, Bonn.

Vivid Economics, 2010, *Climate Change, Adaptation and Economic Growth*, Paper prepared for the UK Department of International Development, Vivid Economics, London

World Bank, 2010a, *The Costs to Developing Countries of Adapting to Climate Change*: The Global Report of the Economics of Adaptation to Climate Change Study, World Bank, Washington, DC.

World Bank, 2010b, *World Development Report 2010: Development and Climate Change*, World Bank, Washington, DC.

12 Beyond climate finance

From accountability to productivity in addressing the climate challenge

Simon Zadek

12.1 Trouble with climate finance

'Climate finance' refers to those funds that are designed and resourced to address the climate challenge. The reasoning for advancing climate financing is clear and has good intentions: to highlight distinct climate-related concerns that have been hitherto marginalized or misunderstood, and to create a basis for catalysing new flows of funds to meet the associated investment needs. Climate finance has been a call to arms that has gone beyond the more familiar 'development' paradigm, and made a powerful case for accelerating the use of clean energy and the need for technology transfer. And beyond this call to arms, climate finance has become the fulcrum around which estimates are made of volumes required, along with definitions and estimates of investment performance. Over time, climate finance has been subdivided according to distinct categories (mitigation and adaptation), and has established in the public mind (or at least as far as policy is concerned) an awareness of the fight against deforestation and land use transformation, and also technology transfer, as distinct investment categories.

Crucially, a climate finance lens has become key to international climate change negotiations. It provides the conceptual framework for determining, at least in theory, what are (and therefore who will pay for) the 'incremental costs' associated with mitigation- and adaptation-focused investments, thereby seeking to distinguish them from other forms of publicly funded programmes and commercial investments and associated returns. To facilitate this, climate finance has become the analytic norm for thinking about resourcing the challenge of climate change, exemplified by 'climate cost-curves', mainstreamed (although not invented) by McKinsey, which provide quantified estimates of these incremental costs.

The political economy of climate finance has, however, proved to be problematic in practice. Attractive conceptual differences between problem-solving categories, notably adaptation and mitigation, have reinforced and legitimized rigid negotiating channels. Developing countries, for example, have argued that 'additionality' implies that international development aid should not count against developed-country obligations to fund action on climate. The place of private, commercial financing has suffered most as a result of this focus through the climate finance lens.

Developing-country negotiators have sought to exclude any discussion of the role of the private sector in funding climate action, even though a growing number of studies have highlighted productive roles for private finance (Forstater *et al.*, 2009).

The UN Secretary General's High-Level Advisory Group on Climate Change Financing (AGF) was mandated following Copenhagen to design innovative means of securing US$100 billion a year by 2020 (United Nations, 2010). Given this, it might have been expected that the Group would explore how the finance might be mobilized to fund the fundamental transition of economies and nations towards a low-carbon existence. Indeed, Project Catalyst estimates that there will be a need for infrastructure investment worldwide of about US$7 trillion per annum by 2020, of which US$1.5 trillion is energy-related (Project Catalyst, 2010). Of this, it is estimated that about US$290 billion per annum by 2020 of this total capital investment is needed for low-carbon infrastructure in developing countries. Instead, the AGF brought together some of the world's best minds and expended considerable political capital in exploring the far narrower question of how to mobilize climate finance, which was interpreted, as in this chapter, as the funds for climate action for which developed nations, and in particular their governments, could be held accountable.

The climate-finance lens has also arguably made it more difficult for international cooperation to leverage much-needed investment funds, especially at a time when developed countries face considerable budgetary pressures (WEF, 2010).[1]

Oft-quoted by those highlighting the challenges in securing the necessary finances is the comparative level of official development assistance, currently running at about US$110 billion annually. Against this benchmark, mobilizing another US$100 billion a year or more has been established as an unrealistically high bar to reach. However, such a basis for comparison is part of the problem, focused as it is on climate finance as one-way, zero-return resource transfers, effectively part of an international social security system. Nothing of course is further from the truth, given the scientific predictions as best as we can understand, alongside predictions of economic losses and the associated political and social dislocations arising from unmitigated climate change. More relevant benchmarks must therefore be economic, as Lord Stern and many others have pointed out. More relevant perhaps would be US Treasury Secretary Tim Geithner's estimate of global lost output as a result of the recession, of the order of US$3–4 trillion in just one year, or the estimated US$5 trillion of taxpayers' money spent on stimulus packages across the world. Such political benchmarking is, however, unlikely as long as the underlying architecture of the debate concerns climate and the redlined policy instrument of climate finance.

12.2 Curse of carbon

Climate finance has become the core currency in the political debate concerning the accountability of developed nations to developing nations, rather than an organizing principle for delivering the capital needed to drive forward effective climate management for the public good. Accountability is, of course, an important part of the equation. Most would agree that developed countries have benefited enormously from the 'carbon era' and should pay their fair share in mitigating the problem for today's and future generations. However, not only are relevant levels of funding unlikely to flow over any relevant time period, as mentioned above, but whatever does may well prove less than effective as a direct result of the manner in which it is framed and delivered.

Criticism of the 'development industry' is well established in political, academic and indeed popular debate. The view that large-scale, international public resource transfers have failed in addressing underlying development challenges (or often even shorter-term humanitarian imperatives) has transferred towards mainstream thinking in policy circles and academic debate (Easterly, 2007). Indeed, there is a growing view that development aid is core to sustained under-development, mainly because of its perverse impacts in incentivizing political and economic actors to focus on rent-seeking rather than real wealth creation (Litovsky *et al.*, 2007; Moyo, 2009). Most of all, the substantial body of evidence that political economies dependent on natural resources (the so-called 'resource curse') have historically under-performed is essentially now accepted wisdom (Collier, 2009).

The implications of this debate, and the growing consensus about the development 'god that failed' (Koestler, 1949), have not been adequately grasped by the climate community. Quite the reverse, in fact, as the design of a new generation of climate-financing institutions offers the prospect of a comparable shortfall in expectations in years to come. The difference from twentieth-century models of development institutions lies in the greater involvement of developing-country governments in the design and governance of 'green funds', such as the newly established Adaptation Fund. Although a welcome innovation in principle, in practice this is likely to be a disappointment, as the underlying institutional design flaws of the old development paradigm have largely been replicated in new clothes. A lack of competition between funds arising from centralization in the pursuit of political capital and accountability, the vertical integration of financing institutions, and the use of existing development institutions, are but three of the design features that are already embedded in climate-financing thinking.

A high-level review of these issues and challenges was provided by Project Catalyst in the run-up to COP-15 in Copenhagen (Zadek, 2009). The review raised concerns that channelling billions of dollars through government coffers to mitigate carbon and address adaptation would most probably induce one or more of the institutional flaws so apparent across the international development community, euphemistically named, the 'five institutional horses of the Apocalypse': political leakage, gaming, rent-seeking, bureaucratization and corruption (Figure 12.1). These flaws are already in evidence. Most apparent is the endemic fraud revealed in a series of assessments of the market for carbon offsets, seen by many as the jewel in the crown of specialized climate-finance mechanisms, including the AGF (United Nations, 2010). Civil society organizations such as Global Witness have raised similar concerns in other areas of climate finance, including REDD (Reducing Emissions from Deforestation and

Forest Degradation).[2] Proposals to remedy such actual and potential problems have been forthcoming, but most actors have focused on monitoring and compliance, which are essentially the very same mechanisms that have proved inadequate within the international development paradigm.

Political leakage will certainly shape capital allocation, all the more so with such highly politicized governing arrangements. The World Bank's allocation of climate funds to the South African state-owned energy monopoly, Eskom, was seen by most as an expedient attempt to defuse international anger over the far larger package of financing to support the commissioning in South Africa of the Medupi Power Station, one of the world's largest coal-fired power stations. Such anger has been amplified by Eskom's early signalling that it intends to access the carbon market to benefit from the relative improvement of the carbon efficiency of the new coal-fired power station over those it is intended to replace.[3] Climate finance does not necessarily erode domestic institutions nor deliver ineffective specific outcomes in terms of climate management. As in the case of development assistance, strong leadership, robust institutions, innovative design and often plain good luck can, and almost certainly will, provide often inspiring, one-off successes. The early experience of the Amazon Fund is arguably a case in point, where strong social entrepreneurship has succeeded in advancing a fairly radical design that combines private and public players, and blends innovative collaborative governance with the delivery strengths of Brazil's powerful development bank (Zadek *et al.*, 2009). Yet even in this case, the bad habits of 'development assistance' have begun to take root. The most recent assessment, of what was hoped to be an exemplar of new thinking and practice, has raised significant concerns as to its performance and likely future success (Zadek *et al.*, 2010a).

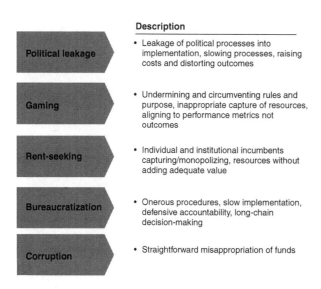

Figure 12.1 Institutional horses of the Apocalypse.

Climate finance tends to reinforce a backward-looking institutional design and practice. In encouraging centralized resource flows, a focus on subsidizing investments rather than a flow of outcomes, and a rent-taking role for the private sector, it unintentionally (one hopes) promotes shortfalls in carbon mitigation and support for climate adaptation. Moreover, and more seriously, it can actively accelerate the deterioration in the public and private institutional environment, thereby damaging nations' capabilities to develop self-managed resilience, adaptability and internal accountability (Zadek and Burgis, 2006). Climate finance might in this sense precipitate a 'curse of carbon' for those countries in receipt of significant public funding, similar in many respects to the well-documented corrupting effects of the 'resource curse', undermining public institutions and distorting the economy.

12.3 From climate finance to financing green growth

Climate finance is the wrong lens through which to understand, let alone design, solutions to the climate challenge. That is not to claim that public funds are not needed to address the climate challenge, nor that wealthier countries should not play a significant role in meeting these costs. Incremental costs are, after all, very real, and the need to support the adaptation of poorer communities is becoming more apparent by the day. Yet, even in this sphere, the climate finance lens has restricted, for example, consideration of innovations in how the private sector can play a profitable role in climate adaptation (Forstater *et al.,* 2009). Also, where there is a role for straightforward public funding, integration into broader development strategies and programmes is more likely to deliver the necessary safeguards and transformation opportunities for vulnerable communities than redlined finance for adaptation. Combating deforestation, on the surface, appears to run counter to this argument, with the relatively successful establishment of REDD+ funds. However, even in this case the jury is out. At COP-16 in Cancun, the REDD+ debates increasingly resembled debates about development assistance, often in an almost Orwellian manner, in focusing on programmatic approaches formulated by businesses, non-governmental organizations (NGOs) and public agencies seeking grant support. Publicly funded projects, some of which, of course, might be effective on their own terms, largely took the place of addressing the core political and policy issues: the need to overcome associated corruption and the imperative to develop scalable enterprise alternatives that are not dependent for their profitability on either an insecure flow of grants or unstable carbon offset markets.

Meaningful alternatives to a climate finance lens cannot merely be conceptually attractive, but need to have the prospect of delivering a different, and better, result on the ground. The starting point for defining an alternative lens and associated approach must be to shift the core end goal, in effect away from addressing climate change with its associated problems, as outlined above. In fact, there is already some evidence that a refocusing is taking place on the ground, far away from the machinations of the climate negotiations. In the USA, most obviously, the language of climate change has been almost completely supplanted by that of energy security. Conversely, China's appetite to use the climate frame has increased, but in many ways only to dilute the obvious fact that it sees the low-carbon economy as its opportunity to take leadership in tomorrow's global economy, beyond its recent experience of dirty and cheap-labour-dependent export competitiveness (Halle and Long, 2010). South Korea, and to a lesser extent Brazil, Mexico and other fast-growing nations, have embraced the rhetoric of 'green growth', declaring it to be the core target zone for future investment and growth. Europe, today's most carbon- and energy-efficient, large developed economy, has similarly understood this economic opportunity, despite the now familiar challenges it faces in translating its potential into concrete advantage.

The refocusing from climate management as 'least-cost mitigation + adaptation' towards economic opportunity is noticeable in a spate of recent reports. Whereas the 'low-carbon growth plans', prepared in effect as pitches for climate finance, focused on the more limiting goal of 'least-cost mitigation + adaptation' (Forstater and Zadek, 2009), the United Nations Environment Programme's (UNEP) recently launched report on green growth, and the European Climate Foundation's 'Europe 2020' report, to name two, focus almost exclusively on investment, jobs and competitiveness. Indeed, the title alone of Project Catalyst's latest paper (Project Catalyst, 2010), launched in Cancun, 'From Climate Finance to Financing Green Growth', similarly signals this refocusing process. Drawing on Project Catalyst's own summarized core message:

> Finance to address 'only' climate is likely to be a moderate proportion of the funds needed and available to pay for the transition of economies onto low carbon trajectories. Reality on the ground is that finance for green growth and development is already coming, and will continue to come in many shapes and forms, from domestic policy measures, reconfigured international development assistance, local banks through to international private equity players. That does not mean that economic opportunities, and associated national self-interest, will always and everywhere exist. And negative impacts of climate change on vulnerable communities will remain a core issue that needs to be addressed with new public money from the international community. But even in such cases, specialized climate finance is so far playing a relatively small, remedial role, and the challenge and opportunity is to leverage what is out there to better effect. That is, to remain within a 'climate finance' paradigm is self-limiting given what needs to happen on the ground
>
> (Project Catalyst, 2010: 45)[4]

Starting with a green growth and development goal is far more than a rhetorical device in that it engages different political and economic actors, and can achieve more effective progress by aligning their plans, interests and leadership. Furthermore, it allows for a more diverse set of financing options to be considered in the light of both the financial opportunities for private actors and delivering economic and development outcomes for public actors. Aligning to a green growth and development agenda also allows for very different enabling institutional configurations, with greater leadership at the national level (rather than the focus being on nations as recipients of international finance), and more private actors in the driving seat, allowing for greater decentralization and competition (which in turn can reduce, for instance, bureaucratization and rent-seeking behaviour).

Renewables provide a case in point. There are no major investments in renewables using dedicated climate finance (i.e. finance with the primary goal of addressing climate change). Instead, significant renewables ramp-up, whether in Germany, Spain and the Canadian province of Ontario in the developed world, or in Brazil and (soon) India, has been associated with industrial opportunities and energy security. The following section focuses on one case in point, the situation of South Africa and the specifics of the South African Renewables Initiative (SARi), which, although still in development, illustrates the potential benefits and associated challenges of the lens shift advocated above.

12.4 South African renewables[5]

South Africa has one of the world's highest levels of carbon intensity per income (GDP) with an economy driven by low-quality coal. The economy is very energy-inefficient and is perceived as being dependent on cheap energy. Its exports are dominated by energy- and carbon-intensive commodities, with exporting industries using about 40 per cent of all electricity generated. Inefficient use of energy is encouraged by electricity tariffs that are significantly less than the full financial cost of coal-fired power generation. Tariff increases, although embraced in Government policies and practices, are unsurprisingly deeply unpopular in domestic and business circles, making rapid change difficult.

Energy security is a major concern for South Africa. Only the current economic recession has delayed increased demand, and economic and social disruptions will arise from inadequate electricity capacity. As a result, the South African Government has considered diverse options for addressing the energy security imperative, including coal, nuclear and renewables. In late 2009, the South African Government initiated an examination, through the Industrial Policy Action Plan, of the relevance of renewables to its industrial strategy, and concluded that the development of renewables was a key economic imperative, independent of direct climate risks or any broader commitment to combat global climate change (SARi, 2010).

South Africa has world-class potential for renewables generation, especially in relation to on-shore wind and solar (Winkler and Marquand, 2009). Although estimates differ, a broad consensus exists that the technical potential for at least 15 per cent of the current grid would be feasible, or about 20 GW. Achieving this level of renewables generation would enable 1.2 billion tons of carbon to be mitigated over the investment's life, and contribute about one-third of South Africa's international commitments under the Copenhagen Accord.

Renewables could support South Africa's medium-term energy security needs; needs that will not conceivably be addressed through other energy sources for a decade or more. Economic disruption costs arising through discontinuities in energy supply do not exist, but were highlighted, in various roundtables held in South Africa, as being dangerously high. Such costs will have been a key rationale for the World Bank's support for the development of Eskom's Medupi Power Station, and the controversy surrounding it exemplifies the policy challenges in balancing energy security, energy prices and subsidies, and international carbon mitigation commitments.

Renewables offer the opportunity to improve value chain localization, and it is estimated in SARi (2010) that 35,000–50,000 jobs could be created (not including regional export potential or positive macro-economic impacts). Renewables could also protect the nation's exports in the face both of the growing carbon sensitivity of international markets and of the likely emergence of both statutory carbon border adjustments and private standards that would otherwise disadvantage South Africa's energy- and carbon-intensive exports (SARi, 2010). Although prospects in this policy area remain highly uncertain, estimates based on the current debate and South Africa's export profile suggest that US$8.5 billion of its current exports would be vulnerable to statutory carbon border tariffs, with still far more being subject to private carbon and energy standards.[6]

South Africa has already established some of the institutional arrangements required to advance renewables. A feed-in tariff has been put in place offering generous tariffs to independent power providers. In practice, however, little progress has occurred in implementation; current renewables generation capacity feeding the grid is insignificant, and the Government has been unwilling either to fast-track projects or to raise its modest targets to realize the country's potential. Investors and technology providers, although enthusiastic in theory, have expressed concerns at numerous practical levels. Private players remain on the sidelines because of perceived weak policy commitment, inadequate institutional arrangements and the associated insecurity concerning the capacity and will of the Government and the state-owned Eskom to deliver on financing and technical pre-conditions for economically viable projects.

Underlying this disappointing lack of progress are the incremental costs of renewables. As with other projects, these are significantly above the full financial cost of coal-fired generation, especially for solar, and are likely to remain so over the next decade, before technology costs are expected to reduce. These incremental costs are well understood by the Government, and recent tariff increases have incorporated the element required to cover these costs up to the current modest target. Beyond this, however, such incremental costs would be too prohibitively high to finance domestically, and this has influenced the Government's unwillingness to increase renewables targets closer to the technical potential.

South Africa faces significant economic challenges by virtue of its location, its low labour productivity (by international standards), the perceived political risk, and institutional weaknesses. It is imperative to address the high and persistent levels of unemployment and inequality through diversification and improved international competitiveness. Although the South African Government is engaging with climate change, in this context, as a global challenge, it takes second place, at best, to domestic economic imperatives.

Addressing this economic imperative, the South African Government's analysis of the role of renewables from an industrial policy perspective concluded that what was required was a radical change in the level of renewables, and an accelerated, credible timetable for achieving this. Localizing the value chain requires a critical mass of renewables purchases to be assured at an acceptable price, which in turn will allow for localization criteria to be introduced to the power and technology providers. Similarly, protecting the nation's exports by greening their power source requires far more renewables in the mix, as does any effective strategy to use renewables to meet part of the short- to medium-term energy supply gap.

Financing this critical mass has from the outset been identified as the key challenge (Zadek *et al.*, 2010b). In straightforward commercial terms, building 20 GW or more of renewables in South Africa, based on a mix of on-shore wind and solar, will cost in the order of US$55–60 billion. Put differently, generating electricity from this installed capacity of renewables will cost approximately US$9 billion more, over the period to 2025, than it will (at full financial cost) to generate the same power from coal-fired stations.[7]

Overcoming the financing challenge is therefore key to unlocking the critical mass in renewables. Accordingly, the South African Government has set out to establish a basis for securing the financing required to catalyze the critical mass of renewables needed to deliver the economic and broader social benefits, with a viable and acceptable domestic burden to the South African economy, citizens and public budgets. Core to the framework governing the search and design of such a financing mechanism has been the assumption that it is unlikely that significant climate finance, funds with the prime purpose of addressing the climate challenge, will be available. At the same time, political considerations dictate equally that any solution proposed should not impose any significant burden on the domestic taxpayer or the South African economy.

Climate finance, in a nutshell, will not form the core foundation of any proposed financing mechanism. Planning has progressed considerably, but not to a definitive design proposal, and not to the point of being formally adopted by the South African Government. However, the design-in-progress already offers useful insights that broadly support this chapter's underlying thesis.

The incremental costs could be financed through a blend of the following sources of finance (Figure 12.2): low-cost project finance, essentially sub-commercial debt, drawn from multilateral and bilateral development, and export and investment promotion institutions that would, alongside political risk and currency hedges, bring down the financing gap to 2025 by over 30 per cent to about US$6.4 billion. The residual gap could be financed in a number of ways. One possible approach is to develop a shared burden model between South Africa and international actors (Figure 12.3). One financing scenario under this approach is for the domestic contribution, as far as possible, to be designed to be fiscally

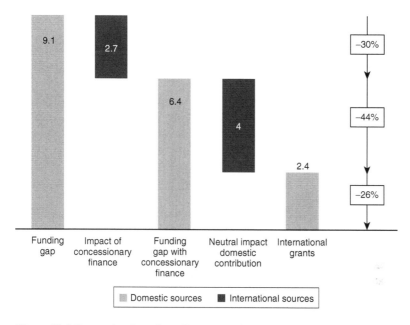

Figure 12.2 Innovative financing of incremental costs.

neutral, with public sector contributions being set at a level commensurate with predicted inflows of tax revenues associated with the increased investment, and economically neutral, which would involve a green purchase obligation for energy-intensive exporters set to be commensurate with the gains that they might thereby make in international markets.

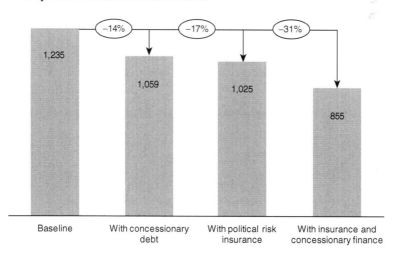

Figure 12.3 Reducing financing costs.

Under this scenario, residual financing requirements could fall to US$2.4 million, just 26 per cent of the original level. This is a comparatively small sum to be financed over the 15-year period to 2025. If financed through international public transfer, in effect an element of climate finance, the implied cost will be about US$5 per ton of carbon. Alternatively, such international support would be a highly efficient use of public funds from an economic development perspective, as it would also be if funded bilaterally from countries co-benefiting from the arising industrial development opportunities (Figure 12.4, Table 12.1).

SARi is currently a policy design option under consideration by the South African Government and potential international partners. There are, however, many barriers to advancing such an ambitious initiative to implementation. There are significant technology-related risks, especially in relatively untested areas such as concentrated solar, which in turn create energy-pricing challenges and also raise doubts as to the contribution that renewables can make in practice to the nation's energy security. The energy sector's institutional configuration has also been the subject of much debate. Eskom, for example, is a state-owned monopoly dominating the electricity sector in South Africa; it has a weak balance sheet, and is anything but flexible in its approach to change. Its history is rooted in coal, and its institutional imagination is focused on highly centralized energy options, with no experience of dealing with independent power providers.

Refocusing from climate and energy to economics thus makes a great deal of sense, but is a challenge in practice. The main challenge is to achieve critical mass to secure the potential economic benefits. Without a commitment to scale, localization of parts of the global value chain of renewables will not be possible;

- **Employment:** 35,000–50,000 new jobs created
- **Decarbonization of South African exports:** greenhouse gas intensity of exports reduced by 35% by 2020

- **Private investment:** directly $55bn–$60bn in renewables capacity by 2020–2025, with a public : private leverage of 1:6
- **International public sources** finance grant of US$171–855m a year, or US$2.4–6.4bn (discounted) to 2025 (maximum $5.5 per ton), plus $23bn of concessional debt
- **Total incremental cost** per carbon ton mitigated of US$7.85 (discounted) or $14.85 (undiscounted)
- **South Africa finances incremental costs** to a maximum of US$4.0bn to 2025

- **Renewables generation:** 20GW by for 15% grid generation by 2020, or 23GW for 15% by 2025
- **Carbon mitigated:** 1.2bn t by 2045 or 60 Mt per annum at full ramp-up
- **Reduction from Business as Usual:** 1.5% below energy sector BAU by 2020 (22% of South Africa's target (Copenhagen Accord)).

Figure 12.4 South African renewables initiative scorecard.

Table 12.1 South African renewables initiative: co-benefits framework

Collaborator	Benefits
South African Government	The gross fiscal cost of US$3.1 billion delivers an estimated 40,000 full-time equivalent jobs, excluding any arising through second-order export opportunities and economic benefits associated with increased energy security and export protection. Moreover, the net fiscal cost is far less than the gross costs taking into account additional tax revenues, estimated at US$2.9 billion over the same period.
South African business	Economic opportunities associated with renewables development will be open to large and small South African businesses. Mitigating risks of blackouts is core to the interests of every business, and so the upside energy security benefits count for a lot. Beyond this, the principal financial impact is on energy-intensive exporters, and in return they receive a credible, certified reduction in their carbon intensity of up to 39% by 2025, enabling them to extract real value from increased costs in international markets.
Business investors	The interest of technology and finance providers and those in the business of generation are not identical, but have some core common elements. Key would be adequate, state-guaranteed prices for renewables, together with predictable and significant growth in the overall renewables mix, both of which would be provided in this approach, reinforced by the involvement of international public partners.
International cooperation partners	Concessionary finance might in part come from multilateral sources, but in the main would be expected to come from bilateral public sources tasked at least in part to advance the economic interests of their domestic business communities. The most obvious countries that fit this would be Germany, the USA and possibly Denmark (for wind), and in addition major emerging exporters such as China and South Korea.
Climate partners	The element of grant channelled through the feed-in tariff might well come from the same governments acting as promoters of industrial joint venture interests, as the grant would in effect benefit the supply-side businesses selling renewables power into the grid. However, even as a straight 'climate' play, the economics of the initiative do not make any use of carbon markets, making the carbon cost per ton equivalent attractive for developed-country governments with mitigation commitments that require in part the financing of off-shore mitigation. Indeed, cash-strapped grant providers might choose to strike a deal, allowing them to cash-in some portion of the 1.2 Mt of carbon emitted over the period.

the economic upsides will be unavailable; the political interest in renewables will not be forthcoming; the institutional transformations required to attract investment will not be made; the risk premiums will be too high; and South Africa will not be able to or wish to finance renewables. The South African Government must therefore set a far higher target for renewables, which in turn requires them to be confident that they can finance the incremental cost without an unacceptable domestic burden (not just for the first tranche, but for the whole target). Such confidence will make the economic potential realizable, secure political support, and enable the institutional changes required to attract private and international public investment at a reasonable cost, making the underlying approach advocated here fundable.

Achieving this is certainly possible, and SARi has already progressed a considerable way in the right direction. However, the players involved are not accustomed to such demanding design conditions. In particular, development finance institutions, such as private investors, are accustomed to a project-by-project approach, allowing for investment-specific assessments of risk-adjusted returns. What is needed, however, is confidence from the outset that the broader targets, spread over multiple investments over a decade-and-a-half (if not more), can and will be achieved. In the case of China, and now India through its 'solar mission' initiative, there is already sufficient confidence that ambitious targets will be achieved, largely because incremental costs will be funded through domestic public financing. Such confidence is also readily apparent in the Canadian province of Ontario, with its large-scale commitment to renewables development and the associated localization of production and services by Samsung. Although Morocco's hugely ambitious renewables programme requires international support, the prospects of such energy being made available to the European community makes high-level political commitment and associated large-scale financing far easier to envisage and, indeed, secure.

12.5 Strategic adaptation

'Adaptation' in a climate context has been misconceived in that it requires 'mitigation' to be understood as a class of action and associated investment, in pursuit of reduced emissions, and implying the need for climate finance. What is needed, rather, is a lens focused on the need for strategic adaptation imperatives and opportunities of the country or community in question. 'Adaptation', in this way, loses the connotation of being about helping victims of climate change, and becomes the organizing principle around which societies mobilize their assets in support of their own development. Furthermore, in discarding the distinction between mitigation and the traditional view of adaptation as goals, operational initiatives or financing targets, it becomes easier to frame investments focused on the creation of value rather than on the mitigation of risk and the consequences of failure.

Repositioning the analytic and design lens from climate finance towards strategic adaptation, underpinned by economic growth and development, can provide insights that are both conceptual and analytic, and inform the design of financing mechanisms. The case of South Africa, albeit a work-in-progress, illustrates the practical consequences and potential benefits of such a reset and refocus. Refocusing on strategic adaptation pathways to a global, low-carbon economy involves a different mindset in addressing the climate challenge. Crucially, just as the currency is economic development, not climate, the unit of ambition and the engine of action is national, rather than the international community and associated agreements and financing commitments and mechanisms. It is national (and, perhaps in some cases, sub-national and regional) leadership and ambition that will drive progress. This does not mean that there is no role for international cooperation; quite the reverse. Political alignment, industrial joint ventures and the self-interested provision of cross-border financing can play a key role in enabling and indeed catalyzing ambitious national initiatives. Concerns that such an approach will deliver too little, too late, from a climate perspective are misconceived. Far from it – such approaches are aligned exactly to those domestic political economies that in practice make things happen. Once a small number come to be of visible national benefit, they will be emulated rapidly and improvements made.

Acknowledgements

This chapter has benefited from the work and comments of Saliem Fakir, Maya Forstater, Joerg Haas, Jon Kornik and Edwin Ritchkin, as well as the many people associated with Project Catalyst, especially Andreas Merkl and Jeremy Oppenheim. Financial support for the underlying research and engagement has been generously provided by Climate Works Foundation, the Department for International Development of the UK Government, and the European Climate Foundation. Errors and omissions are of course the sole responsibility of the author.

Notes

1 George Soros, reflecting in China Daily on the modest advances made in Cancun, has pointed out, alongside others, that even the modest Fast-Start finance of US$30 billion committed by developed countries in Copenhagen in December 2009 has not proved to be additional to funds already allocated as international transfers under existing programmes.
2 See www.globalwitness.org/media_library_detail.php/983/en/report
3 On a different tack, billionaire financier, George Soros, stepped in with a proposed intermediary financing mechanism to handle funding to combat Indonesian deforestation when it became clear that the World Bank's proposal to manage the funds would involve it taking a significant portion as a management fee.
4 Italics added for emphasis.
5 This sections draws extensively from SARi (2010).
6 Estimates made by the International Institute of Sustainable Development in an unpublished commissioned report for the South African Renewables Initiative.
7 Or about US$1.3 billion annually discounted at 6 per cent.

References

Collier, P., 2009, *The Plundered Planet: How to Reconcile Prosperity with Nature*, Allen Lane, London.
Easterly, W., 2007, *The White Man's Burden: Why the West's Efforts to Aid the Rest Have Done So Much Ill And So Little Good*, Oxford University Press, Oxford.

Forstater, M., Zadek, S., 2009, *Low Carbon Growth Plans: Assessing Current Practice*, European Climate Foundation and Project Catalyst, London.

Forstater, M., Huq, S., Zadek, S., 2009, *Business of Adaptation,* AccountAbility, London.

Halle, M., Long, G. (eds), 2010, *Elements of a Sustainable Trade Strategy for China*, International Institute for Sustainable Development, Geneva.

Koestler, A., 1949, *The God that Failed, Colombia University Press*, Washington, DC.

Litovsky, A., McGillivray, A., Zadek, S., 2007, Development as Accountability, Account-Ability, London.

Moyo, D., 2009, *Dead Aid: Why Aid is Not Working and How There is Another Way for Africa*, Penguin, London.

Project Catalyst, 2010, *From Climate Finance to Financing Green Growth*, Project Catalyst Briefing Paper, Brussels.

SARi, 2010, *Unlocking South Africa's Green Growth Potential, the South African Renewables Initiative*, Department of Trade and Industry, Government of Republic of South Africa, Pretoria.

United Nations, 2010, *Report of the Secretary-General's High-Level Advisory Group on Climate Change Financing*, United Nations, New York.

WEF, 2010, *Scaling Up Low Carbon Infrastructure Investment in Developing Countries: the Critical Mass Initiative*, World Economic Forum, Cologny, Geneva.

Winkler, H., Marquand, A., 2009, 'Changing development paths: from an energy-intensive to low-carbon economy in South Africa', *Climate & Development* 1(1), 47–65.

Zadek, S., 2009, *Institutional Arrangements for Advancing Low Carbon Growth and Development*, Project Catalyst, London.

Zadek, S., Burgis, T., 2006, *Reinventing Accountability for the 21st Century*, Account-Ability, London.

Zadek, S., Forstater, M., Polacow, F., Boffino, J., 2009, *Radical Simplicity in Designing National Climate Institutions: Lessons from the Amazon Fund*, AccountAbility, London.

Zadek, S., Forstater, M., Polacow, F., 2010a, *The Amazon Fund: Radical Simplicity and Bold Ambition – Insights for Building National Institutions for Low Carbon Development*, Avina Foundation, Sao Paolo.

Zadek, S., Ritchkin, E., Fakir, S., Forstater, M., 2010b, *The South African Renewables Initiative: Advancing South Africa's Low Carbon Industrial and Economic Strategy*, Department of Trade and Industry, Government of the Republic of South Africa, Pretoria.

13 Recent developments related to international climate change finance

Erik Haites and Preety Bhandari

13.1 Introduction

The genesis of the agreements on climate finance over the last few years is the Stern review on the economics of climate change (2006), which highlighted that the costs of stabilising climate are high but manageable. If the global community could act collectively the costs of reducing emissions to avoid worst impacts could be restricted to 1 per cent of global GDP per year by 2050 while failure could lead to a loss of 5 to 20 per cent of global GDP per year. The Stern review also examined the locus of action and asserted that even if developed countries took on responsibilities for absolute cuts in emissions of 60–80 per cent by 2050, developing countries would need to take significant action too. However, it asserted that developing countries need to be supported to bear the costs of action. Climate finance needs to be transformed and increased to match the scale of flows required.

The Stern review was followed by an analysis of investment and financial flows to address climate change by the United Nations Framework Convention on Climate Change (UNFCCC 2007), which showed that mitigation measures needed to return global GHG emissions to 2005 levels in 2030 required an increase in global investment and financial flows of US$200–210 billion in 2030. For adaptation, the study estimated that the additional investment and financial flows needed in 2030 would amount to several tens of billions of United States dollars. The study also noted that funding available under the Convention primarily relied upon voluntary contributions which might prove to be inconsequential compared to the needs. Finally, it highlighted the role of private sector investment given its predominance in global investment and financial flows.

The discourse on climate finance, its urgency to spur action, the scale and likely sources of funding and the role of different actors – state, private, carbon markets, IFIs – was initiated by these two seminal pieces of work. The Bali Action Plan, agreed in December 2007, launched a two-year negotiating process covering, *inter alia*, enhanced provision of financial resources and investment to support mitigation and adaptation in developing countries. Two years later the negotiations produced the Copenhagen Accord, which although widely supported, was not adopted by the Conference of the Parties (COP) to the UNFCCC.

This chapter reviews the commitments related to international climate change finance that are the core of the Copenhagen Accord. Then it tracks their integration into the UNFCCC process by COP 16 (Cancun, 2010) and progress toward implementation by COP 17 (Durban, 2011). In particular it discusses fast-start finance, the creation of the Green Climate Fund and the establishment of a Standing Committee to advise the COP on issues related to climate finance.

13.2 The Copenhagen accord

After two years of negotiations under the ambit of the Bali Action Plan agreed at COP 13, COP 15 was expected to adopt a new international agreement to address climate change in Copenhagen in December 2009. The new agreement was expected to cover the five building blocks of the Bali Action Plan:[1]

- a shared vision for long-term cooperative action, including a long-term global goal for emission reductions;
- enhanced action on mitigation of climate change by all countries;
- enhanced action on adaptation;
- enhanced action on technology development and transfer to support action on mitigation and adaptation;
- enhanced action on the provision of financial resources and investment to support action on mitigation and adaptation and technology cooperation.

The new agreement, after ratification by a sufficient number of countries, was expected to take effect in 2013 upon conclusion of the 2008–2012 emissions limitation commitments for developed countries in the Kyoto Protocol.

Agreement on a new climate deal could not be sealed.

Rather, President Obama and a small number of other heads of government negotiated the Copenhagen Accord.[2] The Copenhagen Accord was taken note of, but not adopted by, the Conference of the Parties, so it has no official status under the UNFCCC (UNFCCC 2009). However, over 140 countries subsequently "associated" themselves with the Accord, so has substantial international support.

The Copenhagen Accord reflects a different approach to national emissions limitation commitments than the Kyoto Protocol. The Kyoto Protocol incorporates internationally negotiated national emissions limitation commitments with several trading mechanisms (Clean Development Mechanism, Joint Implementation and international emissions trading) to reduce compliance costs and international review of compliance and penalties for non-compliance.[3] The Copenhagen Accord establishes a "pledge and review" system of nationally proposed commitments, with possible co-existence of national and international trading mechanisms, and international review of performance but no penalties for non-attainment.

In a pledge and review architecture international climate finance plays a larger role in supporting mitigation measures in developing countries due to the diminished role of international trading mechanisms. The Copenhagen Accord, accordingly, includes several commitments related to international climate change finance.

Copenhagen accord: commitments on climate finance

- A collective commitment by developed countries to provide new and additional resources, including forestry and investments through international institutions, approaching US$30 billion for the period 2010–2012 with balanced allocation between adaptation and mitigation with adaptation funding to be prioritized for the most vulnerable developing countries, such as the least developed countries, small island developing States and Africa;
- In the context of meaningful mitigation actions and transparency on implementation, a commitment by developed countries to a goal of mobilizing jointly US$100 billion dollars a year by 2020 to address the needs of developing countries from a wide variety of sources, public and private, bilateral and multilateral, including alternative sources of finance;
- Establishment of a High Level Panel under the guidance of and accountable to the Conference of the Parties to study the contribution of the potential sources of revenue, including alternative sources of finance, towards meeting this goal;
- Establishment of a Copenhagen Green Climate Fund as an operating entity of the financial mechanism of the Convention to support projects, programme, policies and other activities in developing countries related to mitigation including REDD-plus, adaptation, capacity-building, technology development and transfer; and
- Delivery of the new multilateral funding for adaptation through effective and efficient fund arrangements, with a governance structure providing for equal representation of developed and developing countries with a significant portion flowing through the Copenhagen Green Climate Fund.

13.3 Fast-start finance

Early in 2010 developed countries began announcing their contributions to the US$30 billion of "fast-start" finance. The commitments were tracked by several organizations including the UNFCCC, Netherlands government, Bloomberg New Energy Finance, Heinrich Böll Foundation North America, Project Catalyst, and World Resources Institute.[4] The sum of the announced pledges is about US$ 30 billion.[5] By July 2011 about US$13.4 billion had been requested or committed by developed countries and of this US$8.5 billion allocated to funds or projects.[6]

Non-governmental organizations questioned whether some of the pledges should count toward the commitment.[7] For example, should the US$5 billion of private funds included in Japan's commitment count? Should loans, approximately one-third of the pledges, be measured at face value or on a "grant-equivalent" basis?[8] Expressing the loans on a grant-equivalent basis reduces the pledged amount by about US$3 billion.[9]

The announced pledges also triggered questions as to whether they were "new and additional" as promised.[10] There is no agreed way to assess whether financial resources are "new and additional". Some countries explain the basis on which they consider their pledge to be "new and additional" while others do not. Researchers have proposed various criteria, which when applied to the pledges, indicate that proportions ranging from virtually none to almost all are new and additional.[11]

The allocation of funds to mitigation and adaptation also has been a matter of some interest, especially to vulnerable developing countries. Historically, over 80 per cent of climate funding has been directed to mitigation (including REDD).[12] The fast-start commitment promised balanced funding for mitigation and adaptation. Data on commitments through June 2011 indicate that 21 per cent has been directed to adaptation.[13]

Most of the allocated funds (51 per cent) are being disbursed bilaterally by the contributing country.[14] Of the money being disbursed through multilateral channels (41 per cent), most is going Climate Investment Funds managed by the World Bank and the regional development banks. Very little of the total is going through the financial mechanism of the UNFCCC operated by the Global Environment Facility.

13.4   UN secretary-general's high-level advisory group of the on climate change financing

In February 2010 Secretary General Ban Ki-moon announced the establishment of a High Level Advisory Group on Climate Change Financing (AGF). Although it was not accountable to or under the guidance of the Conference of the Parties, the mandate of the AGF was essentially identical to that of the High Level Panel promised in the Copenhagen Accord.

Specifically, the AGF was tasked with developing practical proposals on how to significantly scale-up long-term financing for mitigation and adaptation in developing countries from various public and private sources with a particular focus on the need for new and innovative long-term sources of finance.

The report of the AGF, released in November 2010, concludes that it is challenging but feasible to reach the goal of mobilising US$100 billion annually for climate actions in developing countries by 2020 (see Chapter 7).[15]

Based on a carbon price of US$20–25 per ton of CO_2 equivalent, the AGF estimated the revenue potential in 2020 for various sources of climate finance (see Chapter 7, Table 7.1). No single source generates US$100 billion per year, so the AGF considered "bundles" of mutually supportive and internally consistent sources to meet the revenue target. A bundle built around the principle of carbon efficiency, for example, would generate revenues through carbon markets and taxing emissions thus helping to reduce emissions as well (see Chapter 7, Figure 7.1).

The AGF noted that several of the sources examined could be operational relatively quickly while others need more time to be implemented. Some of the sources, such as carbon markets and private finance, are better suited to mitigation leaving adaptation more reliant on public sources.

13.5 COP 16 Cancun: the watershed

The Copenhagen Accord, not formally adopted by the UNFCCC but supported by a large number developed and developing countries, was a sensitive subject for COP 16 at Cancun in November 2010. Some of the Accord's commitments relating to climate finance were brought into the UNFCCC structure while others remained separate.

Fast-start finance remained separate. Developed countries noted that the commitment was independent of the UNFCCC and that it was already being implemented. Many developed countries provided reports on progress they had made in implementing their commitments. The COP decision simply recognized the commitment and invited developed countries to submit reports on implementation to the secretariat for compilation into an annual report.[16]

The COP also noted the AGF report but accorded it no official status in the UNFCCC process.[17]

The goal of jointly mobilizing US$100 billion per year by 2020 was accorded UNFCCC status.[18] The COP decided that scaled-up, new and additional, predictable and adequate funding was needed for developing countries. In that context, it "recognized" the Copenhagen Accord commitment by developed countries to a goal of mobilizing jointly US$100 billion per year by 2020 to address the needs of developing countries. Acknowledgment that funds provided to developing countries may come from a wide variety of sources, public and private, bilateral and multilateral, including alternative sources, is based on the Bali Action Plan rather than the Copenhagen Accord.

COP 16 established a Green Climate Fund, to be designated as an operating entity of the financial mechanism of the Convention with a 24 member board with equal representation from developing and developed countries consistent with the Copenhagen Accord.[19] The decision also confirmed the Accord's commitment that a significant share of new multilateral funding for adaptation should flow through the Green Climate Fund.[20]

To design the Green Climate Fund, the COP 16 decision established a 40 member Transitional Committee with a mandate to develop operational documents for consideration by COP 17 that address, *inter alia*:[21]

- the legal and institutional arrangements for the establishment and operationalization of the Green Climate Fund;
- the rules of procedure of the Board and other governance issues related to the Board;
- methods to manage large financial resources from a number of sources and deliver them through a variety of financial instruments, funding windows and

access modalities, including direct access, with the objective of achieving balanced allocation between adaptation and mitigation;

- the financial instruments that the Fund can use to achieve its priorities;
- methods to enhance complementarity between the Fund's activities and those of other bilateral, regional and multilateral funding mechanisms and institutions;
- the role of the secretariat and the procedure for selecting and/or establishing the secretariat;
- a mechanism to ensure periodic independent evaluation of the Fund's performance;
- mechanisms to ensure financial accountability and to evaluate the performance of activities supported by the Fund, to ensure the application of environmental and social safeguards, as well as internationally accepted fiduciary standards and sound financial management to the Fund's activities;
- mechanisms to ensure appropriate expert and technical advice, including from relevant thematic bodies established under the Convention;
- mechanisms to ensure stakeholder input and participation.

Finally, COP 16 decided to establish a Standing Committee to assist the Conference of the Parties in exercising its functions with respect to the financial mechanism of the Convention in terms of improving coherence and coordination in the delivery of climate change financing, rationalization of the financial mechanism, mobilization of financial resources and measurement, reporting and verification of support provided to developing countries.[22] The composition of the Standing Committee and further definition of its role and functions were deferred to COP 17. Although the name is different, the role of the Standing Committee is similar to that of the High Level Panel mentioned in the Copenhagen Accord.

Some developed countries were reluctant to establish a new Committee to deal with climate finance, arguing that existing processes for review of the financial mechanism of the UNFCCC could discharge the functions being accorded to the Standing Committee. However, developing countries felt that an expert body is needed to assess the needs of developing countries for climate finance and to provide an overview of funding flows through channels inside and outside the Convention (especially the latter) to assist the Conference of the Parties to take informed decisions.

13.6 G20 report

G20 Finance Ministers requested the World Bank Group, in partnership with the IMF, the OECD and the Regional Development Banks, to explore options for scaled up finance for climate change adaptation and mitigation in developing countries building upon and extending the work of the High Level Advisory Group on Climate Finance (AGF) (see Chapter 8).[23]

The report notes that there is no internationally agreed definition of climate finance.

The report recommends the removal of subsidies for fossil-fuel use in Annex II countries;[24] implementation of a comprehensive carbon charge or emissions trading with full auctioning of allowances in Annex II countries; a global carbon charge or emissions trading with full auctioning of allowances for international aviation and maritime bunker fuels; expanded carbon offset markets, such as the Clean Development Mechanism; a modest package of public sources, multilateral development bank flows and carbon offset flows to leverage climate-related private flows; and increased capital contributions to multilateral development banks.

The report notes that some sources can be implemented more quickly than others and that some are better suited to supporting mitigation measures.

13.7 Transitional committee

The Transitional Committee commenced its work in 2011 and clustered its work on the governing instrument for the Green Climate Fund (GCF) into four streams:

- scope, guiding principles and cross-cutting issues;
- governance and institutional arrangements;
- operational modalities;
- monitoring and evaluation.

This is reflected in the governing instrument prepared by the Committee. The instrument was not supported by all members of the Transitional Committee.

The Transitional Committee recommended to COP 17 that it approve the governing instrument of the GCF, invite regional groups and constituencies to nominate their Board members, request Parties to submit expressions of interest to host the GCF, invite voluntary contributions for the start-up of the GCF, and establish an interim secretariat support to the Board until the independent secretariat of the GCF is fully operational.

The governing instrument incorporates some features that hitherto have not been available through the financial mechanism of the UNFCCC, including different financing modalities (loans, grants, guarantees), a private sector facility to leverage private funding, and direct access to funding through national implementing agencies. The instrument strikes a delicate balance between the independence of the Board of the GCF and the guiding role of the COP but leaves the exact nature of the relationship to be defined.[25]

13.8 COP 17 Durban

COP 17, held in Durban in November 2011, finalized the institutional arrangements for climate finance under the UNFCCC. A decision to make the Green Climate Fund operational was adopted and the Standing Committee was established. But this was accomplished only after long, intense negotiations. Negotiations on the Green Climate Fund decision were particularly difficult because the governing instrument was not supported by all members of the Transitional Committee.

The decision on the Green Climate Fund approves the governing instrument prepared by the Transitional Committee, invites constituencies to nominate Board members, requests the Board to operationalize the Fund in an expedited manner, sets out a process to select the location for the Fund, outlines the arrangements for the interim secretariat, defines the process for selecting the trustee, specifies the locations of the first two board meetings, and solicits contributions to the Fund.[26]

A compilation of the information developed countries provided to the secretariat on their fast start finance commitments during 2010 had been prepared. Some developing countries expressed displeasure at how funds had been allocated (see section 13.3). Developed countries repeated that fast-start finance was part of the Copenhagen Accord and not subject to the UNFCCC. In the end, the COP decision welcomes the finance and the information provided and urges developed countries to enhance the transparency of their reporting.[27]

The decision defined the composition and functions of the Standing Committee.[28] The Committee will have ten members from developed countries and ten members from developing countries with defined regional representation. The functions of the Committee include:

- organizing a forum for communication and continued exchange of information among bodies and entities dealing with climate change finance to promote linkages and coherence;
- providing to the Conference of the Parties draft guidance for the operating entities of the financial mechanism of the Convention, with a view to improving the consistency and practicality of such guidance;
- making recommendations on how to improve the coherence, effectiveness and efficiency of the operating entities of the financial mechanism;
- providing expert input, including through independent reviews and assessments, into the preparation and conduct of the periodic reviews of the financial mechanism by the Conference of the Parties;
- preparing a biennial overview and assessment of climate finance.

During 2012 the Standing Committee is expected to prepare a work programme for approval by COP 18.

COP 17 also approved a work programme on long-term finance in 2012, including workshops, under the direction of two co-chairs.[29] The work programme will analyze options for the mobilization of resources from a wide variety of sources and relevant analytical work on climate-related financing needs of developing countries. The analysis will draw upon relevant reports including that of the High-level Advisory Group on Climate Financing (AGF) and the report on mobilizing climate finance for the G20. The co-chairs will prepare a report on the workshops for consideration by COP 18.

Although the scope of the work programme is consistent with the functions of the Standing Committee, it was established as a separate process. The work programme, and the Standing Committee's ability to draw upon all relevant material, provide a mechanism to formally bring information from non-UNFCCC sources, such as the AGF and G20 reports, into the UNFCCC.

13.9 Epilogue

A new institutional architecture for international climate finance under the UNFCCC has been agreed. Both the Green Climate Fund and the Standing Committee should become operational in 2013. How will this change the landscape of international climate finance?

The existing bilateral and multilateral funding channels outside the UNFCCC will continue. If additional funds are provided for climate change, more institutions may be created. The Standing Committee's mandate to organize a forum for exchange of information among the bodies and entities dealing with climate change finance may improve coherence and efficiency. But each body/entity is independent so cooperation must be voluntary and be perceived by each participant to be in its own interest.

One more fund added to the numerous bilateral and multilateral funding channels that already exist will not increase the complexity of the system noticeably. The Standing Committee's mandate to recommend improvements to the coherence, effectiveness and efficiency of the operating entities of the financial mechanism could, in principle, lead to closure or consolidation of the Special Climate Change Fund and Least Developed Countries Fund, and possibly even the Adaptation Fund. This would not simplify the existing system noticeably.

The fate of the Climate Investment Funds also hangs in balance. The sunset clause indicates that each fund will conclude its operations once a new financial architecture is effective.[30] However, there are suggestions that it could act as a bridging fund till the Board of the GCF designs a business model for the GCF that is robust enough to attract funding. There have been some suggestions of folding in the constituent funds of CIFs into the GCF, which could have wider ramifications for the business model and sub-governance structures of GCF.

The Green Climate Fund could be quite small (about US$1 billion of disbursements per year[31]) if it is funded solely through contributions from developed countries. Those countries all have their own bilateral institutions so each multilateral institution competes for funds with the bilateral institution and other multilateral organizations. If most new funding for adaptation is bilateral, a small Green Climate Fund could, as promised, still account for a substantial share of the multilateral funding.

A large Green Climate Fund (over US$50 billion per year[32]) would have a significant impact on international climate finance. It would be the largest single fund by a substantial margin. It could adjust its funding allocation to complement that of other channels, so its policies would influence the overall pattern of climate finance. A large Green Climate Fund is more likely if its resources come from dedicated sources of international funding, such as revenue from the regulation of international aviation and shipping emissions. Further, how the Fund engages and leverages the private sector could also determine its scale of operations.

After some delays, the members of the Board of the GCF were appointed and the first meeting was held in Switzerland on August 23–25, 2012 with a second meeting in Korea scheduled in October. The first two meetings will be devoted mainly to procedural matters including selection of the co-chairs, procedures for adopting Board decisions in the absence of consensus, the role of alternate members, adoption of a work plan, process for recruitment of an Executive Director, and the process for selection of the host country for the Fund.[33]

Two important tasks will need to be addressed in time for consideration by COP 18 at Doha in November 2012. The first is the Fund's relationship with the COP. Those arrangements need to be consistent with the mandate of the Durban GCF decision to ensure that the Fund is accountable to and functions under the guidance of the COP (UNFCCC 2011b). The second is to recommend a host country for the Fund; Germany, Switzerland, Republic of Korea, Mexico, Namibia, and Poland have expressed interest in hosting the GCF.

At present there are great expectations that the GCF meets the aspiration of being a Fund that will "promote the paradigm shift towards low emission and climate resilient development pathways" and "channel new, additional, adequate, predictable financial resources to developing countries and will catalyse finance, both public and private and at the international and national levels" being "scalable and flexible". In essence GCF is likely to engender transformations at an ambitious scale that address climate change in a comprehensive and balanced manner, a gigantic task that the 24 members of its Board have to undertake.

Notes

1 UNFCCC (2007), Bali Action Plan.
2 More heads of government attended COP 15 than any meeting on any issue before or since.
3 Decision 24/CP.7, section XV, paragraph 5 specifies that the consequences for excess emissions by an Annex I party include deduction of 1.3 times the excess emissions from the Party's assigned amount for the second commitment period.
4 See for example, http://unfccc.int/cooperation_support/financial_mechanism/fast_start_finance/items/5646.php and http://pdf.wri.org/climate_finance_pledges_2011-11-18.pdf
5 Fallasch and De Marez (2010) estimates the total at US$31.2 billion; WRI (2010) estimates the total at over US$31 billion; Project Catalyst (2010) p. 13, estimates the amount at approximately US$28 billion; Bloomberg New Energy Finance (2011) estimates the amount pledged at US$27.3 billion.
6 Brown *et al.* (2011).
7 Roberts *et al.* (2010); Schalatek *et al.* (2010).
8 Project Catalyst (2010), p. 14.
9 WRI (2010).
10 Fallasch and De Marez, 2010; Bloomberg New Energy Finance (2011).
11 Brown *et al.* (2010); Stadelmann *et al.* (2010).
12 Project Catalyst (2010), p. 17.

13 Brown *et al.*, (2011).
14 Brown *et al.* (2011).
15 AGF (2010).
16 UNFCCC (2010), paragraphs 95 and 96.
17 UNFCCC (2010), paragraph 101.
18 UNFCCC (2010), paragraphs 97 through 99.
19 UNFCCC (2010), paragraphs 102 through 108.
20 UNFCCC (2010), paragraph 100.
21 UNFCCC (2010), paragraphs 109 through 111.
22 UNFCCC(2010), paragraph 112.
23 World Bank *et al.* (2011).
24 The member countries of the OECD as of 1992 listed in Annex II of the UNFCCC that agreed to provide financial support for climate mitigation and adaptation actions in developing countries.
25 UNFCCC (2011b), Annex II.A, paragraph 6.
26 UNFCCC, (2011b).
27 UNFCCC, (2011a), paragraph 127.
28 UNFCCC, (2011a), paragraphs 115 to 120.
29 UNFCCC, (2011a), paragraphs 121 to 126.
30 Climate Investment Funds, 2011. The Governance Framework contains the following sunset clause. "Recognizing that the establishment of the CTF is not to prejudice the on-going UNFCCC deliberations regarding the future of the climate change regime, including its financial architecture, the CTF will take necessary steps to conclude its operations once a new financial architecture is effective. The Trustee will not enter into any new agreement with contributors for contributions to the CTF once the agreement providing for the new financial architecture is effective. The CTF Trust Fund Committee will decide the date on which it will cease making allocations from the outstanding balance of the CTF."
31 By way of comparison, the Global Environment Facility disburses about US$0.5 billion per year.
32 By way of comparison, the World Bank currently disburses about US$40 billion per year.
33 Schalatek (2012) notes that the GCF decision (UNFCCC, 2011b) and the governing instrument specify more than fifty distinct tasks for the Board.

Bibliography

Bloomberg New Energy Finance, 2011. *Have developed nations broken their promise on $30bn 'fast-start' finance?*, Bloomberg New Energy Finance.

Brown, J., N. Bird, and L. Schalatek, 2010. *Climate finance additionality: emerging definitions and their implications*, Heinrich Böll Foundation North America.

Brown, J., M. Stadelmann, and L. Hornlein, 2011. *Fast-start-finance to address climate change: what we know at the mid point*, Overseas Development Institute, London.

Climate Investment Funds, 2011. *Governance Framework for the Clean Technology Fund*, Adopted November 2008 and amended December 2011. Available at: http://www.climateinvestmentfunds.org/cif/sites/climateinvestmentfunds.org/files/CTF%20Governance%20Framework-FINAL.pdf

Fallasch, F., and L. De Marez, 2010. *New and Additional? An assessment of fast-start finance commitments of the Copenhagen Accord*, Climate Analytics.

High-level Advisory Group of the UN Secretary-General on Climate Change Financing, (AGF) 2010. *Final Report*. Available at: http://www.un.org/wcm/webdav/site/climatechange/shared/Documents/AGF_reports/AGF%20Report.pdf

Project Catalyst, 2010. *Making Fast Start Finance Work*, Briefing Paper, Project Catalyst.

Roberts, J.T., M. Stadelmann, and S. Huq, 2010. *Copenhagen's Climate Finance Promises: Six Key Questions*, International Institute for Environment and Development (IIED), London.

Schalatek, L., 2012. *Regaining Momentum Priority Tasks for the Green Climate Fund at its First Board Meeting*, Heinrich Böll Stiftung, Washington, D.C.

Schalatek, L., N. Bird, and J. Brown, 2010. *Where's the Money? The Status of Climate Finance Post Copenhagen*, Heinrich Böll Foundation North America.

Stadelmann, M., J.T. Roberts, and A. Michaelowa, 2010. *Keeping a big promise: options for baselines to assess "new and additional" climate finance*, Center for Comparative and International Studies (CIS), University of Zurich, Zurich.

Stadelmann, M., J.T. Roberts, and S. Huq, 2010. *Baseline for trust: defining 'new and additional' climate funding*, International Institute for Environment and Development (IIED), London.

Stern, N., 2006. *Stern Review on the Economics of Climate Change*, HM Treasury, London.

United Nations Framework Convention on Climate Change (UNFCCC), 2007. *Bali Action Plan*, Decision 1/CP.13, UNFCCC, Bonn.

United Nations Framework Convention on Climate Change (UNFCCC), 2009. *Copenhagen Accord*, Decision 2/CP.15, UNFCCC, Bonn.

United Nations Framework Convention on Climate Change (UNFCCC), 2010. *Outcome of the work of the Ad Hoc Working Group on long-term Cooperative Action under the Convention*, Decision 1/CP.16, UNFCCC, Bonn.

United Nations Framework Convention on Climate Change (UNFCCC), 2011b. *Launching the Green Climate Fund*, Decision 3/CP.17, UNFCCC, Bonn.

United Nations Framework Convention on Climate Change (UNFCCC), 2011a. *Outcome of the work of the Ad Hoc Working Group on Long-term Cooperative Action under the Convention*, Decision 2/CP.17, UNFCCC, Bonn.

World Bank, International Monetary Fund, Organization for Economic Cooperation and Development, African Development Bank, Asian Development Bank, European Bank for Reconstruction and Development, European Investment Bank, and Inter-American Development Bank, (2011), *Mobilizing Climate Finance,* Paper prepared at the request of G-20 Finance Ministers. Available at http://climatechange.worldbank.org/content/mobilizing-climate-finance.

World Resources Institute (WRI), 2010. *Summary of Climate Finance Pledges Put Forward by Developed Countries*, World Resources Institute, Washington, D.C.

Index